GREAT

AMERICAN

SAILING

STORIES

LYONS PRESS CLASSICS

GREAT AMERICAN SAILING STORIES

EDITED BY

TOM MCCARTHY

GUILFORD
CONNECTICUT

An imprint of Globe Pequot

Distributed by NATIONAL BOOK NETWORK

British Library Cataloguing in Publication Information Available

Library of Congress Cataloging-in-Publication Data

ISBN 978-1-4930-3373-7 (paperback)
ISBN 978-1-4930-3374-4 (e-book)

♾™ The paper used in this publication meets the minimum requirements of American National Standard for Information Sciences—Permanence of Paper for Printed Library Materials, ANSI/NISO Z39.48-1992.

Printed in the United States of America

To Maggie and Britta—
Great American Daughters

CONTENTS

ACKNOWLEDGMENTS

To my sailing friends who suggested these stories because you are not only great sailors, but great readers. You know who you are.

INTRODUCTION

TOM MCCARTHY

There is nothing more American than a romping good sea story.

Here are eighteen unexpected pleasures—from masters like Melville and London and Dana, who celebrated the uniqueness of the American character so eloquently that their writing has never faded from public view. But here also are other writers who produced hidden jewels that simply slipped away quietly. It's time to revive them all.

Great American Sailing Stories offers first and foremost adventure. But there is much more to this collection than mere adventure. Here is

history, and drama, intrigue, well-paced tales, and colorful characters—all available to enjoy as you sit back in the comfort of a warm
and cozy (and I hope, dry) reading chair anchored to your living room
floor. I hope you will soon be pulled into the story and happy you
are home and safe. That's the magic of a good sea story tale and why
some of the best writers choose the sea as a backdrop.

This is not just a collection of stirring writing by wonderful writers. Here also are frank and—one must admit—inspiring stories of
adventure from authors who by luck—or, more often than not, bad
luck—found themselves alone on a boat in devastating circumstances.
Read the first-person accounts of William Lay and Cyrus M. Hussey
on board the ship *Globe* out of Nantucket, who witnessed the bloody
carnage of a mutiny. Or perhaps Lewis Holmes's account of a whaler's frozen voyage. Or Owen Chase's understated but eloquent tale of
survival.

Great American Sailing Stories is about courage and resoluteness, the
very characteristics on which the young United States grew and flour-
ished.

This, of course, leads to a question: What is it about the sea that
lends itself to so many indelibly classic stories?

The sea itself is easy pickings for writers looking for a backdrop
rich in metaphor or symbolism. It's dark, or brooding, or deep. It's
serene, mysterious, unforgiving. It's angry, seductive, cruel. The pos-
sibilities are nearly endless. The sea is a wonderful stage on which to
unroll a dramatic narrative or introduce a heroic character. And writers of both the truly memorable works and the wretchedly clichéd
clunkers have availed themselves of the sea as a setting. Richness of
backdrop aside, any sea story worthy of being in this inspiring collec-

tion must offer much more than mere adventure. The stories included here do so, I hope.

The most difficult aspect of this most enjoyable task was eliminating stories I had selected as "sure things." Such is the volume of wonderful writing available that I could have easily filled another book of similar size with those stories I reluctantly dropped. It is the nature of anthologies to spark debate over the selections, and indeed, any discussion about the contents herein might well focus on what isn't here rather than what is. In the end, my selections were governed by a decidedly personal criterion—I was moved by the story and enriched and informed by its content.

In selecting these stories, I tried for balance, to offer a collection rich in both drama and history, perhaps both. And while each of these stories is above everything else enduring, each I hope also offers something unique. You'll find here a good mixture of fact and fiction, of unvarnished true accounts and of polished, robust fiction oftentimes based on true accounts. The former selections are poignant in their chilling reality, and the latter in their depth and richness of character, and their dramatic pacing.

Fact or fiction, sea stories are, plain and simple, wonderful springboards for vicarious adventure. Few people would want to sail on a small storm-tossed boat with Joshua Slocum or watch with Owen Chase as an angry whale sends his ship to the bottom thousands of miles from the nearest land. But these incidents are certainly fun to read about. Slocum's and Chase's stoic accounts are stronger and more dramatic for their total lack of affectation, their frankness, and their absence of ego. Their gripping stories are custom made for the imaginative reader who seeks adventure in a more controlled environment, safe and warm at home.

Here is a small sampling of what you will find:

"The Capture," by Aaron Smith is a true account of the author's abduction by Cuban pirates while on route from Jamaica to England in 1822. Smith subsequently gained his freedom, but his bad karma continued when he was later arrested as a pirate in Havana, returned to England in chains, and put on trial for his life. Another firsthand account of the travails of life at sea is Owen Chase's chilling retelling of watching his whaler, the *Essex* out of Nantucket, being rammed by a white whale and sunk. Chase was only one of eight crew to survive an ordeal that included spending ninety-three days adrift in a whaleboat after the ship was sunk. Chase's 1821 narrative inspired Melville to write *Moby Dick*, a portion of which appears here. Of Chase's story Melville wrote, "The reading of this wondrous story upon the landless sea, and very close to the latitude of the shipwreck has a surprising effect on me." Melville, the icon, appears here also with "Rounding Cape Horn," from his 1850 work, *White-Jacket*. Melville's contemporary Richard Henry Dana presents an interesting glimpse into the highly superstitious life of a sailor in "Loss of a Man—Superstition," from *Two Years before the Mast*.

Joshua Slocum, who at one point commanded some of the finest tall ships of his era, became in 1898 the first man to sail around the world single-handedly, in his small sloop *Spray*—a 46,000-mile trip he began three years earlier at age 51. "Yammerschooner" is taken from his incomparable *Sailing Alone around the World*.

"MS Found in a Bottle," included here in its entirety, brings us brooding Edgar Allan Poe at his best. Poe not surprisingly has a darker take on a sea journey. After Poe won a $50 prize for this story, he began a career as a magazine writer.

It might strike some as unusual to see a piece by James Fenimore Cooper—an author better known for the landlocked Natty Bumppo and *The Last of the Mohicans*—in a collection of sea stories. But Cooper was a longtime aficionado of the U.S. Navy. His account of the early days of the USS *Constitution* appears in "Young Ironsides."

I hope readers find this collection broad, balanced, and interesting. These stories, having stood the test of time, are classics indeed. But more than anything else, they're good reading.

1

AN AMERICAN SEALER IN THE RUSSIAN SEA

JACK LONDON

"But they won't take excuses. You're across the line, and that's enough. They'll take you. In you go, Siberia and the salt mines. And as for Uncle Sam, why, what's he to know about it? Never a word will get back to the States. 'The *Mary Thomas*,' the papers will say, 'the *Mary Thomas* lost with all hands. Probably in a typhoon in the Japanese seas.' That's what the papers will say, and people, too. In you go, Siberia and the salt mines. Dead to the world and kith and kin, though you live fifty years."

In such manner John Lewis, commonly known as the "sea-lawyer," settled the matter out of hand.

It was a serious moment in the forecastle of the *Mary Thomas*. No sooner had the watch below begun to talk the trouble over, than the watch on deck came down and joined them. As there was no wind, every hand could be spared with the exception of the man at the wheel, and he remained only for the sake of discipline. Even "Bub" Russell, the cabin-boy, had crept forward to hear what was going on.

However, it was a serious moment, as the grave faces of the sailors bore witness. For the three preceding months the *Mary Thomas* sealing schooner had hunted the seal pack along the coast of Japan and north to Bering Sea. Here, on the Asiatic side of the sea, they were forced to give over the chase, or rather, to go no farther; for beyond, the Russian cruisers patrolled forbidden ground, where the seals might breed in peace.

A week before she had fallen into a heavy fog accompanied by calm. Since then the fog-bank had not lifted, and the only wind had been light airs and catspaws. This in itself was not so bad, for the sealing schooners are never in a hurry so long as they are in the midst of the seals; but the trouble lay in the fact that the current at this point bore heavily to the north. Thus the *Mary Thomas* had unwittingly drifted across the line, and every hour she was penetrating, unwillingly, farther and farther into the dangerous waters where the Russian bear kept guard.

How far she had drifted no man knew. The sun had not been visible for a week, nor the stars, and the captain had been unable to take observations in order to determine his position. At any moment a cruiser might swoop down and hale the crew away to Siberia. The fate of other poaching seal-hunters was too well known to the men of the *Mary Thomas*, and there was cause for grave faces.

"Mine friends," spoke up a German boat-steerer, "it vas a pad piziness. Shust as ve make a big catch, und all honest, somedings go wrong, und der Russians nab us, dake our skins and our schooner, und send us mit der anarchists to Siberia. Ach! a pretty pad piziness!"

"Yes, that's where it hurts," the sea-lawyer went on. "Fifteen hundred skins in the salt piles, and all honest, a big pay-day coming to every man Jack of us, and then to be captured and lose it all! It'd be different if we'd been poaching, but it's all honest work in open water."

"But if we haven't done anything wrong, they can't do anything to us, can they?" Bub queried.

"It strikes me as 'ow it ain't the proper thing for a boy o' your age shovin' in when 'is elders is talkin'," protested an English sailor, from over the edge of his bunk.

"Oh, that's all right, Jack," answered the sea-lawyer. "He's a perfect right to. Ain't he just as liable to lose his wages as the rest of us?"

"Wouldn't give thruppence for them!" Jack sniffed back. He had been planning to go home and see his family in Chelsea when he was paid off, and he was now feeling rather blue over the highly possible loss, not only of his pay, but of his liberty.

"How are they to know?" the sea-lawyer asked in answer to Bub's previous question. "Here we are in forbidden water. How do they know but what we came here of our own accord? Here we are, fifteen hundred skins in the hold. How do they know whether we got them in open water or in the closed sea? Don't you see, Bub, the evidence is all against us. If you caught a man with his pockets full of apples like those which grow on your tree, and if you caught him in your tree besides, what'd you think if he told you he couldn't help it, and had just been sort of blown there, and that anyway those apples came from some other tree—what'd you think, eh?"

Bub saw it clearly when put in that light, and shook his head despondently.

"You'd rather be dead than go to Siberia," one of the boat-pullers said. "They put you into the salt-mines and work you till you die. Never see daylight again. Why, I've heard tell of one fellow that was chained to his mate, and that mate died. And they were both chained together! And if they send you to the quicksilver mines you get salivated. I'd rather be hung than salivated."

"Wot's salivated?" Jack asked, suddenly sitting up in his bunk at the hint of fresh misfortunes.

"Why, the quicksilver gets into your blood; I think that's the way. And your gums all swell like you had the scurvy, only worse, and your teeth get loose in your jaws. And big ulcers forms, and then you die horrible. The strongest man can't last long a-mining quicksilver."

"A pad piziness," the boat-steerer reiterated, dolorously, in the silence which followed. "A pad piziness. I vish I vas in Yokohama. Eh? Vot vas dot?"

The vessel had suddenly heeled over. The decks were aslant. A tin pannikin rolled down the inclined plane, rattling and banging. From above came the slapping of canvas and the quivering rat-tat-tat of the after leech of the loosely stretched foresail. Then the mate's voice sang down the hatch, "All hands on deck and make sail!"

Never had such summons been answered with more enthusiasm. The calm had broken. The wind had come which was to carry them south into safety. With a wild cheer all sprang on deck. Working with mad haste, they flung out topsails, flying jibs and staysails. As they worked, the fog-bank lifted and the black vault of heaven, bespangled with the old familiar stars, rushed into view. When all was shipshape, the *Mary Thomas* was lying gallantly over on her side to a beam wind and plunging ahead due south.

"Steamer's lights ahead on the port bow, sir!" cried the lookout from his station on the forecastle-head. There was excitement in the man's voice.

The captain sent Bub below for his night-glasses. Everybody crowded to the lee-rail to gaze at the suspicious stranger, which already began to loom up vague and indistinct. In those unfrequented waters the chance was one in a thousand that it could be anything else than a Russian patrol. The captain was still anxiously gazing through the glasses, when a flash of flame left the stranger's side, followed by the loud report of a cannon. The worst fears were confirmed. It was a patrol, evidently firing across the bows of the *Mary Thomas* in order to make her heave to.

"Hard down with your helm!" the captain commanded the steersman, all the life gone out of his voice. Then to the crew, "Back over the jib and foresail! Run down the flying jib! Clew up the foretopsail! And aft here and swing on to the main-sheet!"

The *Mary Thomas* ran into the eye of the wind, lost headway, and fell to courtesying gravely to the long seas rolling up from the west.

The cruiser steamed a little nearer and lowered a boat. The sealers watched in heartbroken silence. They could see the white bulk of the boat as it was slacked away to the water, and its crew sliding aboard. They could hear the creaking of the davits and the commands of the officers. Then the boat sprang away under the impulse of the oars, and came toward them. The wind had been rising, and already the sea was too rough to permit the frail craft to lie alongside the tossing schooner; but watching their chance, and taking advantage of the boarding ropes thrown to them, an officer and a couple of men clambered aboard. The boat then sheered off into safety and lay to its oars, a young midshipman, sitting in the stern and holding the yoke-lines, in charge.

The officer, whose uniform disclosed his rank as that of second lieutenant in the Russian navy, went below with the captain of the *Mary Thomas* to look at the ship's papers. A few minutes later he emerged, and upon his sailors removing the hatch-covers, passed down into the hold with a lantern to inspect the salt piles. It was a goodly heap which confronted him—fifteen hundred fresh skins, the season's catch; and under the circumstances he could have had but one conclusion.

"I am very sorry," he said, in broken English to the sealing captain, when he again came on deck, "but it is my duty, in the name of the tsar, to seize your vessel as a poacher caught with fresh skins in the closed sea. The penalty, as you may know, is confiscation and imprisonment."

The captain of the *Mary Thomas* shrugged his shoulders in seeming indifference, and turned away. Although they may restrain all outward show, strong men, under unmerited misfortune, are sometimes very close to tears. Just then the vision of his little California home, and of the wife and two yellow-haired boys, was strong upon him, and there was a strange, choking sensation in his throat, which made him afraid that if he attempted to speak he would sob instead.

And also there was upon him the duty he owed his men. No weakness before them, for he must be a tower of strength to sustain them in misfortune. He had already explained to the second lieutenant, and knew the hopelessness of the situation. As the sea-lawyer had said, the evidence was all against him. So he turned aft, and fell to pacing up and down the poop of the vessel over which he was no longer commander.

The Russian officer now took temporary charge. He ordered more of his men aboard, and had all the canvas clewed up and furled snugly away. While this was being done, the boat plied back and forth between the two vessels, passing a heavy hawser, which was made fast to the great towing-bitts on the schooner's forecastle-head. During all this work the sealers stood about in sullen groups. It was madness to think of resisting, with the guns of a man-of-war not a biscuit-toss away; but they refused to lend a hand, preferring instead to maintain a gloomy silence.

Having accomplished his task, the lieutenant ordered all but four of his men back into the boat. Then the midshipman, a lad of sixteen, looking strangely mature and dignified in his uniform and sword, came aboard to take command of the captured sealer. Just as the lieutenant prepared to depart his eye chanced to alight upon Bub. Without a word of warning, he seized him by the arm and dropped him over the rail into the waiting boat; and then, with a parting wave of his hand, he followed him.

It was only natural that Bub should be frightened at this unexpected happening. All the terrible stories he had heard of the Russians served to make him fear them, and now returned to his mind with double force. To be captured by them was bad enough, but to be carried off by them, away from his comrades, was a fate of which he had not dreamed.

"Be a good boy, Bub," the captain called to him, as the boat drew away from the *Mary Thomas's* side, "and tell the truth!"

"Aye, aye, sir!" he answered, bravely enough by all outward appearance. He felt a certain pride of race, and was ashamed to be a coward before these strange enemies, these wild Russian bears.

"Und be politeful!" the German boat-steerer added, his rough voice lifting across the water like a fog-horn.

Bub waved his hand in farewell, and his mates clustered along the rail as they answered with a cheering shout. He found room in the stern-sheets, where he fell to regarding the lieutenant. He didn't look so wild or bearish after all—very much like other men, Bub concluded, and the sailors were much the same as all other man-of-war's men he had ever known. Nevertheless, as his feet struck the steel deck of the cruiser, he felt as if he had entered the portals of a prison.

For a few minutes he was left unheeded. The sailors hoisted the boat up, and swung it in on the davits. Then great clouds of black smoke poured out of the funnels, and they were under way—to Siberia, Bub could not help but think. He saw the *Mary Thomas* swing abruptly into line as she took the pressure from the hawser, and her side-lights, red and green, rose and fell as she was towed through the sea.

Bub's eyes dimmed at the melancholy sight, but—but just then the lieutenant came to take him down to the commander, and he straightened up and set his lips firmly, as if this were a very commonplace affair and he were used to being sent to Siberia every day in the week. The cabin in which the commander sat was like a palace compared to the humble fittings of the *Mary Thomas*, and the commander himself, in gold lace and dignity, was a most august personage, quite unlike the simple man who navigated his schooner on the trail of the seal pack.

Bub now quickly learned why he had been brought aboard, and in the prolonged questioning which followed, told nothing but the plain truth. The truth was harmless; only a lie could have injured his cause. He did not know much, except that they had been sealing far to the south in open water, and that when the calm and fog came down upon them, being close to the line, they had drifted across. Again and again he insisted that they had not lowered a boat or shot a seal in the week they had been drifting about in the forbidden sea; but the commander chose to consider all that he said to be a tissue of falsehoods, and adopted a bullying tone in an effort to frighten the boy. He threatened and cajoled by turns, but failed in the slightest to shake Bub's statements, and at last ordered him out of his presence.

By some oversight, Bub was not put in anybody's charge, and wandered up on deck unobserved. Sometimes the sailors, in passing, bent curious glances upon him, but otherwise he was left strictly alone. Nor could he have attracted much attention, for he was small, the night dark, and the watch on deck intent on its own business. Stumbling over the strange decks, he made his way aft where he could look upon the side-lights of the *Mary Thomas*, following steadily in the rear.

For a long while he watched, and then lay down in the darkness close to where the hawser passed over the stern to the captured schooner. Once an officer came up and examined the straining rope to see if it were chafing, but Bub cowered away in the shadow undiscovered. This, however, gave him an idea which concerned the lives and liberties of twenty-two men, and which was to avert crushing sorrow from more than one happy home many thousand miles away.

In the first place, he reasoned, the crew were all guiltless of any crime, and yet were being carried relentlessly away to imprisonment in Siberia—a living death, he had heard, and he believed it implicitly. In the second place, he was a prisoner, hard and fast, with no chance to escape. In the third, it was possible for the twenty-two men on the *Mary Thomas* to escape. The only thing which bound them was a four-inch hawser. They dared not cut it at their end, for a watch was sure to be maintained upon it by their Russian captors; but at this end, ah! at his end—

Bub did not stop to reason further. Wriggling close to the hawser, he opened his jack-knife and went to work. The blade was not very sharp, and he sawed away, rope-yarn by rope-yarn, the awful picture of the solitary Siberian exile he must endure growing clearer and more terrible at every stroke. Such a fate was bad enough to undergo with one's comrades, but to face it alone seemed frightful. And besides, the very act he was performing was sure to bring greater punishment upon him.

In the midst of such somber thoughts, he heard footsteps approaching. He wriggled away into the shadow. An officer stopped where he had been working, half-stooped to examine the hawser, then changed his mind and straightened up. For a few minutes he stood there, gazing at the lights of the captured schooner, and then went forward again.

Now was the time! Bub crept back and went on sawing. Now two parts were severed. Now three. But one remained. The tension upon this was so great that it readily yielded. Splash the freed end went over-board. He lay quietly, his heart in his mouth, listening. No one on the cruiser but himself had heard.

He saw the red and green lights of the *Mary Thomas* grow dimmer and dimmer. Then a faint hallo came over the water from the Russian prize crew. Still nobody heard. The smoke continued to pour out of the cruiser's funnels, and her propellers throbbed as mightily as ever.

What was happening on the *Mary Thomas*? Bub could only surmise; but of one thing he was certain: his comrades would assert themselves and overpower the four sailors and the midshipman. A few minutes later he saw a small flash, and straining his ears heard the very faint report of a pistol. Then, oh joy! both the red and green lights suddenly disappeared. The *Mary Thomas* was retaken!

Just as an officer came aft, Bub crept forward, and hid away in one of the boats. Not an instant too soon. The alarm was given. Loud voices rose in command. The cruiser altered her course. An electric search-light began to throw its white rays across the sea, here, there, everywhere; but in its flashing path no tossing schooner was revealed.

Bub went to sleep soon after that, nor did he wake till the gray of dawn. The engines were pulsing monotonously, and the water, splash-ing noisily, told him the decks were being washed down. One sweep-ing glance, and he saw that they were alone on the expanse of ocean. The *Mary Thomas* had escaped. As he lifted his head, a roar of laughter went up from the sailors. Even the officer, who ordered him taken below and locked up, could not quite conceal the laughter in his eyes. Bub thought often in the days of confinement which followed that they were not very angry with him for what he had done.

He was not far from right. There is a certain innate nobility deep down in the hearts of all men, which forces them to admire a brave act, even if it is performed by an enemy. The Russians were in nowise different from other men. True, a boy had outwitted them; but they could not blame him, and they were sore puzzled as to what to do with him. It would never do to take a little mite like him in to represent all that remained of the lost poacher.

So, two weeks later, a United States man-of-war, steaming out of the Russian port of Vladivostok, was signaled by a Russian cruiser. A boat passed between the two ships, and a small boy dropped over the rail upon the deck of the American vessel. A week later he was put ashore at Hakodate, and after some telegraphing, his fare was paid on the railroad to Yokohama.

From the depot he hurried through the quaint Japanese streets to the harbor, and hired a sampan boatman to put him aboard a certain vessel whose familiar rigging had quickly caught his eye. Her gaskets were off, her sails unfurled; she was just starting back to the United States. As he came closer, a crowd of sailors sprang upon the forecastle-head, and the windlass-bars rose and fell as the anchor was torn from its muddy bottom.

"'Yankee ship come down the ribber!'" the sea-lawyer's voice rolled out as he led the anchor song.

"'Pull, my bully boys, pull!'" roared back the old familiar chorus, the men's bodies lifting and bending to the rhythm.

Bub Russell paid the boatman and stepped on deck. The anchor was forgotten. A mighty cheer went up from the men, and almost before he could catch his breath he was on the shoulders of the captain, surrounded by his mates, and endeavoring to answer twenty questions to the second.

The next day a schooner hove to off a Japanese fishing village, sent ashore four sailors and a little midshipman, and sailed away. These men did not talk English, but they had money and quickly made their way to Yokohama. From that day the Japanese village folk never heard anything more about them, and they are still a much-talked-of mystery. As the Russian government never said anything about the incident, the United States is still ignorant of the whereabouts of the lost poacher, nor has she ever heard, officially, of the way in which some of her citizens "shanghaied" five subjects of the tsar. Even nations have secrets sometimes.

2

THE CAPTURE: A TRUE ACCOUNT

AARON SMITH

At two o'clock, p.m., while walking the deck in conversation with Captain Cowper, I discovered a schooner standing out towards us from the land; she bore a very suspicious appearance, and I immediately went up aloft with my telescope to examine her more closely. I was instantly convinced that she was a pirate, and mentioned it to Captain Cowper, who coincided with me, and we deemed it proper to call Mr. Lumsden from below & inform him. When he came on deck we pointed out the schooner and stated our suspicions, recommending him to alter his course and avoid her. We were at this moment about six leagues from Cape Roman, which bore S.E. by E. Never did ignorance, with its concomitant obstinacy, betray itself more strongly than on this occasion; he rejected our advice and refused to alter his course, and was infatuated enough to suppose, that, because he bore the English flag, no one would dare to molest him. To this obstinacy and infatuation I must attribute all my subsequent misfortunes—the unparalleled cruelties which I have suffered—the persecutions and prosecutions which I have undergone—the mean and wanton insults which have been heaped upon me—and the villany and dishonesty to which I have been exposed from the author of them all; who, not satisfied with having occasioned my sufferings, would have basely taken advantage of them to defraud my friends of what little of my property had escaped the general plunder. In about half an hour after this conversation, we began to discover that the deck of the schooner was full of men, and that she was beginning to hoist out her boats. This circumstance greatly alarmed Mr. Lumsden, and he ordered the course to be altered two points, but it was then too late, for the stranger was within gunshot. In a short time she was within hail, and, in English, ordered us to lower our stern boat and send the captain on board of her. Mr. Lumsden either did not understand the order, or pretended not to do so, and the corsair, for such she now proved to be, fired a volley of musketry. This increased his terror, which he expressed in hurried exclamations of Aye, aye! Oh, Lord God! and then gave orders to lay the main yard aback. A boat from the pirate now boarded the *Zephyr*, containing nine or ten men, of a most ferocious aspect, armed with muskets, knives, and cutlasses, who immediately took charge of the brig, and ordered Captain Cowper, Mr. Lumsden, the ship's carpenter, and myself, to go on board the pirate, hastening our departure by repeated blows with the flat part of their cutlasses over our backs, and threatening to shoot us. The rapidity of our movements did not give us much time for consideration; and, while we were rowing towards the corsair, Mr. Lumsden remarked that he had been very careless in leaving the books, which contained the account of all the money on board, on the cabin table. The captain of the pirate ordered us on deck immediately on our arrival. He was a man of most uncouth and sav-

age appearance, about five feet six inc[h]
tion, with an aquiline nose, high cheek
large full eyes. His complexion was sa[
appeared to be about two and thirty ye[ars]
very much resembled an Indian, and[
his father was a Spaniard and his m[other]
addressed Mr. Lumsden, & inquired[
sels were that he saw ahead. On bein[g]
merchantmen, he gave orders for all hands to go in chase. The [
was observed in the mean time to make sail and stand in the direction
of Cape Roman.

The captain now addressed himself to Mr. Lumsden on the subject
of his cargo, which he was informed consisted of sugars, rum, coffee,
arrow root, dye woods, & co. He then severally inquired who and what
we were; and then whether we had spoken any vessel on our passage.
On being informed of the schooner from New Brunswick, he asked if
we thought she had specie on board. We told him that those vessels in
general sold their cargoes for cash and he seemed very anxious to learn
whether she was ahead or astern of us, and whether she was armed.
Mr. Lumsden now entreated the captain to make a signal to the *Zephyr*
not to stand nearer to the land, as he was apprehensive of her going
on shore, and was told that he need not be under any alarm, as there
was a very experienced pilot on board of her. He was, however, dissatisfied with this reply, and repeated his entreaty, when the other, in
a menacing tone, enjoined silence, and went forward. In a short time
he returned and questioned Mr. Lumsden as to what money he had on
board, and when told that there was none, he replied, 'Do not imagine
that I am a fool, Sir; I know that all vessels going to Europe have specie
on board; & if you will give up what you have, you shall proceed on
your voyage without further molestation.' Mr. Lumsden repeated his

ate declared that if the money was not produced, the *Zephyr*, throw her cargo overboard, and, if any concealed, he would burn her with every soul belonging to then asked whether there were any candles, wine, or porter, board; and Mr. Lumsden foolishly replied, not any that he could spare, without appearing to consider that we were in his power, and that he could if he pleased possess himself of any thing he might wish without consulting his convenience.

The night was at this time fast approaching, and the breeze had begun to die away. The captain appeared to despair of coming up with his chase, which we could not clearly perceive to be a ship and a brig, and asked Captain Cowper and myself whether he should be able to overtake them before dark. We replied in the negative, and he then gave orders to shorten sail and stand towards the *Zephyr*. The pirates then began to prepare for supper, and were very liberal in serving out spirits to our boat's crew, and also offered us a share, or wine if we preferred it, but we declined both.

The captain now turned to me and said, that, as he was in a bad state of health and none of his ship's company understood navigation, he should detain me for the purpose of navigating the schooner. I tried as much as possible to conceal my emotions at this intimation, and endeavoured to work upon his feelings by telling him that I was married and had three children—that they, together with my wife and aged parents, were anxiously expecting me at home; and represented, in as pathetic language as I could, the misery & distraction which it would cause them, beseeching him to spare my wife and children, and not bring down the grey hairs of my unfortunate parents with sorrow to the grave. But I appealed to a monster, devoid of all feeling, inured to crime, and hardened in iniquity. Mr. Lumsden in the mean time interfered, and hoped that he would not deprive him of my services:

but he savagely told him, 'If I do not keep him, I shall keep you.' This threat evidently alarmed and agitated him, and he seemed to regret the part he had taken.

A few minutes, however, displayed the unfeeling & selfish character of this man in the strongest light. 'Mr. Smith,' said he, turning to me, 'for God's sake do not importune the captain, or he will certainly take me: you are a single man, but I have a large family dependent upon me, who will become orphans and be utterly destitute. The moment I am liberated, I shall proceed to the Havannah, and despatch a man of war in search of the corsair, and at the same time publish to the world the manner in which you have been forcibly detained. Nay, I will represent the whole affair at Lloyd's; and, should the pirate be captured hereafter, and you found on board, no harm shall befall you. Whatever property you have shall be safely delivered to your family, and mine will for ever bless you for the kind and generous act.' During this address he was much affected, and the tears streamed from his eyes. I sympathized in his feelings, and replied, that I hoped that neither of us would be detained; but if the lot must fall upon one, under these circumstances, and on these conditions, I could consent to become the victim. This declaration calmed his agitated spirits; but little did I think of the treachery and duplicity that had been masked beneath them, and which subsequent events have too clearly demonstrated.

Supper having been prepared, the captain and his officers, six or seven in number, sat down to it, and invited us to join them, which, for fear of giving offence and exciting their brutality, we did. Our supper consisted of garlic and onions chopped fine and mixed up with bread in a bowl, for which there was a general scramble, every one helping himself as he pleased, either with his fingers or any instrument with which he happened to be supplied.

During supper Mr. Lumsden begged to be allowed to go on board the *Zephyr* to the children, as he was fearful that they would be alarmed at our absence and the presence of strangers, in which request I joined; but he replied, that no one would injure them, and that, as soon as the two vessels came to an anchor, he would accompany us on board.

The corsair was at this time fast approaching the *Zephyr*, when the captain ordered a musket to be fired, and then tacked in shore; the signal was immediately answered, & the brig followed our movements. One of our boat's crew was then ordered to the lead, with directions to give notice the moment he found soundings, and the captain then inquired if we had any Americans on board as seamen. He expressed himself very warmly against them, and declared he would kill all belonging to that nation in revenge for the injuries that he had sustained at their hands, one of his vessels having been lately taken and destroyed by them; adding, at the same time, that if he discovered that we had concealed the fact from him, he would punish us equally. To the Americans he said that he should never give quarter; but as all nations were hostile to Spain, he would attack all.

The man at the lead, during this conversation, gave notice of soundings in fourteen fathoms, and the captain ordered the boat down, and told Mr. Lumsden he would accompany him on board his vessel. The men we had brought were ordered into the boat, but Captain Cowper, the carpenter, and myself, were not allowed to go into her. The boat then proceeded towards the *Zephyr*, with Mr. Lumsden and the captain of the corsair, and shortly after returned with some of the men whom the pirate had put on board; who brought with them Captain Cowper's watch, the ship's spyglass, and my telescope, together with some of my clothes, and a goat. The goat had no sooner reached the deck, than one of these inhuman wretches cut its throat, and proceeded to flay it while it was yet alive, telling us at the same time, that we should all be served in the same manner if no money was found on board. The corsair had then got into four fathoms' water and came to an anchor, as also did the *Zephyr*, about fifty yards from her, and the pirates that were on board began hailing their companions, & congratulating one another at their success.

The watch on board the corsair was now set, and Captain Cowper, the carpenter, and myself, were ordered to sleep on the Companion. Thither we repaired; but to sleep was impossible. The carpenter then took an opportunity of informing us that there was specie on board, and expressed his apprehension, that, if discovered, the cruel threat would be put into execution. Captain Cowper and myself, however, were ignorant of the circumstance, and felt rather inclined to believe that the carpenter was mistaken, but he assured us that such was the case, and that Mr. Lumsden had consulted him a day or two before about a place for its concealment. The expression which had dropped from him in the boat then occurred to us; but we still felt inclined to believe that it was some private money of his own. The whole night was passed in giving way to various conjectures, and hope and fear and the dread of assassination completely drove sleep away. Each reflected on what might be his future fate, and imparted his hopes or his apprehensions to his fellow-sufferers.

At daylight we perceived the pirates on board beating the *Zephyr*'s crew with their cutlasses, & began to tremble for our own safety. After this we perceived the sailors at work hoisting out her boats, and hauling a rope cable from the afterhatchway and coiling it on deck, as if preparing to take out the brig's cargo. The crew of the corsair meanwhile began to take their coffee, and the officers invited us to partake of some, which we willingly did, & found it very refreshing after a night spent in sleepless apprehension.

At seven o'clock the captain hailed his crew from the *Zephyr*, where he had passed the night, and ordered the boat to be sent, in which he returned in a short time, with some curiosities belonging to myself. On his arrival, he approached me, and, brandishing a cutlass over my head, told me to go on board the *Zephyr*, & bring every thing necessary for the purposes of navigation, as it was his determination to keep me. To this mandate I made no reply; so, brandishing his cutlass again, he asked me, with an oath, if I heard him. I replied that I did, when, with a ferocious air, he said, 'Mind and obey me then, or I will take off your skin.' At this threat I went into the boat, and pulled towards the *Zephyr*, and on my arrival found Mr. Lumsden at the gangway. I told him the nature of my visit, at which he expressed his sorrow, but advised me not to oppose the pirate, lest it might produce bad usage, as he seemed bent upon detaining me. He then informed me that they had taken possession of every thing, and that he himself had narrowly escaped assassination on account of his watch.

On entering my cabin, I found my chest broken to pieces, & contents taken away, with two diamond rings and some articles of value. From a seaman, I received my gold watch, sextant, and some other valuable things, which I had previously given to him to conceal; and with these I returned to my own stateroom, and proceeded to pack up what few clothes had been left by the plunderers. My books, parrot, and various other articles, I gave in charge to Mr. Lumsden, who engaged to deliver them safely into the hands of my friends, should he reach England.

The corsair had, during the interim, weighed anchor and hauled alongside of the *Zephyr*; and, having made fast, the crew had commenced moving all the trunks on board of her. Among these was the desk of Captain Cowper, containing all his papers and vouchers, which he begged me to claim as mine and recover for him, for which purpose he gave me the key. Well aware of the serious loss he would sustain, I undertook the dangerous task; and, passing into the corsair, informed the captain that my desk had been taken, and begged, as it only contained papers, which were of importance to my family, that it might be restored. He ordered me to open it, and, having examined the interior, he granted my request; and I had the pleasure of obliging Captain Cowper, who, in return, promised to represent my case to the underwriters at Lloyd's.

The pirates next commenced taking out the *Zephyr*'s cargo, at which Mr. Lumsden & myself were compelled to assist; but the former was soon after removed on board the schooner, in consequence of the crying of the children, who, the captain said, had been instigated by him to do so. There he was employed in striking the cargo into the hatchways. The pirates in the mean time became intoxicated, and gave way to the most violent excesses. All subordination was at an end, and quality seemed to be the order of the day. Mr. Lumsden was now called on board the *Zephyr*, and questioned as to the cargo down the main hatchway, when he read & explained the manifesto. Orders were immediately given to four sailors and myself to prepare for hoisting the cargo up, and to clear away the dye wood that was in our way. Mr. Lumsden directed us to throw it overboard, which we commenced doing, and threw some over; but this was prevented by the captain, who said that he only wanted to throw the ship's cargo overboard, in order to say that it was taken from him, and defraud the underwriters. We continued our occupation until we had hoisted up two scroons of indigo, a quantity of arrow root, and as much coffee as they thought sufficient. The seamen were then ordered to send down the foretop gallant mast and yard, both of which were taken on board the pirate, with whatever spars they thought would be of utility. Even the playful innocence of the children could not protect them from the barbarity of these ruffians; their earrings were taken out of their ears, and they were left without a bed to lie upon or a blanket to cover them.

They next commenced taking out the ship's stores, with all the live stock and some water; and Mr. Lumsden and Captain Cowper were then ordered on the quarter deck, and told that if they did not either produce the money or tell where it was concealed, the *Zephyr* should be burned and they with her. On this occasion the same answer was given as before, and the inhuman wretch instantly prepared to put his threat into execution, by sending the children on board the schooner, and ordering those two gentlemen to be taken below decks and to be locked to the pumps. The mandate was no sooner issued than it was obeyed by his fiendlike myrmidons, who even commenced piling combustibles round them. The apparent certainty of their fate extorted a confession from Lumsden, who was released and taken on deck, where he went to the round house and produced a small box of doubloons, which the pirate exhibited with an air of exultation to the crew. He then insisted that there was more; and, notwithstanding that the other made the most solemn asseverations to the contrary, and that even what he had given was not his own, he was again lashed to the pumps. The question was then applied to Captain Cowper, and fire was ordered to be put to the combustibles piled round him. Seeing his fate inevitable, he offered to surrender all he had, and, being released, he gave them about nine doubloons, declaring that what he had produced was all he had, and had been entrusted to his care for a poor woman, who, for aught he knew, might at this moment be in a state of starvation.

"Do not speak to me of poor people," exclaimed the fiend, "I am poor, and your countrymen and the Americans have made me so; I know there is more money, and will either have it, or burn you and the vessel."

The unfortunate man was then once more ordered below and fire directed to be applied. In vain did they protest that he had got all; he persisted in his cruelty. The flames now began to approach their persons, and their cries were heart-rending, while they implored him to turn them adrift in a boat, at the mercy of the waves, rather than torture them thus, and keep the *Zephyr*; when, if there was money, he would surely find it.

Finding that no further confession was extorted, he began to believe the truth of these protestations, & ordered his men to throw water below and quench the flames. The unfortunate sufferers were then released and taken into the round house, and the seamen, children, and myself, allowed to go on board the brig. There we were left for a while at liberty, while the pirates caroused and exulted over their booty.

When they had finished their meal, the captain told them that it was now time to return to their own vessel, and ordered me to accompany them. I hesitated at first to obey; but he was not to be thwarted, and, drawing his knife, threatened with an oath to cut my head off if I did not move instanter. I thought it best to pretend ignorance of his order, and said that I had not heard him at first, and hoped, as I had some accounts to settle with Mr. Lumsden, that he would give me time to do so before he took me away. He complied, with some difficulty. I then requested Mr. Lumsden to sign a written bill of lading for the two tierces of coffee belonging to me on board, consigned to Mr. Watson, ship-chandler, in London, and also a promissory note for eighteen pounds ten shillings, payable to the same person, on account of monies due to me.

Having made these arrangements, I returned on board the schooner, and the captain asked me if I had my watch. I answered in the affirmative; he took it from me and looked at it, and, admiring it, gave very strong hints that he should like to have it. I took no notice of the hint, and said that it was a gift from my aged mother, whom I never expected to see again, and should like to send it to her by Mr. Lumsden; but I was afraid that his people would take it away from that person, if I gave it into his hands.

"Your people have a very bad opinion of us," he replied; "but I will convince you that we are not so bad as we are represented to be; come along with me, and your watch shall go safely home."

Saying this, he took me on board the *Zephyr*, with the watch in his hand, and gave it to Mr. Lumsden, and desired his people not to take it from him on any account. I then asked to remain awhile, & bid farewell to the children and crew; which he, with some difficulty, allowed me to do. In this interval, the owner's son, who was on board learning navigation, said that his quadrant and all his clothes had been taken away, and begged me to recover them for him, if possible. I promised him I would do my best, and represented to the pirate that he was the son of poor parents, and could ill afford the loss, and begged that they might be restored. He sulkily replied, that I was presuming too much, but this must be my last request; and the lad might have his things, with the exception of checked shirts, which must be left for his crew. Having performed this good office, the captain became impatient for my return, and I was obliged to take a hasty but affecting leave of my former messmates, to become one of a desperate banditti. The inhuman wretch thought even this affecting ceremony too long, and drove me on board at the point of his knife.

When I had reached the deck of the corsair, he asked me if I had got every instrument necessary to the purposes of navigation; and if not, to go and get them, for he would have no excuses by and by, and if I made any he would kill me. I answered, that I had got all that was necessary, and he then gave orders to cast loose from the *Zephyr*, and told Mr. Lumsden he might proceed on his voyage, but on no account to steer for the Havannah; for, if he overtook him on that course, he would destroy him and his vessel together. He promised that he would not touch there, and the vessels were accordingly cast loose, in a short time afterwards. Mr. Lumsden, Captain Cowper, & the children, stood on the gangway and bade me adieu, and my heart sunk within me as the two vessels parted.

The horrors of my situation now rushed upon my mind; I looked upon myself as a wretch, upon whom the world was closed for ever: exposed to the brutality of a ferocious and remorseless horde of miscreants—doomed to destruction and death, and, perhaps, to worse, to disgrace and ignominy; to become the partaker of their enormities, and be compelled, I knew not how soon, to embrue my hands in the blood of a fellow-creature, and, perhaps, a fellow-countryman. The distraction, grief, and painful apprehensions of my parents, and of one to whom I was under the tenderest of all engagements, filled my mind with terror. I could no longer bear to look upon the scene my fancy presented to me, and I would have sought a refuge from my own miserable thoughts, in self-destruction; but my movements were watched, and I was secured, and a guard set over me. The captain then addressed me, and told me that if I made a second attempt I should be lashed to a gun, and there left to die through hunger; and, for the sake of security, ordered me below; but, at my earnest entreaty, I was allowed to remain on deck till it was dark.

3

THE PROUD NARRAGANSETT'S ESCAPE

JAMES BARNES

"Twenty of those confounded Yankees give me more trouble than three decks full of Frenchmen," remarked Captain Brower of the prison-ship *Spartan*, one of the fleet of dismantled battle-ships that thronged the harbor of Plymouth, England.

Lieutenant Barnard, commanding the neat little sloop of war *Sparrow*, then on the guard station, laughed.

"They are troublesome beggars, sure enough," he said; "but the funny thing is that they behave almost exactly the way our fellows do, or at least would under the same circumstances; that I verily believe."

"Well, such insolence and impudence I never saw in my life," returned Brower. "I shall be glad when I get rid of this last batch and will rest easy when they have been sent ashore to Dartmoor. You should have seen the way they behaved about two weeks ago. Let me see, it was the evening of the fourth, I believe. In fact the whole day through they were at it—skylarking and speech-making and singing."

It was July, 1814. Many vessels in the government service of Great Britain, returning from America, or from the high seas, brought into Plymouth crews of American vessels, and not a few of the troops captured about the Lakes and on the Canadian frontier had been brought over also. They were usually kept on board one of the prison hulks for three or four months; sometimes it was a year or more before they were transferred to the military prisons, the largest of which was situated at Dartmoor, and the second in size at Stapleton, not far from the town of Gloucester. Although the prison-ships and the prisons themselves were crowded with Frenchmen, the Yankees were three or four times as much trouble to control and to command. When they were not planning to escape, they were generally bothering the sentinels, drawing up petitions, or having some row or other, if only for the fun of turning out the guard.

"I wish somebody else had this position," grumbled Captain Brower, pouring out a glass of port. "I don't think that I was made for it. When I am left alone, I am liable to become too lenient, and when I am angered, perhaps I may be too hasty. . . . At any rate, I wish some one else was here in my place. . . . I had to laugh the other day, though; you know old Bagwigge of the *Germanicus*, here alongside, what a hot-tempered, testy old fellow he is?

"Well, the other day he was walking up and down his old quarter-deck, and about fourscore of my Yankee prisoners were up on deck for air and exercise. Suddenly they began singing. Now, I don't object to that; if they'd never do anything worse, I'd be happy. They've only cut four holes through different parts of this ship, and once well-nigh scuttled her; but never mind; to go on: Bagwigge, he walks to the side and shouts across to my vessel: 'Hi, there! you confounded Yankees!

avast that everlasting row.' I didn't see that it was any of his business, as it was on my own ship; but the Yankees—I wish you had seen them, Barnard, upon my soul."

"What did they do? Slanged him, I suppose, terrible."

"Well, you see," continued Captain Brower, "the potatoes had just been given out for the use of the prison mess cooks, and three big baskets of them lay there on the deck. One of the Yankees threw a potato that caught old Captain B. fair and square on the side of his head, capsizing his hat and nearly fetching away his ear. 'You insolent villains!' he cried, almost jumping up on the rail, 'I'll make you sweat your blood for this.' Well, ha, ha, not only one potato was thrown this time, but about half a bushel. I' faith, but those rascals were good shots. Old Bagwigge, he was raked fore and aft. Turning, he ran for it, and dove in the cabin."

The younger man laughed. The officer about whom the tale had been told was not popular in the service. He had had no Americans on board his prison hulk, and the Frenchmen who were temporarily his guests trembled at his frown and cringed at his gesture. He was an overbearing, hot-tempered martinet, and was hated accordingly. But this was not the end of Captain Brower's story, and as soon as the Lieutenant had stopped laughing, he resumed:—

"Let me go on, for I haven't finished yet. When Bagwigge returned, he had with him a file of marines. Up he marches 'em, and the Yankees greeted them with a cheer, and then seeing that the Captain was going to speak to them, they desisted to let him talk.

"'Now,' he said, 'you impudent scoundrels, below with you; every mother's son of you, or I'll——' He hadn't got any farther than that when the same fellow who threw the first potato hit him again. He was only about forty feet away, you know, and with such force was the vegetable thrown that it nearly took his head off his shoulders. 'Fire!'

he roared. 'Fire at them!' I doubt whether the marines could have taken aim, they were so busy dodging potatoes, and as for Bagwigge himself, he was jumping, bubbling, and sizzling like a blob of butter in a skillet. I rushed forward and jumped on to the forecastle rail.

"'If you dare fire, Captain Bagwigge,' I cried, 'you'll swing for it!' At this, he dove down the companionway again, with his marines after him. I turned to the prisoners and ordered them below, where they went readily enough. As to Bagwigge, I don't suppose that I'll hear from him again; I hope that he will attend to his own vessel and leave mine alone."

All this conversation, or at least the relation of Captain Brower's story, had taken place in the *Spartan*'s cabin, and when the two officers left, a detail of the prisoners was on the deck, walking briskly back and forth under the eyes of armed sentries, who guarded the gangways and patrolled narrow board walks, raised some two or three feet above the hammock-nettings.

"Do you see that tall, brown fellow, there?" asked Captain Brower, pointing. "He is the one who did such sharp shooting with the potatoes."

"A strange-looking creature, surely," responded the Commander of the *Sparrow*. "He looks a half-tamed man. Well, I wish you less trouble and all success. Good day to you; I have to return to my ship."

Brower turned and went back into his cabin. Although he did not know it, and would have denied it if he had been told the truth, he was exactly the man for the position, for he was just and painstaking, humane and careful. Although there had been all sorts of attempts to escape formulated among the Yankees, and almost carried into successful execution, Brower had not lost a single prisoner, and his presence among them could restore order and quell a disturbance better than the parading of a file of soldiers.

They were a strange lot, these captives. They came from all walks of life, and from every sort of place. Raw militiamen, who had been surrendered by Hull (the army Hull, mark you, not the brave Commodore), privateersmen, captured in all sorts of crafts and dressed in all fashions, but now principally in rags, and men-of-warsmen who had given themselves up while serving on board English ships rather than fight against their country. These last held themselves rather aloof from the others and messed by themselves. Poor devils, they had never had the satisfaction, even, of having struck a blow. They had turned from one kind of slavery to another; that was all.

The tall, odd-looking figure that Captain Brower had pointed out, belonged to the wildest mess on the orlop deck. His appearance might, perhaps, be called startling; he was far from ill-looking, with straight aquiline features, deep-set and quick black eyes that could laugh or look cruel almost at the same moment. His teeth were beautifully white and even, and although he was not heavy or compact looking, he was as strong almost as any two other men on board the ship. He spoke English without an accent, but with an odd form and phrasing that would have attracted attention to him anywhere. His clear skin was the color of new copper sheathing, and his straight black hair that was gathered sailor fashion into a queue was as coarse as a horse's mane. The grandson of a chief he was, a descendant of the line of kings that had ruled the Narragansett tribes—a full-blooded Indian. But he rejoiced in no fine name.

A sailor before the mast he had been since his sixteenth year, and he had appeared on the books of the privateer brig *Teaser* as John Vance, A.B. It is a wrong supposition that an Indian will never laugh or that he is not a fun-maker. John Vance was constantly skylarking, and he was a leader in that, as he was in almost all the games of skill or strength. Every one liked him, and to a certain extent he was feared, for a tale was told in which John and a knife figured extensively. The flash that would come into his eye gave warning often when the danger limit was being approached, yet he was popular, and even the detested marine guard treated him with some deference. In the last attempt to escape, the Narragansett had been captured after he had swum half-way to the shore and had dived more than twenty times to escape musket-balls from the guard-ships. Suddenly the order came "Prisoners below"—and the ship-bell struck eight sonorous strokes. As the last four or five men left the deck, the Indian touched one of them upon the shoulder.

"Watch me," he said, "and say nothing."

There was a narrow door in a bulkhead close to the companionway, but out of reach unless there was something like a box or barrel on which to stand. It was closed by a padlock thrust through two iron staples. As John descended, he caught the combing of the hatch and drew himself up to a level with his chin. Holding himself there with one arm, he reached forward and caught the padlock in his brown, sinewy fingers. Slowly he turned his hand. The iron bent and gave a little. A grin crossed his face. Swinging himself forward, he landed on a man's shoulders beneath him, and with a wild warwhoop he tumbled a half-dozen down the rest of the ladder, and they sprawled in a heap on the deck. Disdaining to notice the half-humorous curses, he sprang to his feet. Three other men who belonged to his mess followed him.

"Can you do it, Red?" asked one.

"Yes, surely," John replied. "So I can to-night."

The whole of the gun-deck forward of the forecastle hatch had been divided, by a strong partition, into a sort of storeroom. There was one entrance into it from above from the topgallant forecastle, where part of the marine guard were stationed, and the other opening onto the hatchway, to be used in case of emergency.

It was just past the midnight watch when four stealthy figures crept out from the shadows into the light of the dingy lantern that hung at the foot of the companionway. At night there was only one sentry stationed there, and he generally sat halfway up the ladder, and it was impossible for the prisoners to tell without crossing the dead-line that was drawn at night whether he was asleep or not. This was the risk that had to be undertaken; for if the man should see any one pass beneath that old rope that was drawn across the deck, he would have a right to fire. If the fellow was asleep, yet to gain the deck above, the venturesome prisoner would have to pass within arm's length of him.

Perhaps John Vance had inherited from his long line of red ancestors the peculiar knack of moving without sound, the art of crawling on his belly like a snake, perhaps he had acquired it by constant practice since he had been a prisoner. For it was his boast, and one that had been proved to be true, that contrary to rules he had visited every part of the ship, and after hours; as has been told, he had been retaken a number of times when just on the point of making good his escape.

The three seamen who accompanied him on this occasion could see the legs of the sentry from the knee down, as he sat on the steps of the ladder leading to the berth-deck above. They could also see the butt of his musket as it rested beside him. Vance had disappeared in the black shadow that lay along the starboard side, and now the watchers saw a curious thing take place. The sentry's musket suddenly tilted forward, as if of its own volition, and then disappeared backward into the darkness, without a sound, much in the manner of a vanishing slide in a magic lantern. The man's legs did not move.

"He is asleep," whispered Ned Thornton to Bill Pratt.

"He's asleep," reiterated Bill Pratt to Gabe Sackett, who made the fourth one of the "constant plotters," as they were termed by the other prisoners.

But in one minute that sentry was seen to be very wide awake indeed. That is, if movement signified wakefulness. His legs shot out in two vicious and sudden kicks. A hand, with wide-spread, reaching fingers, stretched out as if searching for the missing musket. The man wriggled from one side to another and floundered helplessly, with his body half-way off the edge of the ladder. But not one sound did he utter!

"Red's got hold of him," croaked Thornton, and with the assurance of hunters who had watched their quarry step into the trap that held him fast, they stepped forward without fear or caution.

It was as Thornton had said. The poor sentry's head was wedged against the steps. Around his throat were clasped the fingers of two sinewy, bronze-colored hands that held the victim as closely and in as deadly a clasp as might the strap of the Spanish garrote. The scene was really horrible. Sackett leaned about the edge of the ladder, and then he saw what a wonderful thing the Narragansett had done. The combing of the hatchway was fully six feet from where the sentry sat. Below yawned the black abyss into the mid-hold. Across this Vance had been forced to lean, balancing himself with one hand when he relieved the sentry of his musket, and then springing forward he had caught him from behind, about the throat. There the Indian hung as a man might hang over the mouth of a well. No wonder the unfortunate marine had been unable to cry out!

"Let go of him, Red," whispered Gabe. "You've choked him enough." The Indian stretched out one of his feet and hooked it over the hatch combing. With a supple movement and without a stumble, he stood erect upon the deck. The sentry would have plunged over into the hold, had not the two others grasped him firmly by the shoulders. They carried him to one side and laid him in the deep shadow against a bulkhead. He was breathing, but insensible.

The rest of the escape can be told in a few words: The lock of the door leading into the storeroom was wrenched away, and noiselessly the four entered, closing it behind them. They had been just in time, for they could hear, on the deck above, the new watch coming on. A port on one side of the storeroom was guarded by three flimsy iron bars. There was enough light outside from the young moon to show the direction of the opening.

Vance bent the irons double at the first attempt. They were almost twenty feet above the water, for the old hulk floated high. But everything seemed working for the furtherance of their plan. There was a new coil of rope on the deck, and looking out of the port right beneath them, they could see a ship's dingy with the oars in it. Sackett slid down first; the other two followed, and Vance remained until the last. No sooner had he made the boat in safety than a great hubbub and confusion sounded through the ship. There came a sharp blare of a bugle, the rolling of the alarm drum, and they could hear the slamming of the heavy hatches that prevented communication from one part of the vessel to the other. The prisoners, cooped up below, knew what it all meant. Some one was out, and there in the pitch darkness they fell to cheering.

But to return to the "constant plotters," in the dingy: they had made but a dozen boat's-lengths when they were discovered, for there was light enough to see objects a long distance across the water. There came a quick hail, followed by a spurt of flame.

"Lord!" Pratt, who was pulling stroke oar with Sackett alongside of him, groaned; "I caught that in the shoulder." One of his arms drooped helplessly, but he continued rowing with the other.

"Let go," grunted Sackett; "I can work it alone—lie down in the stern sheets."

There were three or four vessels, mostly prison or sheer hulks, to be passed before they gained the shore. From each one there came a volley. Poor Sackett received a ball through his lungs and fell into the bottom of the boat, bleeding badly. And now the boats were after them!

Vance and Thornton pulled lustily at the oars; but the others gained a foot in every four. The dingy was splintered by the hail of musket-balls. One of the prison hulks—the last they had to pass—let go a carronade loaded with grape. It awoke the echoes of the old town. So close was the charge delivered that it had hardly time to scatter, and churned the water into foam just astern of the little boat as if some one had dumped a bushel of gravel stones into the waters of the harbor. Not three hundred feet ahead of the foremost pursuing boat, the dingy's keel grated on the shingle.

The Narragansett sprang out, Thornton after him. Sackett could not be raised. Pratt, holding his wounded and disabled arm, staggered up the incline towards some stone steps leading to the roadway above. But he had hardly reached the foot when there came another shot. He fell face downward and made no attempt to rise. Sackett and he would join in no more plots; but Vance and Thornton were now running down a side street.

They dodged about a corner into an alley; crossed a small common, and just as they reached the other side they ran, bows on, into a heavy cloaked figure, who, seeing their haste, hailed them peremptorily, and sprang a huge rattle, making much the same noise that a small boy does when he runs down a picket fence with a stick. Thornton was laboring ahead like a wherry in a tideway. But the Indian was striding along like a racehorse, with the easy, springing gait inherited from his own father, "Chief Fleetfoot," who, if the story told be true, could run down a red deer in the woods. He turned to assist his comrade by taking hold of him and giving him a tow. But as he did so, Thornton's foot struck a round stone and he fell forward, and lay there groaning.

"Run on, Red! run on!" he cried breathlessly. "I've broken a leg; something's carried away in my pins; on with you!"

"Come you with me too," answered the Narragansett, pulling Thornton to his feet with one hand; but the poor lad groaned and fell again.

"Run ahead, curse you!" he said. "Don't stay here and be taken!"

The watchman's rattle had attracted the notice of the people in the houses. Windows were opened and heads were thrust forth, and from about a corner came another cloaked figure carrying a lantern, and a big pike was in his hand.

There was nothing else to do, and, obeying Thornton's angry order, the Indian struck out again into his long distance-covering gait. Which way he ran it made little matter to him. He did not know the country; he had no plans; but the feel of the springy earth beneath his feet was good to him. The sight of the stars shining through the branches of the trees overhead—for he had soon reached the open country and left the town behind him—made him breathe the air in long, deep breaths, and tempted him to shout. It was freedom; liberty!

The dim moonlight softened everything, and to his mind he seemed to be flying. He passed by great stone archways leading to private parks and great estates. Twice he had avoided little hamlets of thatched cottages. Once he had run full speed through the streets of a little village, and had been hailed by the watchman, who sprang his harmless rattle. But it was growing light. He must find some place to hide, for travel during the daytime he knew he could not. Leaping a fence, he made his way into an adjoining field and lay down, panting, beneath some bushes.

Soon cocks began to crow; daylight widened; a bell in an ivy-covered tower tolled musically. Insects commenced their morning hum; birds twittered, and people moved out to their toil. From his hiding-place the Narragansett watched the unusual sight. In a field below him—for he lay at the top of a small hill—he could see some men and women working in a field of grain. One of the girls had placed a basket beneath the shade of a bush. The Indian was hungry. It required little trouble to snake himself through the grass and secure the contents of the little hamper, a loaf of bread and a large piece of cheese. Then he carefully replaced the cover and stole back to his former hiding-place. Soon he observed, in the road below him, a man riding along at a fast gait; he pulled in his horse and shouted something to the workers in the field. This done, he rode at top speed into the village. Very soon another horseman appeared, and soon quite a little band of them, among whom was a mounted soldier or two, and three or four in the pink coats of the hunting-field.

But near footsteps sounded. A man in leather gaiters, with a fowling-piece over his shoulder, was coming down a little path from some deep woods on the right. A setter dog played in front of him. The man was reading a freshly printed notice. The ink was smeared from handling. The man spelled it out aloud. "Escaped from the hulks; a dangerous prisoner; a wild American Indian; ten pounds reward," and much more of it.

All of a sudden the dog stopped; then with a short bark, he sprang forward. At the same instant the gamekeeper dropped the printed notice that had been handed to him but a minute previously by a horseman on the road. Surely he could not be mistaken, something had dodged down behind yonder hedge; and as the setter sprang forward, barking viciously, a strange figure arose, a man with a copper-colored face, and streaming, unkempt, black locks; he wore big gold ear-rings, and he was clad in a torn canvas shirt and trousers, with a sailor's neckerchief around his throat.

The dog was bounding forward when suddenly the figure raised its arm. No cricketer that ever played on the village green could throw with such unerring force. A large stone struck the dog and took the fight out of him. Yelping, he sneaked back to his master's heels. The startled gamekeeper raised his gun and fired. Whether it was because of his sudden fright or the quickness with which the agile figure dropped at the flash, the charge whistled harmlessly through the leaves. But the sound of the shot had attracted the attention of the people in the fields. A cry arose, as a weird figure broke from the bushes and dashed down the hill, making for the woods.

"Gone away! gone away! whoop, hi!"—the view hallo of the huntsman.

A man in a red coat had sighted the chase. He leaped a fence, and four or five other horsemen followed. Soon there came the shrill yelping of the dogs as they found the plain trail of the barefoot man running for his life.

It was a great run, that man-hunt, and one remembered to this day. Over fence and hedge, across ditch and stream, the Narragansett led them. No trained hurdler that ever ran across country in the county of Devonshire could have held the pace that Vance kept up. Twice he threw them off the scent by running up a stream and doubling on his tracks. But the whole countryside was out and after him. The dogs were gaining on him swiftly, and at last at the foot of a great oak they had him cornered. He fought them off with a broken branch, and soon the pack surrounded him in a yelping circle, not daring to come nearer.

Up came the huntsmen. They halted at some distance and talked among themselves. Who among them was brave enough to go up and lay hold of this strange wild man? They called off the dogs and waited for the soldiers. Eight or ten yokels and some farmer folks joined the gaping crowd. Five men appeared with muskets, and one with a long coil of rope. But all this time the Narragansett had stood there with his back against an oak tree, with a sneer on his thin lips. They talked aloud as to how they should capture him. Some were for shooting him down at once; but as yet no one had addressed a word to him direct. Surely, he must speak an outlandish foreign tongue! Suddenly, the fugitive took a step forward and raised his hand.

"Englishmen," he said, "listen to me."

All started back in astonishment. Why, this wild man spoke their own language!

"Who is the chief here? Who is the captain?" Every one looked at a middle-aged man astride a sturdy brown cob. He was the Squire, and magistrate of the neighborhood.

"Well, upon my soul," he began, "I suppose—"

But the Narragansett interrupted him. "To you I give myself," he said, advancing. He glanced at the others with supreme contempt. As he came forward, he held out his hand, and involuntarily the man on horseback stretched forth his. It was a strange sight, that greeting. The crowd gave way a little, and three or four mounted dragoons came tearing up hill. They stopped in astonishment.

"You gave us a good run," said the Squire, with some embarrassment, not knowing what to say.

"You are too many; I am your prisoner," was the answer.

No one laid hands on him. Walking beside the Squire's horse down to the road, followed by the gaping, gabbling crowd, who still, however, kept aloof, the Narragansett walked proudly erect. When he reached the highway, he turned. There was a cart standing there. The Squire dismounted from his horse and spoke a few words to the driver.

Then he mounted to the seat. John Vance sprang up beside him. At a brisk pace they started down the road towards Portsmouth, the soldiers and the horsemen trailing on behind them. At the landing where the boat from the old *Spartan* met them—for a horseman had ridden on with the news—was waiting a sergeant of marines. He advanced with a pair of handcuffs.

"None of that!" exclaimed the Squire. "This man has given me his word."

"The word of a chief's son," put in the Narragansett. The two men shook hands again; then proudly John Vance stepped into the boat, and unmanacled sat there in the stern sheets.

In twenty minutes he was once more down in the close, foul-smelling 'tween decks.

The only notice taken of the Narragansett's break for liberty was the fact that he was numbered among the next detail bound for Dartmoor; but the tradition of the man-hunt of Squire Knowlton's hounds, and its curious ending, lives in Devonshire to-day.

4

MUTINY ON BOARD THE SHIP *GLOBE* OF NANTUCKET

WILLIAM LAY AND CYRUS M. HUSSEY

The Ship *Globe*, on board of which vessel occurred the horrid transactions we are about to relate, belonged to the Island of Nantucket; she was owned by Messrs. C. Mitchell, & Co. and other merchants of that place; and commanded on this voyage by Thomas Worth, of Edgartown, Martha's Vineyard. William Beetle, (mate,) John Lumbert, (2d mate,) Nathaniel Fisher, (3d mate,) Gilbert Smith, (boat steerer,) Samuel B. Comstock, do. Stephen Kidder, seaman, Peter C. Kidder, do. Columbus Worth, do. Rowland Jones, do. John Cleveland, do. Constant Lewis, do. Holden Henman, do. Jeremiah Ingham, do. Joseph Ignasius Prass, do. Cyrus M. Hussey, cooper, Rowland Coffin, do. George Comstock, seaman, and William Lay, do.

On the 15th day of December, we sailed from Edgarton, on a whaling voyage, to the Pacific Ocean, but in working out, having carried away the cross-jack-yard, we returned to port, and after having refitted and sent aloft another, we sailed again on the 19th, and on the same day anchored in Holmes' Hole. On the following day a favourable opportunity offering to proceed to sea, we got under way, and after having cleared the land, discharged the pilot, made sail, and performed the necessary duties of stowing the anchors, unbending and coiling away the cables, &c.

On the 1st of January 1823, we experienced a heavy gale from N. W. which was but the first in the catalogue of difficulties we were fated to encounter.—As this was our first trial of a seaman's life, the scene presented to our view, "mid the howling storm," was one of terrific grandeur, as well as of real danger. But as the ship scudded well, and the wind was fair, she was kept before it, under a close reefed main-top-sail and fore-sail, although during the gale, which lasted forty-eight hours, the sea frequently threatened to board us, which was prevented by the skillful management of the helm. On the 9th of January we made the Cape Verd Islands, bearing S. W. twenty-five miles distant, and on the 17th, crossed the Equator. On the 29th of the same month we saw sperm whales, lowered our boats, and succeeded in taking one; the blubber of which, when boiled out, yielded us seventy-five barrels of oil. Pursuing our voyage, on the twenty-third of February we passed the Falkland Islands, and about the 5th of March, doubled the great promontory of South America, Cape Horn, and stood to the Northward.

We saw whales once only before we reached the Sandwich Islands, which we made on the first of May early in the morning. When drawing in with the Island of Hawaii about four in the afternoon, the man at the mast head gave notice that he saw a shoal of black fish on the lee bow; which we soon found to be canoes on their way to meet us. It falling calm at this time prevented their getting along side until night fall, which they did, at a distance of more than three leagues from the land. We received from them a very welcome supply of potatoes, sugar cane, yams, cocoanuts, bananas, fish, &c. for which we gave them in return, pieces of iron hoop, nails, and similar articles. We stood off and on during the next day, and after obtaining a sufficient supply of vegetables and fruit, we shaped our course for Oahu, at which place we arrived on the following day, and after lying there twenty hours, sailed for the coast of Japan, in company with the whaling ships *Palladium* of Boston, and *Pocahontas* of Falmouth; from which ships we parted company when two days out.—After cruising in the Japan seas several months, and obtaining five hundred and fifty barrels of oil, we again shaped our course for the Sandwich Islands, to obtain a supply of vegetables, &c.

While lying at Oahu, six of the men deserted in the night; two of them having been re-taken were put in irons, but one of them having found means to divest himself of his irons, set the other at liberty, and both escaped.

To supply their places, we shipped the following persons, viz: Silas Payne, John Oliver, Anthony Hanson, a native of Oahu, Wm. Humphries, a black man, and steward, and Thomas Lilliston.—Having accommodated ourselves with as many vegetables and much fruit as could be preserved, we again put to sea, fondly anticipating a successful cruise, and a speedy and happy meeting with our friends. After leaving Oahu we ran to the south of the Equator, and after cruising a short time for whales without much success, we steered for Fannings Island, which lies in lat. 3, 49 N. and long. 158, 29 W. While cruising off this Island an event occurred which, whether we consider the want of motives, or the cold blooded and obstinate cruelty with which it was perpetrated, has not often been equalled.

We speak of the want of motives, because, although some occurrences which we shall mention, had given the crew some ground for dissatisfaction, there had been no abuse or severity which could in the least degree excuse or palliate so barbarous a mode of redress and revenge. During our cruise to Japan the season before, many complaints were uttered by the crew among themselves, with respect to the manner and quantity in which they received their *meat*, the quantity sometimes being more than sufficient for the number of men, and at others not enough to supply the ship's company; and it is fair to presume, that the most dissatisfied, deserted the ship at Oahu.

But the reader will no doubt consider it superfluous for us to attempt an unrequired vindication of the conduct of the officers of the *Globe* whose aim was to maintain a correct discipline, which should result in the furtherance of the voyage and be a benefit to all concerned, more especially when he is informed, that part of the men shipped at Oahu, in the room of the deserters, were abandoned wretches, who frequently were the cause of severe reprimands from the officers, and in one instance one of them received a severe flogging.

The reader will also please to bear in mind, that Samuel B. Comstock, the ringleader of the mutiny, was an officer, (being a boat-steerer,) and as is customary, ate in the cabin. The conduct and deportment of the Captain towards this individual, was always decorous and gentlemanly, a proof of intentions long premeditated to destroy the ship. Some of the crew were determined to leave the ship provided she touched at Fannings Island, and we believe had concerted a plan of escape, but of which the perpetration of a deed chilling to humanity, precluded the necessity. We were at this time in company with the ship *Lyra*, of New-Bedford, the Captain of which, had been on board the *Globe* during the most of the day, but had returned in the evening to his own ship. An agreement had been made by him with the Captain of the *Globe*, to set a light at midnight as a signal for tacking.

It may not be amiss to acquaint the reader of the manner in which whalemen keep watch during the night. They generally carry three boats, though some carry four, five, and sometimes six, the *Globe*, however, being of the class carrying three. The Captain, mate, and second mate stand no watch except there is *blubber* to be boiled; the boat-steerers taking charge of the watch and managing the ship with their respective boats crews, and in this instance dividing the night into three parts, each taking a third. It so happened that Smith after keeping the first watch, was relieved by Comstock, (whom we shall call by his surname in contradistinction to his brother George) and the *waist boat's crew*, and the former watch retired below to their berths and hammocks. George Comstock took the helm, and during his *trick*, received orders from his brother to "keep the ship a good full," swearing that the ship was too nigh the wind.

When his time at the helm had expired he took the *rattle*, (an instrument used by whalemen, to announce the expiration of the hour, the watch, &c.) and began to shake it, when Comstock came to him, and in the most peremptory manner, ordered him to desist, saying "if you make the least damn bit of noise I'll send you to hell!" He then lighted a lamp and went into the steerage. George becoming alarmed at this conduct of his unnatural brother, again took the *rattle* for the purpose of alarming some one; Comstock arrived in time to prevent him, and with threatenings dark and diabolical, so congealed the blood of his trembling brother, that even had he possessed the power of alarming the unconscious and fated victims below, his life would have been the forfeit of his temerity!

Comstock, now laid something heavy upon a small work bench near the cabin gangway, which was afterwards found to be a boarding knife. It is an instrument used by whalers to cut the *blubber* when hoisting it in, is about four feet in length, two or three inches wide, and necessarily kept very sharp, and for greater convenience when in use, is two edged.

In giving a detail of this chilling transaction, we shall be guided by the description given of it by the younger Comstock, who, as has been observed, was upon deck at the time, and afterwards learned several particulars from his brother, to whom alone they could have been known. Comstock went down into the cabin, accompanied by Silas Payne or Paine, of Sag-Harbour, John Oliver, of Shields, Eng., William Humphries, (the steward) of Philadelphia, and Thomas Lilliston; the latter, however, went no farther than the cabin gangway, and then ran forward and *turned in*. According to his own story he did not think they would attempt to put their designs in execution, until he saw them actually descending into the cabin, having gone so far, to use his own expression, to show himself as brave as any of them. But we believe he had not the smallest idea of assisting the villains. Comstock entered the cabin so silently as not to be perceived by the man at the helm, who was first apprised of his having begun the work of death, by the sound of a heavy blow with an axe, which he distinctly heard.

The Captain was asleep in a hammock, suspended in the cabin, his state room being uncomfortably warm; Comstock approaching him with the axe, struck him a blow upon the head, which was nearly severed in two by the first stroke! After repeating the blow, he ran to Payne, who it seems was stationed with the before mentioned boarding knife, to attack the mate, as soon as the Captain was killed. At this instant, Payne making a thrust at the mate, he awoke, and terrified, exclaimed, "what! what! what!" "Is this—Oh! Payne! Oh! Comstock!" "Don't kill me, don't;" "have I not always—"

Here Comstock interrupted him, saying, "Yes! you have always been a d—d rascal; you tell lies of me out of the ship will you? It's a d—d good time to beg now, but you're too late," here the mate sprang, and grasped him by the throat. In the scuffle, the light which Comstock held in his hand was knocked out, and the axe fell from his hand; but the grasp of Mr. Beetle upon his throat, did not prevent him from making Payne understand that his weapon was lost, who felt about until he found it, and having given it to Comstock, he managed to strike him a blow upon the head, which fractured his skull; when he fell into the pantry where he lay groaning until despatched by Comstock! The steward held a light at this time, while Oliver put in a blow as often as possible!

The second and third mates, fastened in their state rooms, lay in their berths listening, fearing to speak, and being ignorant of the numerical strength of the mutineers, and unarmed, thought it best to wait the dreadful issue, hoping that their lives might yet be spared.

Comstock leaving a watch at the second mate's door, went upon deck to light another lamp at the binnacle, it having been again accidentally extinguished. He was there asked by his terrified brother, whose agony of mind we will not attempt to portray, if he intended to hurt Smith, the other boat-steerer. He replied that he did; and inquired where he was. George fearing that Smith would be immediately pursued, said he had not seen him.—Comstock then perceiving his brother to be shedding tears, asked sternly, "What are you crying about?" "I am afraid," replied George, "that they will hurt me!" "I *will* hurt you," said he, "if you talk in that manner!"

But the work of death was not yet finished. Comstock, took his light into the cabin, and made preparations for attacking the second and third mates, Mr. Fisher, and Mr. Lumbert. After loading two muskets, he fired one through the door, in the direction as near as he could judge of the officers, and then inquired if either was shot! Fisher replied, "yes, I am shot in the mouth!" Previous to his shooting Fisher,

Lumbert asked if he was going to kill him? To which he answered with apparent unconcern, "Oh no, I guess not."

They now opened the door, and Comstock making a pass at Mr. Lumbert, missed him, and fell into the state room. Mr. Lumbert collared him, but he escaped from his hands. Mr. Fisher had got the gun, and actually presented the bayonet to the monster's heart! But Comstock assuring him that his life should be spared if he gave it up, he did so; when Comstock immediately ran Mr. Lumbert through the body several times!!

He then turned to Mr. Fisher, and told him there was no hope for *him*!!—"You have got to die," said he, "remember the scrape you got me into, when in company with the *Enterprise* of Nantucket." The "scrape" alluded to, was as follows. Comstock came up to Mr. Fisher to wrestle with him.—Fisher being the most athletic of the two, handled him with so much ease, that Comstock in a fit of passion *struck him*. At this Fisher seized him, and laid him upon deck several times in a pretty rough manner.

Comstock then made some violent threats, which Fisher paid no attention to, but which now fell upon his soul with all the horrors of reality. Finding his cruel enemy deaf to his remonstrances, and entreaties, he said, "If there is no hope, I will at least die like a man!" and having by order of Comstock, turned back too, said in a firm voice, "*I am ready!!*"

Comstock then put the muzzle of the gun to his head, and fired, which instantly put an end to his existence!—Mr. Lumbert, during this time, was begging for life, although no doubt mortally wounded. Comstock, turned to him and said, "I am a bloody man! I have a bloody hand and *will* be avenged!" and *again* run him through the body with a bayonet! He then begged for a little water; "I'll give you water," said he, and once more plunging the weapon in his body, left him for dead!

Thus it appears that this more than demon, murdered with his own hand, the whole! Gladly would we wash from "memory's waste" all remembrance of that bloody night. The compassionate reader, however, whose heart sickens within him, at the perusal, as does ours at the recital, of this tale of woe, will not, we hope, disapprove our publishing these melancholy facts to the world. As, through the boundless mercy of Providence, we have been restored, to the bosom of our families and homes, we deemed it a duty we owe to the world, to record our "unvarnished tale."

Smith, the other boat-steerer, who had been marked as one of the victims, on hearing the noise in the cabin, went aft, apprehending an altercation between the Captain and some of the other officers, little dreaming that innocent blood was flowing in torrents. But what was his astonishment, when he beheld Comstock, brandishing the boarding knife, and heard him exclaim, "I am the bloody man, and will have revenge!" Horror struck, he hurried forward, and asked the crew in the forecastle, what he should do.

Some urged him to secrete himself in the hold, others to go aloft until Comstock's rage should be abated; but alas! the reflection that the ship afforded no secure hiding place, determined him to confront the ringleader, and if he could not save his life by fair means, to sell it dearly! He was soon called for by Comstock, who upon meeting him, threw his bloody arms around his neck, and embracing him, said, "you are going to be with us, are you not?" The reader will discover the good policy of Smith when he unhesitatingly answered, "Oh, yes, I will do any thing you require."

All hands were now called to make sail, and a light at the same time was set as a signal for the *Lyra* to tack;—while the *Globe* was kept upon the same tack, which very soon caused a separation of the two ships.

All the reefs were turned out, top-gallant-sails set, and all sail made on the ship, the wind being quite light.

The mutineers then threw the body of the Captain overboard, after wantonly piercing his bowels with a boarding knife, which was *driven with an axe*, until the point protruded from his throat!! In Mr. Beetle, the mate, the lamp of life had not entirely gone out, but he was committed to the deep.

Orders were next given to have the bodies of Mr. Fisher, and Mr. Lumbert brought up. A rope was fastened to Fisher's neck, by which he was hauled upon deck. A rope was made fast to Mr. Lumbert's feet, and in this way was he got upon deck, but when in the act of being thrown from the ship, he caught the plank-shear; and appealed to Comstock, reminding him of his promise to save him, but in vain; for the monster forced him from his hold, and he fell into the sea! As he appeared to be yet capable of swimming, a boat was ordered to be lowered, to pursue and finish him, fearing he might be picked up by the *Lyra*; which order was as soon countermanded as given, fearing, no doubt, a desertion of his murderous companions.

We will now present the reader, with a journal of our passage to the Mulgrave Islands, for which group we shaped our course.

1824, Jan. 26th. At 2 A. M. from being nearly calm a light breeze sprung up, which increased to a fresh breeze by 4 A. M. This day cleaned out the cabin, which was a scene of blood and destruction of which the recollection at this day chills the blood in our veins.—Every thing bearing marks of the murder, was brought on deck and washed.

Lat. 5° 50' N. Long. 159° 13' W.

Jan. 27th. These twenty-four hours commenced with moderate breezes from the eastward. Middle and latter part calm. Employed in cleaning the small arms which were fifteen in number, and making cartridge boxes.

Lat. 3° 45' N. Long. 160° 45' W.

Jan. 28. This day experienced fine weather, and light breezes from N. by W. The black steward was hung for the following crime.

George Comstock who was appointed steward after the mutiny, and business calling him into the cabin, he saw the former steward, now called the purser, engaged in loading a pistol. He asked him what he was doing that for. His reply was, "I have heard something very strange, and I'm going to be ready for it." This information was immediately carried to Comstock, who called to Payne, now mate, and bid him follow him.

On entering the cabin they saw Humphreys, still standing with the pistol in his hand. On being demanded what he was going to do with it, he said he had heard something which made him afraid of his life!

Comstock told him if he had heard any thing, that he ought to have come to him, and let him know, before he began loading pistols. He then demanded to know, what he had heard. Humphreys answered at first in a very suspicious and ambiguous manner, but at length said, that Gilbert Smith, the boat-steerer who was saved, and Peter Kidder, were going to re-take the ship. This appeared highly improbable, but they were summoned to attend a council at which Comstock presided, and asked if they had entertained any such intentions.

They positively denied ever having had conversation upon the subject. All this took place in the evening. The next morning the parties were summoned, and a jury of two men called. Humphreys under a guard of six men, armed with muskets, was arraigned, and Smith and Kidder, seated upon a chest near him. The prisoner was asked a few questions touching his intentions, which he answered but low and indistinctly. The trial, if it may be so called, had progressed thus far, when Comstock made a speech in the following words. "It appears that William Humphreys *has been accused guilty*, of a *treacherous and base act*, in loading a pistol for the purpose of shooting Mr. Payne and myself. Having been tried the jury will now give in their verdict, whether Guilty or Not Guilty. If guilty he shall be hanged to a studding-sail boom, rigged out eight feet upon the fore-yard, but if found not guilty, Smith and Kidder, shall be hung upon the aforementioned gallows!"

But the doom of Humphreys had been sealed the night before, and kept secret *except from the jury*, who returned a verdict of Guilty.— Preparations were immediately made for his execution! His watch was taken from him, and he was then taken forward and seated upon the rail, with a cap drawn over his face, and the rope placed round his neck.

Every man was ordered to take hold of the execution rope, to be ready to run him up when Comstock should give the signal, by ringing the ship's bell!

He was now asked if he had any thing to say, as he had but fourteen seconds to live! He began by saying, "little did I think I was born to come to this—"; the bell struck! and he was immediately swung to the yard-arm! He died without a struggle; and after he had hung a few minutes, the rope was cut, to let him fall overboard, but getting entangled aloft, the body was towed some distance along side, when a *runner hook* was attached to it, to sink it, when the rope was again cut and the body disappeared. His chest was now overhauled, and sixteen dollars in specie found, which he had taken from the Captain's trunk. Thus ended the life of one of the mutineers, while the blood of innocent victims was scarcely washed from his hands, much less the guilty stain from his soul.

Feb. 7th. These twenty-four hours commenced with thick squally weather. Middle part clear and fine weather.—Hove to at 2 A. M., and at 6 made sail, and steered W. by S. At ½ past 8 made an Island ahead, one of the Kingsmill group. Stood in with the land and received a number of canoes along side, the natives in them however having nothing to sell us but a few beads of their own manufacture. We saw some cocoanut, and other trees upon the shore, and discovered many of the natives upon the beach, and some dogs. The principal food of these Islanders is, a kind of bread fruit, which they pound very fine and mix it with fish.

Feb. 8. Commences squally with fresh breezes from the northward.—Took a departure from Kingsmill Island; one of the group of that name, in Lat. 1° 27' N. and Long. 175° 14' E. In the morning passed through the channel between Marshall's and Gilbert's Islands; luffed to and despatched a boat to Marshall's Island, but did not land, as the natives appeared hostile, and those who swam off to the boat, endeavoured to steal from her. When about to leave, a volley of musketry was discharged at them, which probably killed or wounded some of them. The boat then gave chase to a canoe, paddled by two of the natives, which were fired upon when within gunshot, when they immediately ceased paddling; and on the boat approaching them, discovered that one of the natives was wounded. In the most supplicating manner they held up a jacket, manufactured from a kind of flag, and some beads, being all they possessed, giving their inhuman pursuers to understand, that all should be theirs if they would spare their lives! The wounded native laid down in the bottom of the boat, and from his convulsed frame and trembling lip, no doubt remained but that the wound was mortal. The boat then returned on board and we made sail for the Mulgrave Islands. Here was another sacrifice; an innocent child of nature shot down, merely to gratify the most wanton and unprovoked cruelty, which could possibly possess the heart of man. The unpolished savage, a stranger to the more tender sympathies of the human heart, which are cultivated and enjoyed by civilized nations, nurtures in his bosom a flame of revenge, which only the blood of those who have injured him, can damp; and when years have rolled away, this act of cruelty will be remembered by these Islanders, and made the pretext to slaughter every white man who may fall into their hands.

Feb. 11th. Commenced with strong breezes from the Northward. At ½ past meridian made the land bearing E. N. E. four leagues distant. Stood in and received a number of canoes along side. Sent a boat on shore; and brought off a number of women, a large quantity of cocoanuts, and some fish.—Stood off shore most of the night, and

Feb. 12th, in the morning stood in shore again and landed the women.—We then stood along shore looking out for an anchorage, and reconnoitering the country, in the hope of finding some spot suitable for cultivation; but in this we were disappointed, or more properly speaking, they, the mutineers; for we had no will of our own, while our bosoms were torn with the most conflicting passions, in which Hope and Despair alternately gained the ascendency.

Feb. 13th. After having stood off all night, we in the morning stood in, and after coasting the shores of several small Islands, we came to one, low and narrow, where it was determined the Ship should be anchored. When nearly ready to let go, a man was sent into the chains to sound, who pronounced twelve fathoms; but at the next cast, could not get bottom. We continued to stand in, until we got regular sounding, and anchored within five rods of the shore, on a coral rock bottom, in seven fathoms water. The ship was then moored with a kedge astern, sails furled, and all hands retired to rest, except an *anchor watch*.

Feb. 14th, was spent in looking for a landing place. In the morning a boat was sent to the Eastward, but returned with the information that no good landing place could be found, the shore being very rocky. At 2 P. M. she was sent in an opposite direction, but returned at night without having met with better success; when it was determined to land at the place where we lay; notwithstanding it was very rocky.—Nothing of consequence was done, until

Sunday, 15th Feb. 1824, when all hands were set to work to construct a raft out of the spare spars, upon which to convey the provisions, &c. on shore.

The laws by which we were now governed had been made by Comstock, soon after the mutiny, and read as follows:

"That if any one saw a sail and did not report it immediately, he should be put to death! If any one refused to fight a ship he should be put to death; and the manner of their death, this—They shall be bound hand and foot and boiled in the *try pots*, of boiling oil!" Every man was made to seal and sign this instrument, the seals of the mutineers being *black*, and the remainder, *blue* and *white*. The raft or stage being completed, it was anchored, so that one end rested upon the rocks, the other being kept sea-ward by the anchor.

During the first day many articles were brought from the ship in boats, to the raft, and from thence conveyed on shore. Another raft, however, was made, by laying spars upon two boats, and boards again upon them, which at high water would float well up on the shore. The following, as near as can be recollected, were the articles landed from the ship; (and the intention was, when all should have been got on shore, to haul the ship on shore, or as near it as possible and burn her.) One mainsail, one foresail, one mizen-topsail, one spanker, one driver, one maintop gallantsail, two lower studdingsails, two royals, two top-mast-studdingsails, two top-gallant-studdingsails, one mizen-staysail, two mizen-top-gallantsails, one fly-gib, (thrown overboard, being a little torn,) three boat's sails (new,) three or four casks of bread, eight or ten barrels of flour, forty barrels of beef and pork, three or more 60 gal. casks of molasses, one and a half barrels of sugar, one barrel dried apples, one cask vinegar, two casks of rum, one or two barrels domestic coffee, one keg W. I. coffee, one and a half chests of tea, one barrel of pickles, one do. cranberries, one box chocolate, one cask of tow-lines, three or more coils of cordage, one coil rattling, one do. lance warp, ten or fifteen balls spunyarn, one do. worming, one stream cable, one larboard bower anchor, all the spare spars, every chest of clothing, most of the ship's tools, &c. &c. The ship by this time was considerably unrigged.

On the following day, Monday 16th February, Payne the second in the mutiny, who was on board the ship attending to the discharge of articles from her, sent word to Comstock, who with Gilbert Smith and a number of the crew were on shore, attending to the landing of the raft; "That if he did not act differently with regard to the plunder, such as making presents to the natives of the officers' fine clothing, &c. he would do no more, but quit the ship and come on shore."

Comstock had been very liberal to the natives in this way, and his object was, no doubt, to attach them as much as possible to his person, as it must have been suggested to his guilty mind, that however he himself might have become a misanthrope, yet there were those around him, whose souls shuddered at the idea of being forever exiled from their country and friends, whose hands were yet unstained by blood, but who might yet imbrue them, for the purpose of escape from lonely exile, and cruel tyranny.

When the foregoing message was received from Payne, Comstock commanded his presence immediately on shore, and interrogated him, as to what he meant by sending such a message. After considerable altercation, which took place in the tent, Comstock was heard to say, "I helped to take the ship, and have navigated her to this place.—I have also done all I could to get the sails and rigging on shore, and now you may do what you please with her; but if any man wants any thing of *me*, I'll take a musket with him!"

"That is what I want," replied Payne, "and am ready!" This was a check upon the murderer, who had now the offer of becoming a duellist; and he only answered by saying, "I will go on board once more, and then you may do as you please."

He then went on board, and after destroying the paper upon which were recorded the "Laws," returned, went into the tent with Payne, and putting a sword into a scabbard, exclaimed, *"this* shall stand by me as long as I live."

We ought not to omit to mention that during the time he was on board the ship, he challenged the persons there, to fight him, and as he was leaving, exclaimed "I am going to leave you; *Look out for yourselves!"*

After obtaining from Payne permission to carry with him a cutlass, a knife, and some hooks and lines, he took his departure, and as was afterwards ascertained, immediately joined a gang of natives, and endeavoured to excite them to slay Payne and his companions! At dusk of this day he passed the tent, accompanied by about 50 of the natives, in a direction of their village, upwards of a league distant. Payne came on board, and after expressing apprehensions that Comstock would persuade the natives to kill us all, picked out a number of the crew to go on shore for the night, and stationed sentinels around the tent, with orders to shoot any one, who should attempt to approach without giving the countersign. The night, however, passed, without any one's appearing; but early on the morning of the

17th Feb.; Comstock was discovered at some distance coming towards the tent. It had been before proposed to Smith by Payne, to shoot him; but poor Smith like ourselves, dare do no other than remain upon the side of neutrality.

Oliver, whom the reader will recollect as one of the wretches concerned in the mutiny, hurried on shore, and with Payne and others, made preparations to put him to death. After loading a number of muskets they stationed themselves in front of the tent, and waited his approach—a bushy spot of ground intervening, he did not make his appearance until within a short distance of the tent, which, as soon as he saw, drew his sword and walked quick towards it, in a menacing manner; but as soon as he saw a number of the muskets levelled at him, he waved his hand, and cried out, "don't shoot me, don't shoot me! I will not hurt you!" At this moment they fired, and he fell!—Payne fearing he might *pretend* to be shot, ran to him with an axe, and nearly severed his head from his body! There were four muskets fired at him, but only two balls took effect, one entered his right breast, and passed out near the back bone, the other through his head.

Thus ended the life, of perhaps as cruel, blood-thirsty, and vindictive a being as ever bore the form of humanity.

All hands were now called to attend his burial, which was conducted in the same inconsistent manner which had marked the proceedings of the actors in this tragedy. While some were engaged in sewing the body in a piece of canvas, others were employed in digging a grave in the sand, adjacent to the place of his decease, which, by order of Payne, was made five feet deep. Every article attached to him, including his cutlass, was buried with him, except his watch; and the ceremonies consisted in *reading a chapter from the bible over him, and firing a musket!*

Only twenty-two days had elapsed after the perpetration of the massacre on board the ship, when with all his sins upon his head, he was hurried into eternity!

No duty was done during the remainder of the day, except the selection by Payne, of six men, to go on board the ship and take charge of her, under the command of Smith; who had communicated his intentions to a number of running away with the ship. We think we cannot do better than to give an account of their escape in the words of Smith himself. It may be well to remark, that Payne had ordered the two binnacle compasses to be brought on shore, they being the only ones remaining on board, except a hanging compass suspended in the cabin. Secreting one of the binnacle compasses, he took the hanging compass on shore, and the exchange was not discovered.

"At 7 P. M. we began to make preparations for our escape with the ship.—I went below to prepare some weapons for our defence should we be attacked by Payne, while the others, as silently as possible, were employed in clearing the running rigging, for every thing was in the utmost confusion. Having found one musket, three bayonets, and some whale lances, they were laid handy, to prevent the ship being boarded. A handsaw well greased was laid upon the windlass to saw off the cable, and the only remaining hatchet on board, was placed by the mizen mast, to cut the stern moorings when the ship should have sufficiently swung off. Taking one man with me, we went upon the fore-top-sail-yard, loosed the sail and turned out the reefs, while two others were loosing the main-top-sail and main sail. I will not insult the reader's good sense, by assuring him, that this was a duty, upon the success of which seemed to hang our very existence. By this time the moon was rising, which rendered it dangerous to delay, for those who had formed a resolution to swim on board, and accompany us. The *bunts* of the sails being yet confined aloft, by their respective gaskets, I sent a man on the fore-yard and another upon the fore-top-sail-yard, with orders to *let fall*, when I should give the word; one man being at the helm, and two others at the fore tack.

"It was now half past nine o'clock, when I took the handsaw, and in less than two minutes the cable was off!—The ship *payed off* very quick, and when her head was off the land, there being a breeze from that quarter, the hawser was cut and all the sail we could make upon the ship immediately set, a fine fair wind blowing. A raft of iron hoops, which was towing along side, was cut adrift, and we congratulated each other upon our fortunate escape; for even with a vast extent of ocean to traverse, hope excited in our bosoms a belief that we should again embrace our friends, and our joy was heightened by the reflection, that we might be the means of rescuing the innocents left behind, and having the guilty punished."

After a long and boisterous passage the ship arrived at Valparaiso, when she was taken possession of by the American Consul, Michael Hogan, Esq. and the persons on board were put in irons on board a French frigate, there being no American man-of-war in port. Their names were, Gilbert Smith, George Comstock, Stephen Kidder, Joseph Thomas, Peter C. Kidder, and Anthony Henson.

5

ON THE GRAND BANKS

RUDYARD KIPLING

To the end of his days, Harvey will never forget that sight. The sun was just clear of the horizon they had not seen for nearly a week, and his low red light struck into the riding-sails of three fleets of anchored schooners—one to the north, one to the westward, and one to the south. There must have been nearly a hundred of them, of every possible make and build, with, far away, a square-rigged Frenchman, all bowing and courtesying one to the other. From every boat dories were dropping away like bees from a crowded hive; and the clamour of voices, the rattling of ropes and blocks, and the splash of the oars carried for miles across the heaving water. The sails turned all colours, black, pearly-grey, and white, as the sun mounted; and more boats swung up through the mists to the southward.

The dories gathered in clusters, separated, reformed, and broke again, all heading one way; while men hailed and whistled and cat-called and sang, and the water was speckled with rubbish thrown over-board.

"It's a town," said Harvey. "Disko was right. It is a town!"

"I've seen smaller," said Disko. "There's about a thousand men here; an' yonder's the Virgin." He pointed to a vacant space of greenish sea, where there were no dories.

The "We're Here" skirted round the northern squadron, Disko waving his hand to friend after friend, and anchored as neatly as a racing yacht at the end of the season. The Bank fleet pass good seamanship in silence; but a bungler is jeered all along the line.

"Jest in time fer the caplin," cried the Mary Chilton.

"'Salt 'most wet?" asked the King Philip.

"Hey, Tom Platt! Come t' supper to-night?" said the Henry Clay; and so questions and answers flew back and forth. Men had met one another before, dory-fishing in the fog, and there is no place for gossip like the Bank fleet. They all seemed to know about Harvey's rescue, and asked if he were worth his salt yet. The young bloods jested with Dan, who had a lively tongue of his own, and inquired after their health by the town—nicknames they least liked. Manuel's countrymen jabbered at him in their own language; and even the silent cook was seen riding the jib-boom and shouting Gaelic to a friend as black as himself. After they had buoyed the cable—all around the Virgin is rocky bottom, and carelessness means chafed ground-tackle and danger from drifting—after they had buoyed the cable, their dories went forth to join the mob of boats anchored about a mile away. The schooners rocked and dipped at a safe distance, like mother ducks watching their brood, while the dories behaved like mannerless ducklings.

As they drove into the confusion, boat banging boat, Harvey's ears tingled at the comments on his rowing. Every dialect from Labrador to Long Island, with Portuguese, Neapolitan, Lingua Franca, French, and Gaelic, with songs and shoutings and new oaths, rattled round him, and he seemed to be the butt of it all. For the first time in his life he felt shy—perhaps that came from living so long with only the "We're Heres"—among the scores of wild faces that rose and fell with the reeling small craft. A gentle, breathing swell, three furlongs from trough to barrel, would quietly shoulder up a string of variously painted dories. They hung for an instant, a wonderful frieze against the sky-line, and their men pointed and hailed. Next moment the open mouths, waving arms, and bare chests disappeared, while on another swell came up an entirely new line of characters like paper figures in a toy theatre. So Harvey stared. "Watch out!" said Dan, flourishing a dip-net. "When I tell you dip, you dip. The caplin'll school any time from naow on. Where'll we lay, Tom Platt?"

Pushing, shoving, and hauling, greeting old friends here and warning old enemies there, Commodore Tom Platt led his little fleet well to leeward of the general crowd, and immediately three or four men began to haul on their anchors with intent to lee-bow the "We're Heres." But a yell of laughter went up as a dory shot from her station with exceeding speed, its occupant pulling madly on the roding.

"Give her slack!" roared twenty voices. "Let him shake it out."

"What's the matter?" said Harvey, as the boat flashed away to the southward. "He's anchored, isn't he?"

"Anchored, sure enough, but his graound-tackle's kinder shifty," said Dan, laughing. "Whale's fouled it. . . . Dip, Harve! Here they come!"

The sea round them clouded and darkened, and then frizzed up in showers of tiny silver fish, and over a space of five or six acres the cod began to leap like trout in May; while behind the cod three or four broad grey-black backs broke the water into boils.

Then everybody shouted and tried to haul up his anchor to get among the school, and fouled his neighbour's line and said what was in his heart, and dipped furiously with his dip-net, and shrieked cautions and advice to his companions, while the deep fizzed like freshly opened soda-water, and cod, men, and whales together flung in upon the luckless bait. Harvey was nearly knocked overboard by the handle of Dan's net. But in all the wild tumult he noticed, and never forgot, the wicked, set little eye—something like a circus elephant's eye—of a whale that drove along almost level with the water, and, so he said, winked at him. Three boats found their rodings fouled by these reckless mid-sea hunters, and were towed half a mile ere their horses shook the line free.

Then the caplin moved off and five minutes later there was no sound except the splash of the sinkers overside, the flapping of the cod, and the whack of the muckles as the men stunned them. It was wonderful fishing. Harvey could see the glimmering cod below, swimming slowly in droves, biting as steadily as they swam. Bank law strictly forbids more than one hook on one line when the dories are on the Virgin or the Eastern Shoals; but so close lay the boats that even single hooks snarled, and Harvey found himself in hot argument with a gentle, hairy Newfoundlander on one side and a howling Portuguese on the other.

Worse than any tangle of fishing-lines was the confusion of the dory-rodings below water. Each man had anchored where it seemed good to him, drifting and rowing round his fixed point. As the fish struck on less quickly, each man wanted to haul up and get to better ground; but every third man found himself intimately connected with some four or five neighbours. To cut another's roding is crime unspeakable on the Banks; yet it was done, and done without detection, three or four times that day. Tom Platt caught a Maine man in the black act and knocked him over the gunwale with an oar, and Manuel served a fellow-countryman in the same way. But Harvey's anchor-line was cut, and so was Penn's, and they were turned into relief-boats to carry fish to the "We're Here" as the dories filled. The caplin schooled once more at twilight, when the mad clamour was repeated; and at dusk they rowed back to dress down by the light of kerosene-lamps on the edge of the pen.

It was a huge pile, and they went to sleep while they were dressing. Next day several boats fished right above the cap of the Virgin; and Harvey, with them, looked down on the very weed of that lonely rock, which rises to within twenty feet of the surface. The cod were there in legions, marching solemnly over the leathery kelp. When they bit, they bit all together; and so when they stopped. There was a slack time at noon, and the dories began to search for amusement. It was Dan who sighted the Hope of Prague just coming up, and as her boats joined the company they were greeted with the question: "Who's the meanest man in the Fleet?"

Three hundred voices answered cheerily:

"Nick Bra-ady." It sounded an organ chant.

"Who stole the lamp-wicks?" That was Dan's contribution.

"Nick Bra-ady," sang the boats.

"Who biled the salt bait fer soup?" This was an unknown backbiter a quarter of a mile away.

Again the joyful chorus. Now, Brady was not especially mean, but he had that reputation, and the Fleet made the most of it. Then they discovered a man from a Truro boat who, six years before, had been convicted of using a tackle with five or six hooks—a "scrowger," they call it—on the Shoals. Naturally, he had been christened "Scrowger Jim"; and though he had hidden himself on the Georges ever since, he found his honours waiting for him full blown. They took it up in a sort of fire-cracker chorus: "Jim! O Jim! Jim! O Jim! Ssscrowger Jim!" That pleased everybody. And when a poetical Beverly man—he had been making it up all day, and talked about it for weeks—sang, "The Carrie Pitman's anchor doesn't hold her for a cent!" the dories felt that they were indeed fortunate. Then they had to ask that Beverly man how he was off for beans, because even poets must not have things all their own way. Every schooner and nearly every man got it in turn. Was there a careless or dirty cook anywhere? The dories sang about him and his food. Was a schooner badly found? The Fleet was told at full length. Had a man hooked tobacco from a messmate? He was named in meeting; the name tossed from roller to roller. Disko's infallible judgments, Long Jack's market-boat that he had sold years ago, Dan's sweetheart (oh, but Dan was an angry boy!), Penn's bad luck with dory-anchors, Salters's views on manure, Manuel's little slips from virtue ashore, and Harvey's ladylike handling of the oar—all were laid before the public; and as the fog fell around them in silvery sheets beneath the sun, the voices sounded like a bench of invisible judges pronouncing sentence.

The dories roved and fished and squabbled till a swell underran the sea. Then they drew more apart to save their sides, and some one called that if the swell continued the Virgin would break. A reckless Galway man with his nephew denied this, hauled up anchor, and rowed over the very rock itself. Many voices called them to come away, while others dared them to hold on. As the smooth-backed rollers passed to the south-ward, they hove the dory high and high into the mist, and dropped her in ugly, sucking, dimpled water, where she spun round her anchor, within a foot or two of the hidden rock. It was playing with death for mere bravado; and the boats looked on in uneasy silence till Long Jack rowed up behind his countrymen and quietly cut their roding.

"Can't ye hear ut knockin'?" he cried. "Pull for your miserable lives! Pull!"

The men swore and tried to argue as the boat drifted; but the next swell checked a little, like a man tripping on a carpet. There was a deep sob and a gathering roar, and the Virgin flung up a couple of acres of foaming water, white, furious, and ghastly over the shoal sea. Then all the boats greatly applauded Long Jack, and the Galway men held their tongue.

"Ain't it elegant?" said Dan, bobbing like a young seal at home. "She'll break about once every ha'af hour now, 'less the swell piles up good. What's her reg'lar time when she's at work, Tom Platt?"

"Once ivry fifteen minutes, to the tick. Harve, you've seen the greatest thing on the Banks; an' but for Long Jack you'd seen some dead men too."

There came a sound of merriment where the fog lay thicker and the schooners were ringing their bells. A big bark nosed cautiously out of the mist, and was received with shouts and cries of, "Come along, darlin'," from the Irishry.

"Another Frenchman?" said Harvey.

"Hain't you eyes? She's a Baltimore boat; goin' in fear an' tremblin'," said Dan. "We'll guy the very sticks out of her. 'Guess it's the fust time her skipper ever met up with the Fleet this way."

She was a black, buxom, eight-hundred-ton craft. Her mainsail was looped up, and her topsail flapped undecidedly in what little wind was moving. Now a bark is feminine beyond all other daughters of the sea, and this tall, hesitating creature, with her white and gilt figurehead, looked just like a bewildered woman half lifting her skirts to cross a muddy street under the jeers of bad little boys. That was very much her situation. She knew she was somewhere in the neighbourhood of the Virgin, had caught the roar of it, and was, therefore, asking her way. This is a small part of what she heard from the dancing dories:

"The Virgin? Fwhat are you talk in' of'? This is Le Have on a Sunday mornin'. Go home an' sober up."

"Go home, ye tarrapin! Go home an' tell 'em we're comin'."

Half a dozen voices together, in a most tuneful chorus, as her stern went down with a roll and a bubble into the troughs: "Thay-aah—she—strikes!"

"Hard up! Hard up fer your life! You're on top of her now."

"Daown! Hard daown! Let go everything!"

"All hands to the pumps!"

"Daown jib an' pole her!"

Here the skipper lost his temper and said things. Instantly fishing was suspended to answer him, and he heard many curious facts about his boat and her next port of call. They asked him if he were insured; and whence he had stolen his anchor, because, they said, it belonged to the Carrie Pitman; they called his boat a mud-scow, and accused him of dumping garbage to frighten the fish; they offered to tow him and charge it to his wife; and one audacious youth slipped almost under the counter, smacked it with his open palm, and yelled: "Gid up, Buck!"

The cook emptied a pan of ashes on him, and he replied with cod-heads. The bark's crew fired small coal from the galley, and the dories threatened to come aboard and "razee" her. They would have warned her at once had she been in real peril; but, seeing her well clear of the Virgin, they made the most of their chances. The fun was spoilt when the rock spoke again, a half-mile to windward, and the tormented bark set everything that would draw and went her ways; but the dories felt that the honours lay with them.

All that night the Virgin roared hoarsely and next morning, over an angry, white-headed sea, Harvey saw the Fleet with flickering masts waiting for a lead. Not a dory was hove out till ten o'clock, when the two Jeraulds of the Day's Eye, imagining a lull which did not exist, set the example. In a minute half the boats were out and bobbing in the cockly swells, but Troop kept the "We're Heres" at work dressing-down. He saw no sense in "dares"; and as the storm grew that evening they had the pleasure of receiving wet strangers only too glad to make any refuge in the gale. The boys stood by the dory-tackles with lanterns, the men ready to haul, one eye cocked for the sweeping wave that would make them drop everything and hold on for the dear life. Out of the dark would come a yell of "Dory, dory!" They would hook up and haul in a drenched man and a half-sunk boat, till their decks were littered down with nests of dories and the bunks were full. Five times in their watch did Harvey, with Dan, jump at the foregaff where it lay lashed on the boom, and cling with arms, legs, and teeth to rope and spar and sodden canvas as a big wave filled the decks. One dory was smashed to pieces, and the sea pitched the man head first on to the decks, cutting his forehead open; and about dawn, when the racing seas glimmered white all along their cold edges, another man, blue and ghastly, crawled in with a broken hand, asking news of his brother. Seven extra mouths sat down to breakfast: a Swede; a Chatham skipper; a boy from Hancock, Maine; one Duxbury, and three Provincetown men.

There was a general sorting out among the Fleet next day; and though no one said anything, all ate with better appetites when boat after boat reported full crews aboard. Only a couple of Portuguese and an old man from Gloucester were drowned, but many were cut or bruised; and two schooners had parted their tackle and been blown to the southward, three days' sail. A man died on a Frenchman—it was the same bark that had traded tobacco with the "We're Heres." She slipped away quite quietly one wet, white morning, moved to a patch of deep water, her sails all hanging anyhow, and Harvey saw the funeral through Disko's spy-glass. It was only an oblong bundle slid overside. They did not seem to have any form of service, but in the night, at anchor, Harvey heard them across the star-powdered black water, singing something that sounded like a hymn. It went to a very slow tune.

La brigantine Qui va tourner, Roule et s'incline Pour m'entrainer. Oh, Vierge Marie, Pour moi priez Dieu! Adieu, patrie; Québec, adieu!

Tom Platt visited her, because, he said, the dead man was his brother as a Freemason. It came out that a wave had doubled the poor fellow over the heel of the bowsprit and broken his back. The news spread like a flash, for, contrary to general custom, the Frenchman held an auction of the dead man's kit,—he had no friends at St. Malo or Miquelon,—and everything was spread out on the top of the house, from his red knitted cap to the leather belt with the sheath-knife at the back. Dan and Harvey were out on twenty-fathom water in the Hattie S., and naturally rowed over to join the crowd. It was a long pull, and they stayed some little time while Dan bought the knife, which had a curious brass handle. When they dropped overside and pushed off into a drizzle of rain and a lop of sea, it occurred to them that they might get into trouble for neglecting the lines. "Guess 'twon't hurt us any to be warmed up," said Dan, shivering under his oilskins, and they rowed on into the heart of a white fog, which, as usual, dropped on them without warning.

"There's too much blame tide hereabouts to trust to your instinks," he said. "Heave over the anchor, Harve, and we'll fish a piece till the thing lifts. Bend on your biggest lead. Three pound ain't any too much in this water. See how she's tightened on her rodin' already."

There was quite a little bubble at the bows, where some irresponsible Bank current held the dory full stretch on her rope; but they could not see a boat's length in any direction. Harvey turned up his collar and bunched himself over his reel with the air of a wearied navigator. Fog had no special terrors for him now. They fished awhile in silence, and found the cod struck on well. Then Dan drew the sheath-knife and tested the edge of it on the gunwale.

"That's a daisy," said Harvey. "How did you get it so cheap?"

"On account o' their blame Cath'lic superstitions," said Dan, jabbing with the bright blade. "They don't fancy takin' iron frum off of a dead man, so to speak. See them Arichat Frenchmen step back when I bid?"

"But an auction ain't taking anything off a dead man. It's business."

"We know it ain't, but there's no goin' in the teeth o' superstition. That's one o' the advantages o' livin' in a progressive country." And Dan began whistling:

"Oh, Double Thatcher, how are you? Now Eastern Point comes inter view. The girls an' boys we soon shall see, At anchor off Cape Ann!"

"Why didn't that Eastport man bid, then? He bought his boots. Ain't Maine progressive?"

"Maine? Pshaw! They don't know enough, or they hain't got money enough, to paint their haouses in Maine. I've seen 'em. The Eastport man he told me that the knife had been used—so the French captain told him—used up on the French coast last year."

"Cut a man? Heave's the muckle." Harvey hauled in his fish, rebaited, and threw over.

"Killed him! 'Course, when I heard that I was keener 'n ever to get it."

"Christmas! I didn't know it," said Harvey, turning round. "I'll give you a dollar for it when I—get my wages. Say, I'll give you two dollars."

"Honest? D'you like it as much as all that?" said Dan, flushing. "Well, to tell the truth, I kinder got it for you—to give; but I didn't let on till I saw how you'd take it. It's yours and welcome, Harve, because we're dory-mates, and so on and so forth, an' so followin'. Catch a-holt!"

He held it out, belt and all.

"But look at here. Dan, I don't see—"

"Take it. 'Tain't no use to me. I wish you to hev it."

The temptation was irresistible. "Dan, you're a white man," said Harvey. "I'll keep it as long as I live."

"That's good hearin'," said Dan, with a pleasant laugh; and then, anxious to change the subject: "Look's if your line was fast to somethin'."

"Fouled, I guess," said Harve, tugging. Before he pulled up he fastened the belt round him, and with deep delight heard the tip of the sheath click on the thwart. "Concern the thing!" he cried. "She acts as though she were on strawberry-bottom. It's all sand here, ain't it?"

Dan reached over and gave a judgmatic tweak. "Holibut'll act that way 'f he's sulky. Thet's no strawberry-bottom. Yank her once or twice. She gives, sure. 'Guess we'd better haul up an' make certain."

They pulled together, making fast at each turn on the cleats, and the hidden weight rose sluggishly.

"Prize, oh! Haul!" shouted Dan, but the shout ended in a shrill, double shriek of horror, for out of the sea came—the body of the dead Frenchman buried two days before! The hook had caught him under the right armpit, and he swayed, erect and horrible, head and shoulders above water. His arms were tied to his side, and—he had no face. The boys fell over each other in a heap at the bottom of the dory, and there they lay while the thing bobbed alongside, held on the shortened line.

"The tide—the tide brought him!" said Harvey, with quivering lips, as he fumbled at the clasp of the belt.

"Oh, Lord! Oh, Harve!" groaned Dan, "be quick. He's come for it. Let him have it. Take it off."

"I don't want it! I don't want it!" cried Harvey. "I can't find the bu-buckle."

"Quick, Harve! He's on your line!"

Harvey sat up to unfasten the belt, facing the head that had no face under its streaming hair. "He's fast still," he whispered to Dan, who slipped out his knife and cut the line, as Harvey flung the belt far overside. The body shot down with a plop, and Dan cautiously rose to his knees, whiter than the fog.

"He come for it. He come for it. I've seen a stale one hauled up on a trawl and I didn't much care, but he come to us special."

"I wish—I wish I hadn't taken the knife. Then he'd have come on your line."

"Dunno as thet would ha' made any differ. We're both scared out o' ten years' growth. Oh, Harve, did ye see his head?"

"Did I? I'll never forget it. But look at here, Dan; it couldn't have been meant. It was only the tide."

"Tide! He come for it, Harve. Why, they sunk him six mile to south'ard o' the Fleet, an' we're two miles from where she's lyin' now. They told me he was weighted with a fathom an' a half o' chain-cable."

"Wonder what he did with the knife—up on the French coast?"

"Something bad. 'Guess he's bound to take it with him to the Judgment, an' so—What are you doin' with the fish?"

"Heaving 'em overboard," said Harvey.

"What for? We sha'n't eat 'em."

"I don't care. I had to look at his face while I was takin' the belt off. You can keep your catch if you like. I've no use for mine."

Dan said nothing, but threw his fish over again.

"'Guess it's best to be on the safe side," he murmured at last. "I'd give a month's pay if this fog 'u'd lift. Things go abaout in a fog that ye don't see in clear weather—yo-hoes an' hollerers and such like. I'm sorter relieved he come the way he did instid o' walkin'. He might ha' walked."

"Do-on't, Dan! We're right on top of him now. 'Wish I was safe aboard, bein' pounded by Uncle Salters."

"They'll be lookin' fer us in a little. Gimme the tooter." Dan took the tin dinner-horn, but paused before he blew.

"Go on," said Harvey. "I don't want to stay here all night."

"Question is, haow he'd take it. There was a man frum down the coast told me once he was in a schooner where they darsen't ever blow a horn to the dories, becaze the skipper—not the man he was with, but a captain that had run her five years before—he'd drownded a boy alongside in a drunk fit; an' ever after, that boy he'd row alongside too and shout, 'Dory! dory!' with the rest."

"Dory! dory!" a muffled voice cried through the fog. They cowered again, and the horn dropped from Dan's hand.

"Hold on!" cried Harvey; "it's the cook."

"Dunno what made me think o' thet fool tale, either," said Dan. "It's the doctor, sure enough."

"Dan! Danny! Oooh, Dan! Harve! Harvey! Oooh, Haarveee!"

"We're here," sung both boys together. They heard oars, but could see nothing till the cook, shining and dripping, rowed into them.

"What iss happened?" said he. "You will be beaten at home."

"Thet's what we want. Thet's what we're sufferin' for," said Dan. "Anything homey's good enough fer us. We've had kinder depressin' company." As the cook passed them a line, Dan told him the tale.

"Yess! He come for hiss knife," was all he said at the end.

Never had the little rocking "We're Here" looked so deliciously home—like as when the cook, born and bred in fogs, rowed them back to her. There was a warm glow of light from the cabin and a satisfying smell of food forward, and it was heavenly to hear Disko and the others, all quite alive and solid, leaning over the rail and promising them a first-class pounding. But the cook was a black master of strategy. He did not get the dories aboard till he had given the more striking points of the tale, explaining as he backed and bumped round the counter how Harvey was the mascot to destroy any possible bad luck. So the boys came overside as rather uncanny heroes, and every one asked them questions instead of pounding them for making trouble. Little Penn delivered quite a speech on the folly of superstitions; but public opinion was against him and in favour of Long Jack, who told the most excruciating ghost-stories to nearly midnight. Under that influence no one except Salters and Penn said anything about "idolatry" when the cook put a lighted candle, a cake of flour and water, and a pinch of salt on a shingle, and floated them out astern to keep the Frenchman quiet in case he was still restless. Dan lit the candle because he had bought the belt, and the cook grunted and muttered charms as long as he could see the ducking point of flame.

Said Harvey to Dan, as they turned in after watch: "How about progress and Catholic superstitions?"

"Huh! I guess I'm as enlightened and progressive as the next man, but when it comes to a dead St. Malo deck-hand scarin' a couple o' pore boys stiff fer the sake of a thirty-cent knife, why, then, the cook can take hold fer all o' me. I mistrust furriners, livin' or dead."

Next morning all, except the cook, were rather ashamed of the ceremonies, and went to work double tides, speaking gruffly to one another.

The "We're Here" was racing neck and neck for her last few loads against the "Parry Norman"; and so close was the struggle that the Fleet took sides and betted tobacco. All hands worked at the lines or dressing-down till they fell asleep where they stood—beginning before dawn and ending when it was too dark to see. They even used the cook as pitcher, and turned Harvey into the hold to pass salt, while Dan helped to dress down. Luckily a "Parry Norman" man sprained his ankle falling down the fo'c'sle, and the "We're Heres" gained. Harvey could not see how one more fish could be crammed into her, but Disko and Tom Platt stowed and stowed, and planked the mass down with big stones from the ballast, and there was always "jest another day's work." Disko did not tell them when all the salt was wetted. He rolled to the lazarette aft the cabin and began hauling out the big mainsail. This was at ten in the morning. The riding-sail was down and the main- and top-sail were up by noon, and dories came alongside with letters for home, envying their good fortune. At last she cleared decks, hoisted her flag,—as is the right of the first boat off the Banks,—up-anchored, and began to move. Disko pretended that he wished to accommodate folk who had not sent in their mail, and so worked her gracefully in and out among the schooners. In reality, that was his little triumphant procession, and for the fifth year running it showed what kind of mariner he was. Dan's accordion and Tom Platt's fiddle supplied the music of the magic verse you must not sing till all the salt is wet:

Hih! Yih! Yoho!
Send your letters raound!
All our salt is wetted, an' the anchor's off the graound!
Bend, oh, bend your mains'l!, we're back to Yankeeland—
With fifteen hunder' quintal,
An' fifteen hunder' quintal,
'Teen hunder' toppin' quintal,
'Twix' old 'Queereau an' Grand.

The last letters pitched on deck wrapped round pieces of coal, and the Gloucester men shouted messages to their wives and womenfolk and owners, while the "We're Here" finished the musical ride through the Fleet, her head-sails quivering like a man's hand when he raises it to say good-bye.

Harvey very soon discovered that the "We're Here," with her riding-sail, strolling from berth to berth, and the "We're Here" headed west by south under home canvas, were two very different boats. There was a bite and kick to the wheel even in "boy's" weather; he could feel the dead weight in the hold flung forward mightily across the surges, and the streaming line of bubbles overside made his eyes dizzy.

Disko kept them busy fiddling with the sails; and when those were flattened like a racing yacht's, Dan had to wait on the big topsail, which was put over by hand every time she went about. In spare moments they pumped, for the packed fish dripped brine, which does not improve a cargo. But since there was no fishing, Harvey had time to look at the sea from another point of view. The low-sided schooner was naturally on most intimate terms with her surroundings. They saw little of the horizon save when she topped a swell; and usually she was elbowing, fidgeting, and coaxing her steadfast way through grey, grey-blue, or black hollows laced across and across with streaks of shivering foam; or rubbing herself caressingly along the flank of some bigger water-hill. It was as if she said: "You wouldn't hurt me, surely? I'm only the little 'We're Here'." Then she would slide away chuckling softly to herself till she was brought up by some fresh obstacle. The dullest of folk cannot see this kind of thing hour after hour through long days without noticing it; and Harvey, being anything but dull, began to comprehend and enjoy the dry chorus of wave-tops turning over with a sound of incessant tearing; the hurry of the winds working across open spaces and herding the purple-blue cloud-shadows; the splendid upheaval of the red sunrise; the folding and packing away of the morning mists, wall after wall withdrawn across the white floors; the salty glare and blaze of noon; the kiss of rain falling over thousands of dead, flat square miles; the chilly blackening of everything at the day's end; and the million wrinkles of the sea under the moonlight, when the jib-boom solemnly poked at the low stars, and Harvey went down to get a doughnut from the cook.

But the best fun was when the boys were put on the wheel together, Tom Platt within hail, and she cuddled her lee-rail down to the crashing blue, and kept a little home-made rainbow arching unbroken over her windlass. Then the jaws of the booms whined against the masts, and the sheets creaked, and the sails filled with roaring; and when she slid into a hollow she trampled like a woman tripped in her own silk dress, and came out, her jib wet half-way up, yearning and peering for the tall twin-lights of Thatcher's Island.

They left the cold grey of the Bank sea, saw the lumber-ships making for Quebec by the Straits of St. Lawrence, with the Jersey salt-brigs from Spain and Sicily; found a friendly northeaster off Artimon Bank that drove them within view of the East light of Sable Island,—a sight Disko did not linger over,—and stayed with them past Western and Le Have, to the northern fringe of George's. From there they picked up the deeper water, and let her go merrily.

"Hattie's pulling on the string," Dan confided to Harvey. "Hattie an' ma. Next Sunday you'll be hirin' a boy to throw water on the windows to make ye go to sleep. 'Guess you'll keep with us till your folks come. Do you know the best of gettin' ashore again?"

"Hot bath?" said Harvey. His eyebrows were all white with dried spray.

"That's good, but a night-shirt's better. I've been dreamin' o' nightshirts ever since we bent our mainsail. Ye can wiggle your toes then. Ma'll hev a new one fer me, all washed soft. It's home, Harve. It's home! Ye can sense it in the air. We're runnin' into the aidge of a hot wave naow, an' I can smell the bayberries. Wonder if we'll get in fer supper. Port a trifle."

The hesitating sails flapped and lurched in the close air as the deep smoothed out, blue and oily, round them. When they whistled for a wind only the rain came in spiky rods, bubbling and drumming, and behind the rain the thunder and the lightning of mid-August. They lay on the deck with bare feet and arms, telling one another what they would order at their first meal ashore; for now the land was in plain sight. A Gloucester swordfish-boat drifted alongside, a man in the little pulpit on the bowsprit flourishing his harpoon, his bare head plastered down with the wet. "And all's well!" he sang cheerily, as though he were watch on a big liner. "Wouverman's waiting fer you, Disko. What's the news o' the Fleet?"

Disko shouted it and passed on, while the wild summer storm pounded overhead and the lightning flickered along the capes from four different quarters at once. It gave the low circle of hills round Gloucester Harbour, Ten Pound Island, the fish-sheds, with the broken line of house-roofs, and each spar and buoy on the water, in blinding photographs that came and went a dozen times to the minute as the "We're Here" crawled in on half-flood, and the whistling-buoy moaned and mourned behind her. Then the storm died out in long, separated, vicious dags of blue-white flame, followed by a single roar like the roar of a mortar-battery, and the shaken air tingled under the stars as it got back to silence.

"The flag, the flag!" said Disko, suddenly, pointing upward.

"What is ut?" said Long Jack.

"Otto! Ha'af mast. They can see us frum shore now."

"I'd clean forgot. He's no folk to Gloucester, has he?"

"Girl he was goin' to be married to this fall."

"Mary pity her!" said Long Jack, and lowered the little flag half-mast for the sake of Otto, swept overboard in a gale off Le Have three months before.

Disko wiped the wet from his eyes and led the "We're Here" to Wouverman's wharf, giving his orders in whispers, while she swung round moored tugs and night-watchmen hailed her from the ends of inky-black piers. Over and above the darkness and the mystery of the procession, Harvey could feel the land close round him once more, with all its thousands of people asleep, and the smell of earth after rain, and the familiar noise of a switching-engine coughing to herself in a freight-yard; and all those things made his heart beat and his throat dry up as he stood by the foresheet. They heard the anchor-watch snoring on a lighthouse-tug, nosed into a pocket of darkness where a lantern glimmered on either side; somebody waked with a grunt, threw them a rope, and they made fast to a silent wharf flanked with great iron-roofed sheds full of warm emptiness, and lay there without a sound.

Then Harvey sat down by the wheel, and sobbed and sobbed as though his heart would break, and a tall woman who had been sitting on a weigh-scale dropped down into the schooner and kissed Dan once on the cheek; for she was his mother, and she had seen the "We're Here" by the lightning-flashes. She took no notice of Harvey till he had recovered himself a little and Disko had told her his story. Then they went to Disko's house together as the dawn was breaking; and until the telegraph office was open and he could wire to his folk, Harvey Cheyne was perhaps the loneliest boy in all America. But the curious thing was that Disko and Dan seemed to think none the worse of him for crying.

Wouverman was not ready for Disko's prices till Disko, sure that the "We're Here" was at least a week ahead of any other Gloucester boat, had given him a few days to swallow them; so all hands played about the streets, and Long Jack stopped the Rocky Neck trolley, on principle, as he said, till the conductor let him ride free. But Dan went about with his freckled nose in the air, bungful of mystery and most haughty to his family.

"Dan, I'll hev to lay inter you ef you act this way," said Troop, pensively. "Sence we've come ashore this time you've bin a heap too fresh."

"I'd lay into him naow ef he was mine," said Uncle Salters, sourly. He and Penn boarded with the Troops.

"Oho!" said Dan, shuffling with the accordion round the back-yard, ready to leap the fence if the enemy advanced. "Dad, you're welcome to your own jedgment, but remember I've warned ye. Your own flesh an' blood ha' warned ye! 'Tain't any o' my fault ef you're mistook, but I'll be on deck to watch ye. An' ez fer yeou, Uncle Salters, Pharaoh's chief butler ain't in it 'longside o' you! You watch aout an' wait. You'll be ploughed under like your own blamed clover; but me—Dan Troop—I'll flourish like a green bay-tree because I warn't stuck on my own opinion."

Disko was smoking in all his shore dignity and a pair of beautiful carpet-slippers. "You're gettin' ez crazy as poor Harve. You two go araound gigglin' an' squinchin' an' kickin' each other under the table till there's no peace in the haouse," said he.

"There's goin' to be a heap less—fer some folks," Dan replied. "You wait an' see."

He and Harvey went out on the trolley to East Gloucester, where they tramped through the bayberry-bushes to the lighthouse, and lay down on the big red boulders and laughed themselves hungry. Harvey had shown Dan a telegram, and the two swore to keep silence till the shell burst.

"Harve's folk?" said Dan, with an unruffled face after supper. "Well, I guess they don't amount to much of anything, or we'd ha' heard frum 'em by naow. His pop keeps a kind o' store out West. Maybe he'll give you's much as five dollars, dad."

"What did I tell ye?" said Salters. "Don't sputter over your vittles, Dan."

6

YAMMERSCHOONER

JOSHUA SLOCUM

On February 1 the *Spray* rounded Cape Virgins and entered the Strait of Magellan. The scene was again real and gloomy; the wind, northeast, and blowing a gale, sent feather-white spume along the coast; such a sea ran as would swamp an ill-appointed ship. As the sloop neared the entrance to the strait I observed that two great tide-races made ahead, one very close to the point of the land and one farther offshore. Between the two, in a sort of channel, through combers, went the *Spray* with close-reefed sails. But a rolling sea followed her a long way in, and a fierce current swept around the cape against her; but this she stemmed, and was soon chirruping under the lee of Cape Virgins and running every minute into smoother water. However, long trailing kelp from sunken rocks waved forebodingly under her keel, and the wreck of a great steamship smashed on the beach abreast gave a gloomy aspect to the scene.

I was not to be let off easy. The Virgins would collect tribute even from the *Spray* passing their promontory. Fitful rain-squalls from the northwest followed the northeast gale. I reefed the sloop's sails, and sitting in the cabin to rest my eyes, I was so strongly impressed with what in all nature I might expect that as I dozed the very air I breathed seemed to warn me of danger. My senses heard "*Spray* ahoy!" shouted in warning. I sprang to the deck, wondering who could be there that knew the *Spray* so well as to call out her name passing in the dark; for it was now the blackest of nights all around, except away in the southwest where rose the old familiar white arch, the terror of Cape Horn, rapidly pushed up by a southwest gale. I had only a moment to douse sail and lash all solid when it struck like a shot from a cannon, and for the first half-hour it was something to be remembered by way of a gale. For thirty hours it kept on blowing hard. The sloop could carry no more than a three-reefed mainsail and forestaysail; with these she held on stoutly and was not blown out of the strait. In the height of the squalls in this gale she doused all sail, and this occurred often enough.

After this gale followed only a smart breeze, and the *Spray*, passing through the narrows without mishap, cast anchor at Sandy Point on February 14, 1896.

Sandy Point (Punta Arenas) is a Chilean coaling station, and boasts about two thousand inhabitants, of mixed nationality, but mostly Chileans. What with sheep-farming, gold-mining, and hunting, the settlers in this dreary land seemed not the worst off in the world. But the natives, Patagonian and Fuegian, on the other hand, were as squalid as contact with unscrupulous traders could make them. A large percentage of the business there was traffic in "fire-water." If there was a law against selling the poisonous stuff to the natives, it was not enforced. Fine specimens of the Patagonian race, looking smart in the morning when they came into town, had repented before night of ever having seen a white man, so beastly drunk were they, to say nothing about the peltry of which they had been robbed.

The port at that time was free, but a customhouse was in course of construction, and when it is finished, port and tariff dues are to be collected. A soldier police guarded the place, and a sort of vigilante force besides took down its guns now and then; but as a general thing, to my mind, whenever an execution was made they killed the wrong man. Just previous to my arrival the governor, himself of a jovial turn of mind, had sent a party of young bloods to foray a Fuegian settlement and wipe out what they could of it on account of the recent massacre of a schooner's crew somewhere else. Altogether the place was quite newsy and supported two papers—dailies, I think. The port captain, a Chilean naval officer, advised me to ship hands to fight Indians in the strait farther west, and spoke of my stopping until a gunboat should be going through, which would give me a tow. After canvassing the place, however, I found only one man willing to embark, and he on condition that I should ship another "mon and a doog." But as no one else was willing to come along, and as I drew the line at dogs, I said no more about the matter, but simply loaded my guns. At this point in my dilemma Captain Pedro Samblich, a good Austrian of large experience, coming along, gave me a bag of carpet-tacks, worth more than all the fighting men and dogs of Tierra del Fuego. I protested that I had no use for carpet-tacks on board. Samblich smiled at my want of experience, and maintained stoutly that I would have use for them. "You must use them with discretion," he said; "that is to say, don't step on them yourself." With this remote hint about the use of the tacks I got on all right, and saw the way to maintain clear decks at night without the care of watching.

Samblich was greatly interested in my voyage, and after giving me the tacks he put on board bags of biscuits and a large quantity of smoked venison. He declared that my bread, which was ordinary sea-biscuits and easily broken, was not nutritious as his, which was so hard that I could break it only with a stout blow from a maul. Then he gave me, from his own sloop, a compass which was certainly better than mine, and offered to unbend her mainsail for me if I would accept it. Last of all, this large-hearted man brought out a bottle of Fuegian gold-dust from a place where it had been *cached* and begged me to help myself from it, for use farther along on the voyage. But I felt sure of success without this draft on a friend, and I was right. Samblich's tacks, as it turned out, were of more value than gold.

The port captain, finding that I was resolved to go, even alone, since there was no help for it, set up no further objections, but advised me, in case the savages tried to surround me with their canoes, to shoot straight, and begin to do it in time, but to avoid killing them if possible, which I heartily agreed to do. With these simple injunctions the officer gave me my port clearance free of charge, and I sailed on the same day, February 19, 1896. It was not without thoughts of strange and stirring adventure beyond all I had yet encountered that I now sailed into the country and very core of the savage Fuegians.

A fair wind from Sandy Point brought me on the first day to St. Nicholas Bay, where, so I was told, I might expect to meet savages; but seeing no signs of life, I came to anchor in eight fathoms of water, where I lay all night under a high mountain. Here I had my first experience with the terrific squalls, called williwaws, which extended from this point on through the strait to the Pacific. They were compressed gales of wind that Boreas handed down over the hills in chunks. A full-blown williwaw will throw a ship, even without sail on, over on her beam ends; but, like other gales, they cease now and then, if only for a short time.

February 20 was my birthday, and I found myself alone, with hardly so much as a bird in sight, off Cape Froward, the southernmost point of the continent of America. By daylight in the morning I was getting my ship under way for the bout ahead.

The sloop held the wind fair while she ran thirty miles farther on her course, which brought her to Fortescue Bay, and at once among the natives' signal-fires, which blazed up now on all sides. Clouds flew over the mountain from the west all day; at night my good east wind failed, and in its stead a gale from the west soon came on. I gained anchorage at twelve o'clock that night, under the lee of a little island, and then prepared myself a cup of coffee, of which I was sorely in need; for, to tell the truth, hard beating in the heavy squalls and against the current had told on my strength. Finding that the anchor held, I drank my beverage, and named the place Coffee Island. It lies to the south of Charles Island, with only a narrow channel between.

By daylight the next morning the *Spray* was again under way, beating hard; but she came to in a cove in Charles Island, two and a half miles along on her course. Here she remained undisturbed two days, with both anchors down in a bed of kelp. Indeed, she might have remained undisturbed indefinitely had not the wind moderated; for during these two days it blew so hard that no boat could venture out on the strait, and the natives being away to other hunting-grounds, the island anchorage was safe. But at the end of the fierce windstorm fair weather came; then I got my anchors, and again sailed out upon the strait.

Canoes manned by savages from Fortescue now came in pursuit. The wind falling light they gained on me rapidly till coming within hail, when they ceased paddling, and a bow-legged savage stood up and called to me, "Yammerschooner! yammerschooner!" which is their begging term. I said, "No!" Now, I was not for letting on that I was alone, and so I stepped into the cabin, and, passing through the hold, came out at the fore-scuttle, changing my clothes as I went along. That made two men. Then the piece of bowsprit which I had sawed off at Buenos Aires, and which I had still on board, I arranged forward on the outlook, dressed as a seaman, attaching a line by which I could pull it into motion. That made three of us, and we didn't want to "yammerschooner"; but for all that the savages came on faster than before. I saw that besides four at the paddles in the canoe nearest to me, there were others in the bottom, and that they were shifting hands often. At eighty yards I fired a shot across the bows of the nearest canoe, at which they all stopped, but only for a moment. Seeing that they persisted in coming nearer, I fired the second shot so close to the chap who wanted to "yammerschooner" that he changed his mind quickly enough and bellowed with fear, "Bueno jo via Isla," and sitting down in his canoe, he rubbed his starboard cat-head for some time. I was thinking of the good port captain's advice when I pulled the trigger, and must have aimed pretty straight; however, a miss was as good as a mile for Mr. "Black Pedro," as he it was, and no other, a leader in several bloody massacres. He made for the island now, and the others followed him. I knew by his Spanish lingo and by his full beard that he was the villain I had named, a renegade mongrel, and the worst murderer in Tierra del Fuego. The authorities had been in search of him for two years. The Fuegians are not bearded.

So much for the first day among the savages. I came to anchor at midnight in Three Island Cove, about twenty miles along from Fortescue Bay. I saw on the opposite side of the strait signal-fires, and heard the barking of dogs, but where I lay it was quite deserted by natives. I have always taken it as a sign that where I found birds sitting about, or seals on the rocks, I should not find savage Indians. Seals are never plentiful in these waters, but in Three Island Cove I saw one on the rocks, and other signs of the absence of savage men.

On the next day the wind was again blowing a gale, and although she was in the lee of the land, the sloop dragged her anchors, so that I had to get her under way and beat farther into the cove, where I came to in a landlocked pool. At another time or place this would have been a rash thing to do, and it was safe now only from the fact that the gale which drove me to shelter would keep the Indians from crossing the strait. Seeing this was the case, I went ashore with gun and axe on an island, where I could not in any event be surprised, and there felled trees and split about a cord of fire-wood, which loaded my small boat several times.

While I carried the wood, though I was morally sure there were no savages near, I never once went to or from the skiff without my gun. While I had that and a clear field of over eighty yards about me I felt safe.

The trees on the island, very scattering, were a sort of beech and a stunted cedar, both of which made good fuel. Even the green limbs of the beech, which seemed to possess a resinous quality, burned readily in my great drum-stove. I have described my method of wooding up in detail, that the reader who has kindly borne with me so far may see that in this, as in all other particulars of my voyage, I took great care against all kinds of surprises, whether by animals or by the elements. In the Strait of Magellan the greatest vigilance was necessary. In this instance I reasoned that I had all about me the greatest danger of the whole voyage—the treachery of cunning savages, for which I must be particularly on the alert.

The *Spray* sailed from Three Island Cove in the morning after the gale went down, but was glad to return for shelter from another sudden gale. Sailing again on the following day, she fetched Borgia Bay, a few miles on her course, where vessels had anchored from time to time and had nailed boards on the trees ashore with name and date of harbouring carved or painted. Nothing else could I see to indicate the civilized man had ever been before. I had taken a survey of the gloomy place with my spy-glass, and was getting my boat out to land and take notes, when the Chilean gunboat *Huemel* came in, and officers, coming on board, advised me to leave the place at once, a thing that required little eloquence to persuade me to do. I accepted the captain's kind offer of a tow to the next anchorage, at the place called Notch Cove, eight miles farther along, where I should be clear of the worst of the Fuegians.

We made anchorage at the cove about dark that night, while the wind came down in fierce williwaws from the mountains. An instance of Magellan weather was afforded when the *Huemel*, a well-appointed gunboat of great power, after attempting on the following day to proceed on her voyage, was obliged by sheer force of the wind to return and take up anchorage again and remain till the gale abated; and lucky she was to get back!

Meeting this vessel was a little godsend. She was commanded and officered by high-class sailors and educated gentlemen. An entertainment that was gotten up on her, impromptu, at the Notch would be hard to beat anywhere. One of her midshipmen sang popular songs in French, German, and Spanish, and one (so he said) in Russian. If the audience did not know the lingo of one song from another, it was no drawback to the merriment.

I was left alone the next day, for then the *Huemel* put out on her voyage, the gale having abated. I spent a day taking in wood and water; by the end of that time the weather was fine. Then I sailed from the desolate place.

There is little more to be said concerning the *Spray's* first passage through the strait that would differ from what I have already recorded. She anchored and weighed many times, and beat many days against the current, with now and then a "slant" for a few miles, till finally she gained anchorage and shelter for the night at Port Tamar, with Cape Pillar in sight to the west. Here I felt the throb of the great ocean that lay before me. I knew now that I had put a world behind me, and that I was opening out another world ahead. I had passed the haunts of savages. Great piles of granite mountains of bleak and lifeless aspect were now astern; on some of them not even a speck of moss had ever grown. There was an unfinished newness all about the land. On the hill back of Port Tamar a small beacon had been thrown up, showing that some man had been there. But how could one tell but that he had died of loneliness and grief? In a bleak land is not the place to enjoy solitude.

Throughout the whole of the strait west of Cape Froward I saw no animals except dogs owned by savages. These I saw often enough, and heard them yelping night and day. Birds were not plentiful. The scream of a wild fowl, which I took for a loon, sometimes startled me with its piercing cry. The steamboat duck, so called because it propels itself over the sea with its wings, and resembles a miniature side-wheel steamer in its motion, was sometimes seen scurrying on out of danger. It never flies, but, hitting the water instead of the air with its wings, it moves faster than a rowboat or a canoe. The few fur-seals I saw were very shy; and of fishes I saw next to none at all. I did not catch one; indeed, I seldom or never put a hook over during the whole voyage. Here in the strait I found great abundance of mussels of an excellent quality. I fared sumptuously on them. There was a sort of swan, smaller than a Muscovy duck, which might have been brought down with the gun, but in the loneliness of life about the dreary country I found myself in no mood to make one life less, except in self-defence.

7

YOUNG IRONSIDES

JAMES FENIMORE COOPER

The second cruise of Old Ironsides commenced in August, 1799. Her orders were to go off Cayenne, in the first place, where she was to remain until near the close of September, when she was to proceed via Guadeloupe to Cape Francois, at which point, Talbot was to assume the command of all the vessels he found on the station. In the course of the season, this squadron grew to be six sail, three frigates and as many sloops, or brigs.

Two incidents occurred to Old Ironsides, while on the St. Domingo station, that are worthy of being noticed, the first being of an amicable, and the second of a particularly hostile character.

While cruising to windward the island, a strange sail was made, which, on closing, proved to be the English frigate, the _____. The commander of this ship and Com. Talbot were acquaintances, and the Englishman had the curiosity to take a full survey of the new Yankee craft. He praised her, as no unprejudiced seaman could fail to do, but insisted that his own ship could beat her on a wind. After some pleasantry on the subject, the English captain made the following proposition; he had touched at Madeira on his way out, and taken on board a few casks of wine for his own use. This wine stood him in so much a cask—now, he was going into port to refit, and clean his bottom, which was a little foul; but, if he could depend on finding the *Constitution* on that station, a few weeks later he would join her, when there should be a trial of speed between the two ships, the loser to pay a cask of the wine, or its price to the winner.

The bet was made, and the vessels parted. At the appointed time, the _____ reappeared; her rigging overhauled, new sails bent, her sides painted, her bottom cleaned. And, as Jack expressed it, looking like a new fiddle. The two frigates closed, and their commanders dined together, arranging the terms of the cartel for the next day's proceedings. That night, the vessels kept near each other, on the same line of sailing, and under short canvas. The following morning, as the day dawned, the *Constitution* and the _____ each turned up their hands, in readiness for what was to follow.

Just as the lower limb of the sun rose clear of the waves, each fired a gun, and made sail on a bowline. Throughout the whole of that day, did these two gallant ships continue turning to windward, on tacks of a few leagues in length, and endeavoring to avail themselves of every advantage which skill could confer on seamen. Hull sailed the *Constitution* on this interesting occasion and the admirable manner in which he did it, was long the subject of eulogy.

All hands were kept on deck all day, and there were tacks on which the people were made to place themselves to windward, in order to keep the vessel as near upright as possible, so as to hold a better wind. Just as the sun dipped, in the evening, the *Constitution* fired a gun, as did her competitor. At that moment the English frigate was precisely hull down dead to leeward; so much having Old Ironsides, or young Ironsides, as she was then, gained in the race, which lasted about eleven hours! The manner in which the *Constitution* beat her competitor out of the wind, was not the least striking feature of this trial, and it must in great degree be ascribed to Hull, whose dexterity in handling a craft under her canvas, was ever remarkable. In this particular, he was perhaps one of the most skilful seamen of his time, as he was also for coolness in moments of hazard. When the evening gun was fired and acknowledged, the *Constitution* put up her helm, and squared away to join her friend. The vessels joined a little after dark, the Englishman as the leeward ship, first rounding to. The *Constitution* passed under her lee, and threw her maintopsail to the mast. There was a boat out from the _____, which soon came alongside, and in it was the English Captain and his cask of wine; the former being just as prompt to "pay" as to "play."

The other occurrence was the cutting out of the *Sandwich*, a French letter of marque, which was lying in Port Platte, a small harbor on the Spanish side of St. Domingo. While cruising along the coast, the *Constitution* had seized an American sloop called the *Sally*, which had been selling supplies to the enemy.

Hearing that the *Sandwich*, formerly an English packet, but which had fallen into the hands of the French, was filling up with coffee, and was nearly full, Talbot determined to send Hull in, with the *Sally*, in order to cut her out. The sloop had not long before come out of that very haven, with an avowed intention to return, and offered every desirable facility to the success of the enterprise. The great and insuperable objection to its ultimate advantage, was the material circumstance that the Frenchman was lying in a neutral port, as respects ourselves, though watchful of the English who were swarming in those seas.

The *Constitution* manned the *Sally* at sea, near sunset, on the tenth of May, 1800, a considerable distance from Port Platte, and the vessels separated, Hull so timing his movements, as to reach his point of destination about midday of a Sunday, when it was rightly enough supposed many of the French, officers as well as men, would be ashore keeping holiday. Short sail was carried that night on board the *Sally*, and while she was quietly jogging along, thinking no harm, a gun was suddenly heard, and a shot came whistling over the sloop.

On looking around, a large ship was seen in chase, and so near, as to render escape impossible. The *Sally* rounded to, and presently, an English frigate ranged alongside. The boarding Officer was astonished when he found himself among ninety armed men, with officers in naval uniform at their head. On demanding an explanation, Hull told him his business, when the English lieutenant expressed his disappointment, candidly acknowledging that his own ship was waiting on the coast to let the *Sandwich* fill up, and get her sails bent, in order to send a party in, also, in order to cut her out! It was too late, however, as the *Sally* could not be, and would not be, detained, and Hull proceeded.

There have been many more brilliant exploits than this of the *Constitution* in sending in a party against the *Sandwich*, but very few that were more neatly executed, or ingeniously planned. The *Sally* arrived off the port, at the appointed hour, and stood directly in, showing the customary number of hands on deck, until coming near the letter of marque, she ran her aboard forward, and the *Constitution*'s clambered in over the *Sandwich*'s bows, led by Hull in person. In two minutes, the Americans had possession of their prize, a smart brig, armed with four sixes and two nines, with a pretty strong crew, without the loss of a man. A party of marines, led by Capt. Cormick, landed, drove the Spaniards from a battery that commanded the anchorage, and spiked the guns.

All this was against law and right, but it was very ingeniously arranged, and as gallantly executed. The most serious part of the affair remained to be achieved. The *Sandwich* was stripped to a girt line, and the wind blew directly into the harbor. As it was unsafe for the marines to remain in the battery any time, it was necessarily abandoned, leaving to the people of the place every opportunity of annoying their invaders by all the means they possessed.

The battery was reoccupied, and the guns cleared of the spikes as well and as fast as they could be, while the Americans set about swaying up topmasts and yards and bending sails. After some smart exertion, the brig got royal yards across, and, at sunset, after remaining several hours in front of the town, Hull scaled his guns, by way of letting it be known they could be used, weighed, and began to beat out of the harbor. The Spaniards fired a few shots after him, but with no effect.

Although this was one of the best executed enterprises of the sort on record, and did infinite credit to the coolness and spirit of all concerned, it was not quite an illustration of international law or of justice in general. This was the first victory of Old Ironsides in a certain sense, but all men must regret it was ever achieved, since it was a wrong act, committed with an exaggerated, if not an altogether mistaken notion of duty. America was not even at war with France, in the more formal meaning of the term, nor were all the legal consequences of war connected with the peculiar hostilities that certainly did exist; but with Spain she had no quarrel whatever, and the *Sandwich* was entitled to receive all the protection and immunities that of right belonged to her anchored in the neutral harbor of Port-au-Platte. In the end not only was the condemnation of the *Sandwich* resisted successfully, but all the other prize-money made by Old Ironsides in the cruise went to pay damages. The reason why the exploit itself never received the public commendation to which, as a mere military achievement, it was so justly entitled, was connected with the illegality and recklessness of the enterprise in its inception.

It follows that this, which may be termed the *Constitution's* earliest victory, was obtained in the face of law and right. Fortunately the old craft has lived long enough to atone for this error of her youth by many a noble deed achieved in defence of principles and rights that the most fastidious will not hesitate to defend. The *Constitution* returned to Boston in Aug. 1800, her cruise being up, not only on account of her orders, but on account of the short period for which men were then enlisted in the navy, which was one year.

On the 18th Nov., however, she was ordered to sail again for the old station, still wearing the broad pennant of Talbot. Nothing occurred of interest in the course of this cruise; and, early in the spring, orders were sent to recall all the cruisers from the West Indies, in consequence of an arrangement of the difficulties with France.

8

ROUNDING CAPE HORN

HERMAN MELVILLE

And now, through drizzling fogs and vapors, and under damp, double-reefed topsails, our wet-decked frigate drew nearer and nearer to the squally Cape. Who has not heard of it? Cape Horn, Cape Horn—a *horn* indeed, that has tossed many a good ship. Was the descent of Orpheus, Ulysses, or Dante into Hell, one whit more hardy and sublime than the first navigator's weathering of that terrible Cape?

Turned on her heel by a fierce West Wind, many an outward-bound ship has been driven across the Southern Ocean to the Cape of Good Hope—*that* way to seek a passage to the Pacific. And that stormy Cape, I doubt not, has sent many a fine craft to the bottom, and told no tales. At those ends of the earth are no chronicles. What signify the broken spars and shrouds that, day after day, are driven before the prows of more fortunate vessels? or the tall masts, imbedded in icebergs, that are found floating by? They but hint the old story—of ships that have sailed from their port, and never more have been heard of.

Impracticable Cape! You may approach it from this direction or that—in any way you please—from the East or from the West; with the wind astern, or abeam, or on the quarter; and still Cape Horn is Cape Horn. Cape Horn it is that takes the conceit out of fresh-water sailors, and steeps in a still salter brine the saltest. Woe betide the tyro; the fool-hardy, Heaven preserve!

Your Mediterranean captain, who with a cargo of oranges has hitherto made merry runs across the Atlantic, without so much as furling a t'-gallant-sail, oftentimes, off Cape Horn, receives a lesson which he carries to the grave; though the grave—as is too often the case—follows so hard on the lesson that no benefit comes from the experience.

Other strangers who draw nigh to this Patagonia termination of our Continent, with their souls full of its shipwrecks and disasters—top-sails cautiously reefed, and everything guardedly snug—these strangers at first unexpectedly encountering a tolerably smooth sea, rashly conclude that the Cape, after all, is but a bugbear; they have been imposed upon by fables, and founderings and sinkings hereabouts are all cock-and-bull stories.

"Out reefs, my hearties; fore and aft set t'gallantsails! stand by to give her the fore-top-mast stun'-sail!"

But, Captain Rash, those sails of yours were much safer in the sail-maker's loft. For now, while the heedless craft is bounding over the billows, a black cloud rises out of the sea; the sun drops down from the sky; a horrible mist far and wide spreads over the water.

"Hands by the halyard! Let go! Clew up!"

Too late.

For ere the ropes' ends can be cast off from the pins, the tornado is blowing down to the bottom of their throats. The masts are willows, the sails ribbons, the cordage wool; the whole ship is brewed into the yeast of the gale.

And now, if, when the first green sea breaks over him, Captain Rash is not swept overboard, he has his hands full to be sure. In all probability his three masts have gone by the board, and, raveled into list, his sails are floating in the air. Or, perhaps, the ship *broaches to*, or is *brought by the lee*. In either case, Heaven help the sailors, their wives and their little ones; and Heaven help the underwriters.

Familiarity with danger makes a brave man braver, but less daring. Thus with seamen: he who goes the oftenest round Cape Horn goes the most circumspectly. A veteran mariner is never deceived by the treacherous breezes which sometimes waft him pleasantly toward the latitude of the Cape. No sooner does he come within a certain distance of it—previously fixed in his own mind—than all hands are turned to setting the ship in storm-trim; and never mind how light the breeze, down come his t'gallant-yards. He "bends" his strongest storm-sails, and lashes everything on deck securely. The ship is then ready for the worst; and if, in reeling round the headland, she receives a broadside, it generally goes well with her. If ill, all hands go to the bottom with quiet consciences.

Among sea-captains, there are some who seem to regard the genius of the Cape as a wilful, capricious jade, that must be courted and coaxed into complaisance. First, they come along under easy sails; do not steer boldly for the headland, but tack this way and that—sidling up to it. Now they woo the Jezebel with a t'-gallant-studding-sail; anon, they deprecate her wrath with double-reefed-topsails. When, at length, her unappeasable fury is fairly aroused, and all round the dismantled ship the storm howls and howls for days together, they still persevere in their efforts. First, they try unconditional submission; furling every rag and *heaving to*; laying like a log, for the tempest to toss wheresoever it pleases.

This failing, they set a *spencer* or *try-sail*, and shift on the other tack. Equally vain! The gale sings as hoarsely as before. At last, the wind comes round fair; they drop the fore-sail; square the yards, and scud before it; their implacable foe chasing them with tornadoes, as if to show her insensibility to the last.

Other ships, without encountering these terrible gales, spend week after week endeavoring to turn this boisterous world-corner against a continual head-wind. Tacking hither and thither, in the language of sailors they *polish* the Cape by beating about its edges so long.

Le Mair and Schouten, two Dutchmen, were the first navigators who weathered Cape Horn. Previous to this, passages had been made to the Pacific by the Straits of Magellan; nor, indeed, at that period, was it known to a certainty that there was any other route, or that the land now called Tierra del Fuego was an island. A few leagues southward from Tierra del Fuego is a cluster of small islands, the Diegoes; between which and the former island are the Straits of Le Mair, so called in honor of their discoverer, who first sailed through them into the Pacific. Le Mair and Schouten, in their small, clumsy vessels, encountered a series of tremendous gales, the prelude to the long train of similar hardships which most of their followers have experienced. It is a significant fact, that Schouten's vessel, the *Horne*, which gave its name to the Cape, was almost lost in weathering it.

The next navigator round the Cape was Sir Francis Drake, who, on Raleigh's Expedition, beholding for the first time, from the Isthmus of Darien, the "goodlie south Sea," like a true-born Englishman, vowed, please God, to sail an English ship thereon; which the gallant sailor did, to the sore discomfiture of the Spaniards on the coasts of Chili and Peru.

But perhaps the greatest hardships on record, in making this celebrated passage, were those experienced by Lord Anson's squadron in 1736. Three remarkable and most interesting narratives record their disasters and sufferings. The first, jointly written by the carpenter and gunner of the *Wager*; the second by young Byron, a midshipman in the same ship; the third, by the chaplain of the *Centurion*. White-Jacket has them all; and they are fine reading of a boisterous March night, with the casement rattling in your ear, and the chimney-stacks blowing down upon the pavement, bubbling with rain-drops.

But if you want the best idea of Cape Horn, get my friend Dana's unmatchable "Two Years Before the Mast." But you can read, and so you must have read it. His chapters describing Cape Horn must have been written with an icicle.

At the present day the horrors of the Cape have somewhat abated. This is owing to a growing familiarity with it; but, more than all, to the improved condition of ships in all respects, and the means now generally in use of preserving the health of the crews in times of severe and prolonged exposure.

Colder and colder; we are drawing nigh to the Cape. Now gregoes, pea jackets, monkey jackets, reefing jackets, storm jackets, oil jackets, paint jackets, round jackets, short jackets, long jackets, and all manner of jackets, are the order of the day, not excepting the immortal white jacket, which begins to be sturdily buttoned up to the throat, and pulled down vigorously at the skirts, to bring them well over the loins.

But, alas! those skirts were lamentably scanty; and though, with its quiltings, the jacket was stuffed out about the breasts like a Christmas turkey, and of a dry cold day kept the wearer warm enough in that vicinity, yet about the loins it was shorter than a ballet-dancer's skirts; so that while my chest was in the temperate zone close adjoining the torrid, my hapless thighs were in Nova Zembla, hardly an icicle's toss from the Pole.

Then, again, the repeated soakings and dryings it had undergone, had by this time made it shrink woefully all over, especially in the arms, so that the wristbands had gradually crawled up near to the elbows;

and it required an energetic thrust to push the arm through, in drawing the jacket on.

I endeavored to amend these misfortunes by sewing a sort of canvas ruffle round the skirts, by way of a continuation or supplement to the original work, and by doing the same with the wristbands.

This is the time for oil-skin suits, dread-naughts, tarred trousers and overalls, sea-boots, comforters, mittens, woolen socks, Guernsey frocks, Havre shirts, buffalo-robe shorts, and moose-skin drawers. Every man's jacket is his wigwam, and every man's hat his caboose.

Perfect license is now permitted to the men respecting their clothing. Whatever they can rake and scrape together they put on— swaddling themselves in old sails, and drawing old socks over their heads for night-caps. This is the time for smiting your chest with your hand, and talking loud to keep up the circulation.

Colder, and colder, and colder, till at last we spoke a fleet of icebergs bound North. After that, it was one incessant *"cold snap,"* that almost snapped off our fingers and toes. Cold! It was cold as *Blue Flujin*, where sailors say fire freezes.

And now coming up with the latitude of the Cape, we stood southward to give it a wide berth, and while so doing were becalmed; ay, becalmed off Cape Horn, which is worse, far worse, than being becalmed on the Line.

Here we lay forty-eight hours, during which the cold was intense. I wondered at the liquid sea, which refused to freeze in such a temperature. The clear, cold sky overhead looked like a steel-blue cymbal, that might ring, could you smite it. Our breath came and went like puffs of smoke from pipe-bowls. At first there was a long gauky swell, that obliged us to furl most of the sails, and even send down t'-gallant-yards, for fear of pitching them overboard.

Out of sight of land, at this extremity of both the inhabitable and uninhabitable world, our peopled frigate, echoing with the voices of men, the bleating of lambs, the cackling of fowls, the grunting of pigs, seemed like Noah's old ark itself, becalmed at the climax of the Deluge.

There was nothing to be done but patiently to await the pleasure of the elements, and "whistle for a wind," the usual practice of seamen in a calm. No fire was allowed, except for the indispensable purpose of cooking, and heating bottles of water to toast Selvagee's feet. He who possessed the largest stock of vitality, stood the best chance to escape freezing. It was horrifying.

In such weather any man could have undergone amputation with great ease, and helped take up the arteries himself.

Indeed, this state of affairs had not lasted quite twenty-four hours, when the extreme frigidity of the air, united to our increased tendency to inactivity, would very soon have rendered some of us subjects for the surgeon and his mates, had not a humane proceeding of the Captain suddenly impelled us to rigorous exercise.

And here be it said, that the appearance of the Boatswain, with his silver whistle to his mouth, at the main hatchway of the gun-deck, is always regarded by the crew with the utmost curiosity, for this betokens that some general order is about to be promulgated through the ship. What now? is the question that runs on from man to man. A short preliminary whistle is then given by "Old Yarn," as they call him, which whistle serves to collect round him, from their various stations, his four mates. Then Yarn, or Pipes, as leader of the orchestra, begins a peculiar call, in which his assistants join. This over, the order, whatever it may be, is loudly sung out and prolonged, till the remotest corner echoes again. The Boatswain and his mates are the town-criers of a man-of-war.

The calm had commenced in the afternoon: and the following morning the ship's company were electrified by a general order, thus set forth and declared: *"D'ye hear there, fore and aft! all hands skylark!"*

This mandate, nowadays never used except upon very rare occasions, produced the same effect upon the men that Exhilarating Gas would have done, or an extra allowance of "grog." For a time, the wonted discipline of the ship was broken through, and perfect license allowed. It was a Babel here, a Bedlam there, and a Pandemonium everywhere. The Theatricals were nothing compared with it. Then the faint-hearted and timorous crawled to their hiding-places, and the lusty and bold shouted forth their glee.

Gangs of men, in all sorts of outlandish habiliments, wild as those worn at some crazy carnival, rushed to and fro, seizing upon whomsoever they pleased—warrant-officers and dangerous pugilists excepted—pulling and hauling the luckless tars about, till fairly baited into a genial warmth. Some were made fast to and hoisted aloft with a will: others, mounted upon oars, were ridden fore and aft on a rail, to the boisterous mirth of the spectators, any one of whom might be the next victim. Swings were rigged from the tops, or the masts; and the most reluctant wights being purposely selected, in spite of all struggles, were swung from East to West, in vast arcs of circles, till almost breathless. Hornpipes, fandangoes, Donnybrook-jibs, reels, and quadrilles, were danced under the very nose of the most mighty captain, and upon the very quarter-deck and poop. Sparring and wrestling, too, were all the vogue; *Kentucky bites* were given, and the *Indian hug* exchanged. The din frightened the sea-fowl, that flew by with accelerated wing.

It is worth mentioning that several casualties occurred, of which, however, I will relate but one. While the "skylarking" was at its height, one of the fore-top-men—an ugly-tempered devil of a Portuguese, looking on—swore that he would be the death of any man who laid violent hands upon his inviolable person. This threat being overhead, a band of desperadoes, coming up from behind, tripped him up in an instant, and in the twinkling of an eye the Portuguese was straddling an oar, borne aloft by an uproarious multitude, who rushed him along the deck at a railroad gallop. The living mass of arms all round and beneath him was so dense, that every time he inclined one side he was instantly pushed upright, but only to fall over again, to receive another push from the contrary direction. Presently, disengaging his hands from those who held them, the enraged seaman drew from his bosom an iron belaying-pin, and recklessly laid about him to right and left. Most of his persecutors fled; but some eight or ten still stood their ground, and, while bearing him aloft, endeavored to wrest the weapon from his hands. In this attempt, one man was stuck on the head, and dropped insensible. He was taken up for dead, and carried below to Cuticle, the surgeon, while the Portuguese was put under guard. But the wound did not prove very serious; and in a few days the man was walking about the deck, with his head well bandaged.

This occurrence put an end to the "skylarking," further head-breaking being strictly prohibited. In due time the Portuguese paid the penalty of his rashness at the gangway; while once again the officers *shipped their quarterdeck faces.*

Ere the calm had yet left us, a sail had been discerned from the fore-top-mast-head, at a great distance, probably three leagues or more. At first it was a mere speck, altogether out of sight from the deck. By the force of attraction or something else equally inscrutable, two ships in a calm, and equally affected by the currents, will always approximate, more or less. Though there was not a breath of wind, it was not a great while before the strange sail was described from our bulwarks; gradually, it drew still nearer.

What was she, and whence? There is no object which so excites interest and conjecture, and, at the same time, baffles both, as a sail, seen as a mere speck on these remote seas off Cape Horn.

A breeze! a breeze! for lo! the stranger is now perceptibly nearing the frigate; the officer's spy-glass pronounced her a full-rigged ship, with all sail set, and coming right down to us, though in our own vicinity the calm still reigns.

She is bringing the wind with her. Hurrah! Ay, there it is! Behold how mincingly it creeps over the sea, just ruffling and crisping it.

Our top-men were at once sent aloft to loose the sails, and presently they faintly began to distend. As yet we hardly had steerage-way. Toward sunset the stranger bore down before the wind, a complete pyramid of canvas. Never before, I venture to say, was Cape Horn so audaciously insulted. Stun'-sails alow and aloft; royals, moon-sails, and everything else. She glided under our stern, within hailing distance, and the signal-quarter-master ran up our ensign to the gaff.

"Ship ahoy!" cried the Lieutenant of the Watch, through his trumpet.

"Halloa!" bawled an old fellow in a green jacket, clapping one hand to his mouth, while he held on with the other to the mizzen-shrouds.

"What ship's that?"

"The *Sultan*, Indiaman, from New York, and bound to Callao and Canton, sixty days out, all well. What frigate's that?"

"The United States ship *Neversink*, homeward bound."

"Hurrah! hurrah! hurrah!" yelled our enthusiastic countryman, transported with patriotism.

By this time the *Sultan* had swept past, but the Lieutenant of the Watch could not withhold a parting admonition.

"D'ye hear? You'd better take in some of your flying-kites there. Look out for Cape Horn!"

But the friendly advice was lost in the now increasing wind. With a suddenness by no means unusual in these latitudes, the light breeze soon became a succession of sharp squalls, and our sail-proud braggadocio of an India-man was observed to let everything go by the run, his t'-gallant stun'-sails and flying-jib taking quick leave of the spars; the flying-jib was swept into the air, rolled together for a few minutes, and tossed about in the squalls like a foot-ball. But the wind played no such pranks with the more prudently managed canvas of the *Neversink*, though before many hours it was stirring times with us.

About midnight, when the starboard watch, to which I belonged, was below, the boatswain's whistle was heard, followed by the shrill cry of *"All hands take in sail!* Jump, men, and save ship!"

Springing from our hammocks, we found the frigate leaning over to it so steeply, that it was with difficulty we could climb the ladders leading to the upper deck.

Here the scene was awful. The vessel seemed to be sailing on her side. The main-deck guns had several days previous been run in and housed, and the port-holes closed, but the lee carronades on the quarter-deck and forecastle were plunging through the sea, which undulated over them in milk-white billows of foam. With every lurch to leeward the yard-arm-ends seemed to dip in the sea, while forward the spray dashed over the bows in cataracts, and drenched the men who were on the fore-yard. By this time the deck was alive with the whole strength of the ship's company, five hundred men, officers and all, mostly clinging to the weather bulwarks. The occasional phosphorescence of the yeasting sea cast a glare upon their uplifted faces, as a night fire in a populous city lights up the panic-stricken crowd.

In a sudden gale, or when a large quantity of sail is suddenly to be furled, it is the custom for the First Lieutenant to take the trumpet from whoever happens then to be officer of the deck. But Mad Jack had the trumpet that watch; nor did the First Lieutenant now seek to wrest it from his hands. Every eye was upon him, as if we had chosen him from among us all, to decide this battle with the elements, by single combat with the spirit of the Cape; for Mad Jack was the saving genius of the ship, and so proved himself that night. I owe this right hand, that is this moment flying over my sheet, and all my present being to Mad Jack. The ship's bows were now butting, battering, ramming, and thundering over and upon the head seas, and with a horrible wallowing sound our whole hull was rolling in the trough of the foam. The gale came athwart the deck, and every sail seemed bursting with its wild breath.

All the quarter-masters, and several of the forecastle-men, were swarming round the double-wheel on the quarter-deck. Some jumping up and down, with their hands upon the spokes; for the whole helm and galvanized keel were fiercely feverish, with the life imparted to them by the wild tempest.

"Hard *up* the helm!" shouted Captain Claret, bursting from his cabin like a ghost in his night-dress.

"Damn you!" raged Mad Jack to the quarter-masters; "hard *down*— hard *down*, I say, and be damned to you!"

Contrary orders! but Mad Jack's were obeyed. His object was to throw the ship into the wind, so as the better to admit of close-reefing the top-sails, but though the halyards were let go, it was impossible to clew down the yards, owing to the enormous horizontal strain on the canvas. It now blew a hurricane. The spray flew over the ship in floods. The gigantic masts seemed about to snap under the world-wide strain of the three entire top-sails.

"Clew down! Clew down!" shouted Mad Jack, husky with excitement, and in a frenzy, beating his trumpet against one of the shrouds. But, owing to the slant of the ship, the thing could not be done. It was obvious that before many minutes something must go—either sails, rigging, or sticks; perhaps the hull itself, and all hands.

Presently a voice from the top exclaimed that there was a rent in the main-top-sail. And instantly we heard a report like two or three muskets discharged together; the vast sail was rent up and down like the Veil of the Temple. This saved the main-mast; for the yard was now clewed down with comparative ease, and the top-men laid out to stow the shattered canvas. Soon, the two remaining top-sails were also clewed down and close-reefed.

Above all the roar of the tempest and the shouts of the crew, was heard the dismal tolling of the ship's bell—almost as large as that of a village church—which the violent rolling of the ship was occasioning. Imagination cannot conceive the horror of such a sound in a night-tempest at sea.

"Stop that ghost!" roared Mad Jack; "away, one of you, and wrench off the clapper!"

But no sooner was this ghost gagged, than a still more appalling sound was heard, the rolling to and fro of the heavy shot, which, on the gun-deck, had broken loose from the gun-racks, and converted that part of the ship into an immense bowling-alley. Some hands were sent down to secure them; but it was as much as their lives were worth. Several were maimed; and the midshipmen who were ordered to see the duty performed reported it impossible, until the storm abated.

The most terrific job of all was to furl the main-sail, which, at the commencement of the squalls, had been clewed up, coaxed and quieted as much as possible with the bunt-lines and slab-lines. Mad Jack waited some time for a lull, ere he gave an order so perilous to be executed. For to furl this enormous sail, in such a gale, required at least fifty men on the yard; whose weight, superadded to that of the ponderous stick itself, still further jeopardized their lives. But there was no prospect of a cessation of the gale, and the order was at last given.

At this time a hurricane of slanting sleet and hail was descending upon us; the rigging was coated with a thin glare of ice, formed within the hour.

"Aloft, main-yard-men! and all you main-top-men! and furl the main-sail!" cried Mad Jack.

I dashed down my hat, slipped out of my quilted jacket in an instant, kicked the shoes from my feet, and, with a crowd of others, sprang for the rigging. Above the bulwarks (which in a frigate are so high as to afford much protection to those on deck) the gale was horrible. The sheer force of the wind flattened us to the rigging as we ascended, and every hand seemed congealing to the icy shrouds by which we held.

"Up—up, my brave hearties!" shouted Mad Jack; and up we got, some way or other, all of us, and groped our way out on the yard-arms.

"Hold on, every mother's son!" cried an old quarter-gunner at my side. He was bawling at the top of his compass, but in the gale, he seemed to be whispering; and I only heard him from his being right to windward of me.

But his hint was unnecessary; I dug my nails into the *Jack-stays*, and swore that nothing but death should part me and them until I was able to turn round and look to windward. As yet, this was impossible; I could scarcely hear the man to leeward at my elbow; the wind seemed to snatch the words from his mouth and fly away with them to the South Pole.

All this while the sail itself was flying about, sometimes catching over our heads, and threatening to tear us from the yard in spite of all our hugging. For about three quarters of an hour we thus hung suspended right over the rampant billows, which curled their very crests under the feet of some four or five of us clinging to the lee-yard-arm, as if to float us from our place.

Presently, the word passed along the yard from wind-ward that we were ordered to come down and leave the sail to blow; since it could not be furled. A midshipman, it seemed, had been sent up by the offi-cer of the deck to give the order, as no trumpet could be heard where we were.

Those on the weather yard-arm managed to crawl upon the spar and scramble down the rigging; but with us, upon the extreme leeward side, this feat was out of the question; it was, literally, like climbing a precipice to get to windward in order to reach the shrouds; besides, the entire yard was now encased in ice, and our hands and feet were so numb that we dared not trust our lives to them. Nevertheless, by assisting each other, we contrived to throw ourselves prostrate along the yard, and embrace it with our arms and legs. In this position, the stun'-sail-booms greatly assisted in securing our hold. Strange as it may appear, I do not suppose that, at this moment, the slightest sensation of fear was felt by one man on that yard. We clung to it with might and main; but this was instinct. The truth is, that, in circumstances like these, the sense of fear is annihilated in the unutterable sights that fill all the eye, and the sounds that fill all the ear. You become identified with the tempest; your insignificance is lost in the riot of the stormy universe around.

Below us, our noble frigate seemed thrice its real length—a vast black wedge, opposing its widest end to the combined fury of the sea and wind.

At length the first fury of the gale began to abate, and we at once fell to pounding our hands, as a preliminary operation to going to work; for a gang of men had now ascended to help secure what was left of the sail; we somehow packed it away, at last, and came down.

About noon the next day, the gale so moderated that we shook two reefs out of the top-sails, set new courses, and stood due east, with the wind astern.

Thus, all the fine weather we encountered after first weighing anchor on the pleasant Spanish coast, was but the prelude to this one terrific night; more especially, that treacherous calm immediately preceding it. But how could we reach our long-promised homes without encountering Cape Horn? by what possibility avoid it? And though some ships have weathered it without these perils, yet by far the greater part must encounter them. Lucky it is that it comes about midway in the homeward-bound passage, so that the sailors have time to prepare for it, and time to recover from it after it is astern.

But, sailor or landsman, there is some sort of a Cape Horn for all. Boys! beware of it; prepare for it in time. Grey-beards! thank God it is passed. And ye lucky livers, to whom, by some rare fatality, your Cape Horns are placid as Lake Lemans, flatter not yourselves that good luck is judgment and discretion; for all the yolk in your eggs, you might have foundered and gone down, had the Spirit of the Cape said the word.

9

LOSS OF A MAN— SUPERSTITION

RICHARD HENRY DANA

Monday, Nov. 19th. This was a black day in our calendar. At seven o'clock in the morning, it being our watch below, we were aroused from a sound sleep by the cry of "All hands ahoy! a man overboard!" This unwonted cry sent a thrill through the heart of every one, and hurrying on deck we found the vessel hove flat aback, with all her studding-sails set; for the boy who was at the helm left it to throw something overboard, and the carpenter, who was an old sailor, knowing that the wind was light, put the helm down and hove her aback.

The watch on deck were lowering away the quarter-boat, and I got on deck just in time to heave myself into her as she was leaving the side; but it was not until out upon the wide Pacific, in our little boat, that I knew whom we had lost. It was George Ballmer, a young English sailor, who was prized by the officers as an active lad and willing seaman, and by the crew as a lively, hearty fellow, and a good shipmate.

He was going aloft to fit a strap round the main top-mast-head, for ringtail halyards, and had the strap and block, a coil of halyards and a marline-spike about his neck. He fell from the starboard futtock shrouds, and not knowing how to swim, and being heavily dressed, with all those things round his neck, he probably sank immediately. We pulled astern, in the direction in which he fell, and though we knew that there was no hope of saving him, yet no one wished to speak of returning, and we rowed about for nearly an hour, without the hope of doing anything, but unwilling to acknowledge to ourselves that we must give him up. At length we turned the boat's head and made towards the vessel.

Death is at all times solemn, but never so much so as at sea. A man dies on shore; his body remains with his friends, and "the mourners go about the streets"; but when a man falls overboard at sea and is lost, there is a suddenness in the event, and a difficulty in realizing it, which give to it an air of awful mystery. A man dies on shore—you follow his body to the grave, and a stone marks the spot. You are often prepared for the event. There is always something which helps you to realize it when it happens, and to recall it when it has passed.

A man is shot down by your side in battle, and the mangled body remains an object, and a real evidence; but at sea, the man is near you—at your side—you hear his voice, and in an instant he is gone, and nothing but a vacancy shows his loss. Then, too, at sea—to use a homely but expressive phrase—you miss a man so much. A dozen men are shut up together in a little bark, upon the wide, wide sea, and for months and months see no forms and hear no voices but their own, and one is taken suddenly from among them, and they miss him at every turn. It is like losing a limb. There are no new faces or new scenes to fill up the gap. There is always an empty berth in the forecastle, and one man wanting when the small night watch is mustered. There is one less to take the wheel, and one less to lay out with you upon the yard. You miss his form, and the sound of his voice, for habit had made them almost necessary to you, and each of your senses feels the loss.

All these things make such a death peculiarly solemn, and the effect of it remains upon the crew for some time. There is more kindness shown by the officers to the crew, and by the crew to one another. There is more quietness and seriousness. The oath and the loud laugh are gone. The officers are more watchful, and the crew go more carefully aloft. The lost man is seldom mentioned, or is dismissed with a sailor's rude eulogy—"Well, poor George is gone! His cruise is up soon! He knew his work, and did his duty, and was a good shipmate." Then usually follows some allusion to another world, for sailors are almost all believers; but their notions and opinions are unfixed and at loose ends. They say,—"God won't be hard upon the poor fellow," and seldom get beyond the common phrase which seems to imply that their sufferings and hard treatment here will excuse them hereafter,—"To work hard, live hard, die hard, and go to hell after all, would be hard indeed!" Our cook, a simple-hearted old African, who had been through a good deal in his day, and was rather seriously inclined, always going to church twice a day when on shore, and reading his Bible on a Sunday in the galley, talked to the crew about spending their Sabbaths badly, and told them that they might go as suddenly as George had, and be as little prepared.

Yet a sailor's life is, at best, but a mixture of a little good with much evil, and a little pleasure with much pain. The beautiful is linked with the revolting, the sublime with the commonplace, and the solemn with the ludicrous.

We had hardly returned on board with our sad report, before an auction was held of the poor man's clothes. The captain had first, however, called all hands aft and asked them if they were satisfied that everything had been done to save the man, and if they thought there was any use in remaining there longer. The crew all said that it was in vain, for the man did not know how to swim, and was very heavily dressed. So we then filled away and kept her off to her course.

The laws regulating navigation make the captain answerable for the effects of a sailor who dies during the voyage, and it is either a law or a universal custom, established for convenience, that the captain should immediately hold an auction of his things, in which they are bid off by the sailors, and the sums which they give are deducted from their wages at the end of the voyage. In this way the trouble and risk of keeping his things through the voyage are avoided, and the clothes are usually sold for more than they would be worth on shore.

Accordingly, we had no sooner got the ship before the wind, than his chest was brought up upon the forecastle, and the sale began. The jackets and trowsers in which we had seen him dressed but a few days before, were exposed and bid off while the life was hardly out of his body, and his chest was taken aft and used as a store-chest, so that there was nothing left which could be called his. Sailors have an unwillingness to wear a dead man's clothes during the same voyage, and they seldom do so unless they are in absolute want.

As is usual after a death, many stories were told about George. Some had heard him say that he repented never having learned to swim, and that he knew that he should meet his death by drowning. Another said that he never knew any good to come of a voyage made against the will, and the deceased man shipped and spent his advance and was afterwards very unwilling to go, but not being able to refund, was obliged to sail with us. A boy, too, who had become quite attached to him, said that George talked to him during most of the watch on the night before, about his mother and family at home, and this was the first time that he had mentioned the subject during the voyage.

The night after this event, when I went to the galley to get a light, I found the cook inclined to be talkative, so I sat down on the spars, and gave him an opportunity to hold a yarn. I was the more inclined to do so, as I found that he was full of the superstitions once more common among seamen, and which the recent death had waked up in his mind. He talked about George's having spoken of his friends, and said he believed few men died without having a warning of it, which he supported by a great many stories of dreams, and the unusual behavior of men before death. From this he went on to other superstitions, the Flying Dutchman, etc., and talked rather mysteriously, having something evidently on his mind.

At length he put his head out of the galley and looked carefully about to see if any one was within hearing, and being satisfied on that point, asked me in a low tone—

"I say! you know what countryman 'e carpenter be?"

"Yes," said I; "he's a German."

"What kind of a German?" said the cook.

"He belongs to Bremen," said I.

"Are you sure o' dat?" said he.

I satisfied him on that point by saying that he could speak no language but the German and English.

"I'm plaguy glad o' dat," said the cook. "I was mighty 'fraid he was a Fin. I tell you what, I been plaguy civil to that man all the voyage."

I asked him the reason of this, and found that he was fully possessed with the notion that Fins are wizards, and especially have power over winds and storms. I tried to reason with him about it, but he had the best of all arguments, that from experience, at hand, and was not to be moved. He had been in a vessel at the Sandwich Islands, in which the sail-maker was a Fin, and could do anything he was of a mind to. This sail-maker kept a junk bottle in his berth, which was always just half full of rum, though he got drunk upon it nearly every day. He had seen him sit for hours together, talking to this bottle, which he stood up before him on the table. The same man cut his throat in his berth, and everybody said he was possessed.

He had heard of ships, too, beating up the gulf of Finland against a head wind, and having a ship heave in sight astern, overhaul and pass them, with as fair a wind as could blow, and all studding-sails out, and find she was from Finland.

"Oh ho!" said he; "I've seen too much of them men to want to see 'em 'board a ship. If they can't have their own way, they'll play the d—l with you."

As I still doubted, he said he would leave it to John, who was the oldest seaman aboard, and would know, if anybody did. John, to be sure, was the oldest, and at the same time the most ignorant, man in the ship; but I consented to have him called. The cook stated the matter to him, and John, as I anticipated, sided with the cook, and said that he himself had been in a ship where they had a head wind for a fortnight, and the captain found out at last that one of the men, whom he had had some hard words with a short time before, was a Fin, and immediately told him if he didn't stop the head wind he would shut him down in the fore peak, and would not give him anything to eat. The Fin held out for a day and a half, when he could not stand it any longer, and did something or other which brought the wind round again, and they let him up.

"There," said the cook, "what do you think o' dat?"

I told him I had no doubt it was true, and that it would have been odd if the wind had not changed in fifteen days, Fin or no Fin.

"Oh," said he, "go 'way! You think, 'cause you been to college, you know better than anybody. You know better than them as 'as seen it with their own eyes. You wait till you've been to sea as long as I have, and you'll know."

10

A STUDENT'S SEA STORY

HARRIET BEECHER STOWE

Among the pleasantest of my recollections of old Bowdoin is the salt-air flavor of its sea experiences. The site of Brunswick is a sandy plain, on which the college buildings seem to have been dropped for the good old Yankee economic reason of using land for public buildings that could not be used for any thing else. The soil was a fathomless depth of dry, sharp, barren sand, out of whose bosom nothing but pitch-pines and blueberry-bushes emerged, or ever could emerge without superhuman efforts of cultivation. But these sandy plains, these pine forests, were neighbors to the great, lively, musical blue ocean, whose life-giving presence made itself seen, heard, and felt every hour of the day and night. The beautiful peculiarity of the Maine coast, where the sea interpenetrates the land in picturesque fiords and lakes, brought a constant romantic element into the landscape.

White-winged ships from India or China came gliding into the forest recesses bringing news from strange lands, and tidings of wild adventure, into secluded farmhouses, that, for the most part, seemed to be dreaming in woodland solitude. In the early days of my college life the shipping interest of Maine gave it an outlook into all the countries of the earth. Ships and ship-building and ship-launching were the drift of the popular thought; and the very minds of the people by this commerce had apparently "Suffered a sea change into something rare and strange."

There was a quaintness, shrewdness, and vivacity of lonely solitude about these men, (half skipper, half farmer!) that half skip was piquant and enlivening.

It was in the auspicious period of approaching Thanksgiving that my chum and I resolved to antedate for a few days our vacation, and take passage on the little sloop "Brilliant," that lay courtesying and teetering on the bright waters of Maquoit Bay, loading up to make her Thanksgiving trip to Boston.

It was a bright Indian-summer afternoon that saw us all on board the little craft. She was laden deep with dainties and rarities for the festal appetites of Boston nabobs,—loads of those mealy potatoes for which the fields of Maine were justly famed, barrels of ruby cranberries, boxes of solid golden butter (ventures of a thrifty housemother emulous to gather kindred gold in the Boston market). Then there were dressed chickens, turkeys, and geese, all going the same way, on the same errand; and there were sides and saddles of that choice mutton for which the sea islands of Maine were as famous as the South Downs of England.

Every thing in such a stowage was suggestive of good cheer. The little craft itself had a sociable, friendly, domestic air. The captain and mate were cousins: the men were all neighbors, sons of families who had grown up together. There was a kindly home flavor in the very stowage of the cargo. Here were Melissa's cranberries, and by many a joke and wink we were apprised that the mate had a tender interest in that venture. There was Widder Toothacre's butter, concerning which there were various comments and speculations, but which was handled and cared for with the consideration the Maine sailor-boy always gives to "the widder." There was a private keg of very choice eggs, over which the name of Lucindy Ann was breathed by a bright-eyed, lively youngster, who had promised to bring her back the change, and as to the precise particulars of this change many a witticism was expended.

Our mode of living on the "Brilliant" was of the simplest and most primitive kind. On each side the staircase that led down to the cabin, hooped strongly to the partition, was a barrel, which on the one side contained salt beef, and on the other salt pork. A piece out of each barrel, delivered regularly to the cook, formed the foundation of our daily meals; and sea-biscuit and potatoes, with the sauce of salt-water appetites, made this a feast for a king. I make no mention here of gingerbread and doughnuts, and such like ornamental accessories, which were not wanting, nor of nuts and sweet cider, which were to be had for the asking. At meal-times a swing-shelf, which at other seasons hung flat against the wall, was propped up, and our meals were eaten thereon in joyous satisfaction.

A joyous, rollicking set we were, and the whole expedition was a frolic of the first water. One of the drollest features of these little impromptu voyages often was the woe-begone aspect of some unsuspecting land-lubber, who had been beguiled into thinking that he would like a trip to Boston by seeing the pretty "Brilliant" courtesying in the smooth waters of Maquoit, and so had embarked, in innocent ignorance of the physiological resets of such enterprises.

I remember the first morning out. As we were driving ahead, under a stiff breeze, I came on deck, and found the respectable Deacon Muggins, who in his Sunday coat had serenely embarked the day before, now desolately clinging to the railing, very white about the gills, and contemplating the sea with a most suggestive expression of disgust and horror.

"Why, deacon, good-morning! How are you? Splendid morning!" said I maliciously.

He drew a deep breath, surveyed me with a mixture of indignation and despair, and then gave vent to his feelings: "Tell ye what: there was one darned old fool up to Brunswick yesterday! but he ain't there now: he's *here*." The deacon, in the weekly prayer-meeting at Brunswick, used to talk of the necessity of being "emptied of self": he seemed to be in the way of it in the most literal manner at the present moment. In a few minutes he was extended on the deck, the most utterly limp and dejected of deacons, and vowing with energy, if he ever got out o' this 'ere, you wouldn't catch him again. Of course, my chum and I were not seasick. We were prosperous young sophomores in Bowdoin College, and would have scorned to acknowledge such a weakness. In fact, we were in that happy state of self-opinion where we surveyed every thing in creation, as birds do, from above, and were disposed to patronize everybody we met, with a pleasing conviction that there was nothing worth knowing, but what we were likely to know, or worth doing, but what we could do.

Capt. Stanwood liked us, and we liked him: we patronized him, and he was quietly amused at our patronage, and returned it in kind. He was a good specimen of the sea-captain in those early days in Maine: a man in middle life, tall, thin, wiry, and active, full of resource and shrewd mother-wit; a man very confident in his opinions, because his knowledge was all got at first-hand,—the result of a careful use of his own five senses. From his childhood he had followed the seas, and, as he grew older, made voyages to Archangel, to Messina, to the West Indies, and finally round the Horn; and, having carried a very sharp and careful pair of eyes, he had acquired not only a snug competency of worldly goods, but a large stock of facts and inductions, which stood him in stead of an education.

He was master of a thriving farm at Harpswell, and, being tethered somewhat by love of wife and children, was mostly stationary there, yet solaced himself by running a little schooner to Boston, and driving a thriving bit of trade by the means. With that reverence for learning, which never deserts the New-Englander, he liked us the better for being collegians, and amiably conceded that there were things quite worth knowing taught "up to Brunswick there," though he delighted now and then to show his superiority in talking about what he knew better than we.

Jim Larned, the mate, was a lusty youngster, a sister's son whom he had taken in training in the way he should go. Jim had already made a voyage to Liverpool and the East Indies, and felt himself also quite an authority in his own way.

The evenings were raw and cool; and we generally gathered round the cabin stove, cracking walnuts, smoking, and telling stories, and having a jolly time generally. It is but due to those old days to say that a most respectable Puritan flavor penetrated even the recesses of those coasters,—a sort of gentle Bible and psalm-book aroma, so that there was not a word or a joke among the men to annoy the susceptibilities even of a deacon. Our deacon, somewhat consoled and amended, lay serene in his berth, rather enjoying the yarns that we were spinning. The web, of course, was many-colored,—of quaint and strange and wonderful; and, as the night wore on, it was dyed in certain weird tints of the supernatural.

"Well," said Jim Larned, "folks may say what they're a mind to: there are things that there's no sort o' way o' 'countin' for,—things you've jist got to say. Well, here's suthin' to work that I don't know nothin' about; and, come to question any man up sharp, you 'll find he's seen *one* thing o' that sort' himself; and this 'ere I'm going to tell's *my* story:—

"Four years ago I went down to aunt Jerushy's at Fair Haven. Her husband's in the oysterin' business, and I used to go out with him considerable. Well, there was Bill Jones there,—a real bright fellow, one of your open-handed, lively fellows,—and he took a fancy to me, and I to him, and he and I struck up a friendship. He run an oyster-smack to New York, and did a considerable good business for a young man. Well, Bill had a fellow on his smack that I never looks of. He was from the Malays, or foreign crittur, or other; spoke broken English; had eyes set kind o' edgeways 'n his head: homely as sin he was, and I always mistrusted him. 'Bill,' I used to say, 'you look out for that fellow: don't you trust him. If I was you, I'd ship him off short metre.' But Bill, he only laughed. 'Why,' says he, 'I can get double work for the same pay out o' that fellow; and what do I care if he ain't handsome?' I remember how chipper an' cheery Bill looked when he was sayin' that, just as he was going down to New York with his load o' oysters. Well, the next night I was sound asleep in aunt Jerusha's front-chamber that opens towards the Sound, and I was waked right clear out o' sleep by Bill's voice screaming to me. I got up and run to the window, and looked liked the some out, and I heard it again, plain as any thing: 'Jim, Jim! Help, help!' It wasn't a common cry, neither: it was screeched out, as if somebody was murdering him. I tell you, it rung through my head for weeks afterwards."

"Well, what came of it?" said my chum, as the narrator made a pause, and we all looked at him in silence.

"Well, as nigh as we can make it out, that very night poor Bill *was* murdered by that very Malay feller: leastways, his body was found in his boat. He'd been stabbed, and all his money and watch and things taken, and this Malay was gone nobody knew where. That's all that was ever known about it."

"But surely," said my chum, who was of a very literal and rationalistic turn of mind, "it couldn't have been his voice you heard: he must have been down to the other end of the Sound, close by New York, by that time."

"Well," said the mate, "all I know is, that I was waked out of sleep by Bill's voice calling my name, screaming in a real agony. It went through me like lightning; and then I find he was murdered that night. Now, I don't know any thing about it. I know I heard him calling me; I know he was murdered: but *how* it was, or *what* it was, or *why* it was, I don't know."

"These 'ere college boys can tell ye," said the captain. "Of course, they've got into sophomore year, and there ain't nothing in heaven or earth that they don't know."

"No," said I, "I say with Hamlet, 'There are more things in heaven and earth, Horatio, than are dreamed of in your philosophy.'"

"Well," said my chum, with the air of a philosopher, "what shakes my faith in all supernatural stories is, that I can't see any use or purpose in them."

"Wal, if there couldn't nothin' happen nor be except what *you* could see a use in, there wouldn't *much* happen nor be," quoth the captain.

A laugh went round at the expense of my friend.

"Wal, now, I'll tell ye what, boys," piped the thin voice of the deacon, "folks mustn't be too presumptuous: there is providences permitted that we don't see no use in; but they do happen,—yes, they do. Now, what Jim Larned's been a-tell-in' is a good deal like what happened to me once, when I was up to Umbagog, in the lumberin' business."

"Halloo!" called out Jim, "here's the deacon's story! I told you every man had one.—Give it to us, deacon! Speak out, and don't be bashful!"

"Wal, really, it ain't what I like to talk about," said the deacon, in a quavering, uncertain voice; "but I don't know but I may as well, though.

"It was that winter I was up to Umbagog. I was clerk, and kep' the 'counts and books, and all that; and Tom Huly,—he was surveyor and marker,—he was there with me, and we chummed together. And there was Jack Cutter; he was jest out o' college: he was there practising surveyin' with him. We three had a kind o' pine-board sort o' shanty, built out on a plain near by the camp: it had a fire-place, and two windows, and our bunks, and each of us had our tables and books and things.

"Well, Huly, he started with a party of three or four to go up through the woods to look out a new tract. It was two or three days' journey through the woods; and jest about that time the Indians up there was getting sort o' uneasy, and we all thought mabbe 'twas sort o' risky: howsomdever, Tom had gone off in high spirits, and told us to be sure and take care of his books and papers. Tom had a lot of books, and thought every thing of 'em, and was sort o' particular and nice about his papers. His table sot up one side, by the winder, where he could see to read and write. Well, he'd been gone four days, when one night—it was a bright moonlight night—Jack and I were sitting by the fire, reading, and between nine and ten o'clock there came a strong, regular knock on the window over by Tom's table. We were sitting with our backs to the window. 'Halloo!' says Jack, 'who's that?' We both jumped up, and went to the window and looked out, and see there warn't nobody there.

"'This is curious,' said I.

"'Some of the boys trying to trick us,' says he. 'Let's keep watch: perhaps they'll do it again,' says he.

"We sot down by the fire, and 'fore long it came again.

"Then Jack and I both cut out the door, and run round the house,—he one way, and I the other. It was light as day, and nothin' for anybody to hide behind, and there warn't a critter in sight. Well, we come in and sot down, and looked at each other kind o' puzzled, when it come agin, harder'n ever; and Jack looked to the window, and got as white as a sheet.

"'For the Lord's sake, do look!' says he. And you may believe me or not; but I tell you it's a solemn fact: Tom's books was movin',—jest as if somebody was pickin' 'em up, and putting 'em down again, jest as I've seen him do a hundred times.

"'Jack,' says I, 'something's happened to Tom.'

"Wal, there had. That very night Tom was murdered by the Indians. We put down the date, and a week arter the news came."

"Come now, captain," said I, breaking the pause that followed the deacon's story, "give us your story. You've been all over the world, in all times and all weathers, and you ain't a man to be taken in. Did you ever see any thing of this sort?"

"Well, now, boys, since you put it straight at me, I don't care if I say I have,—on these 'ere very waters we're a-sailin' over now, on board this very schooner, in this very cabin."

This was bringing matters close home. We felt an agreeable shiver, and looked over our shoulders: the deacon, in his berth, raised up on his elbow, and ejaculated, "Dew tell! ye don't say so!"

"Tell us about it, captain," we both insisted. "We 'll take your word for most any thing."

"Well, it happened about five years ago. It's goin' on now eight years ago that my father died. He sailed out of Gloucester: had his house there; and, after he died, mother, she jest kep' on in the old place. I went down at first to see her fixed up about right, and after that I went now and then, and now and then I sent money. Well, it was about Thanksgiving time, as it is now, and I'd ben down to Boston, and was coming back pretty well loaded with the things I'd been buying in Boston for Thanksgiving at home,—raisins and sugar, and all sorts of West Ingy goods, for the folks in Harpswell. Well, I meant to have gone down to Gloucester to see mother; but I had so many ways to run, and so much to do, I was afraid I wouldn't be back on time; and so I didn't see her.

"Well, we was driving back with a good stiff breeze, and we'd got past Cape Ann, and I'd gone down and turned in, and was fast asleep in my berth. It was past midnight: every one on the schooner asleep, except the mate, who was up on the watch. I was sleepin' as sound as ever I slept in my life,—not a dream, nor a feelin', no more'n if I had been dead,—when suddenly I waked square up. My eyes flew open like a spring, with my mind clear and wide awake, and, sure as I ever see any thing, I see my father standing right in the middle of the cabin, looking right at me. I rose right up in my berth, and says I,—

"'Father, is that you?'

"'Yes,' says he, 'it is me.'

"'Father,' says I, 'what do you come for?'

"'Sam,' says he, 'do you go right back to Gloucester, and take your mother home with you, and keep her there as long as she lives.'

"And says I, 'Father, I will.' And as I said this he faded out and was gone. I got right up, and run up on deck, and called out, ''Bout ship!' Mr. More—he was my mate then—stared at me as if he didn't believe his ears. ''Bout ship!' says I. 'I'm going to Gloucester.'

"Well, he put the ship about, and then came to me, and says, 'What the devil does this mean? We're way past Cape Ann. It's forty miles right back to Gloucester.'

"'Can't help it,' I said. 'To Gloucester I must go as quick as wind and water will carry me. I've thought of matters there that I *must* attend to, no matter what happens.'

"Well, Ben More and I were good friends always; but I tell you all that day he watched me, in a curious kind of way, to see if I weren't took with a fever, or suthin; and the men, they whispered and talked among themselves. You see, they all had their own reasons for wanting to be back to Thanksgiving, and it was hard on 'em.

"Well, it was just about sun up we got into Gloucester, and I went ashore. And there was mother, looking pretty poorly, jest making her fire, and getting on her kettle. When she saw me, she held up her hands, and burst out crying,—

"'Why, Sam, the Lord must 'a' sent you! I've time, and I've felt as if I couldn't hold our much longer.'

"'Well,' says I, 'mother, pack up your things, and come right aboard the sloop; for I've come to take you home, and take care of you: so put up your things.'

"Well, I took hold and helped her, and we put ben sick and all alone, having a drefful hard things together lively, and packed up her trunks, and tied up the bed and pillows and bedclothes, and took her rocking-chair and bureau and tables and chairs down to the sloop. And when I came down, bringing her and all her things, Ben More seemed to see what I was after; but how or why the idea came into my head I never told him. There's things that a man feels shy of tellin',' and I didn't want to talk about it.

"Well, when we was all aboard, the wind sprung up fair and steady, and we went on at a right spanking pace; and the fellows said the Harpswell girls had got hold of our rope, and was pulling us with all their might; and we came in all right the very day before Thanksgiving. And my wife was as glad to see mother as if she'd expected her, and fixed up the front-chamber for her, with a stove in't, and plenty of kindlings. And the children was all so glad to see grandma, and we had the best kind of a Thanksgiving!"

"Well," said I, "nobody could say there wasn't any use in *that* spirit's coming (if spirit it was): it had a most practical purpose."

"Well," said the captain, "I've been all round the world, in all sorts of countries, seen all sorts of queer, strange things, and seen so many things that I never could have believed if I hadn't seen 'em, that I never say I won't believe this or that. If I see a thing right straight under my eyes, I don't say it couldn't 'a' ben there 'cause college-folks say there ain't no such things."

"How do you know it wasn't all a dream?" said my chum.

"How do I know?' Cause I was broad awake, and I gen'lly know when I'm awake and when I'm asleep. I think Mr. More found me pretty wide awake."

It was now time to turn in, and we slept soundly while the "Brilliant" ploughed her way. By daybreak the dome of the State House was in sight.

"I've settled the captain's story," said my chum to me. "It can all be accounted for on the theory of cerebral hallucination."

"All right," said I; "but it answered the purpose beautifully for the old mother."

11

MS. FOUND IN A BOTTLE

EDGAR ALLAN POE

Qui n'a plus qu'un moment a vivre
N'a plus rien a dissimuler.

—*Quinault—Atys.*

Of my country and of my family I have little to say. Ill usage and length of years have driven me from the one, and estranged me from the other. Hereditary wealth afforded me an education of no common order, and a contemplative turn of mind enabled me to methodize the stores which early study very diligently garnered up. Beyond all things, the study of the German moralists gave me great delight; not from any ill-advised admiration of their eloquent madness, but from the ease with which my habits of rigid thought enabled me to detect their falsities. I have often been reproached with the aridity of my genius; a deficiency of imagination has been imputed to me as a crime; and the Pyrrhonism of my opinions has at all times rendered me notorious. Indeed, a strong relish for physical philosophy has, I fear, tinctured my mind with a very common error of this age—I mean the habit of referring occurrences, even the least susceptible of such reference, to the principles of that science. Upon the whole, no person could be less liable than myself to be led away from the severe precincts of truth by the *ignes fatui* of superstition. I have thought proper to premise thus much, lest the incredible tale I have to tell should be considered rather the raving of a crude imagination, than the positive experience of a mind to which the reveries of fancy have been a dead letter and a nullity.

After many years spent in foreign travel, I sailed in the year 18__, from the port of Batavia, in the rich and populous island of Java, on a voyage to the Archipelago of the Sunda islands. I went as passenger—having no other inducement than a kind of nervous restlessness which haunted me as a fiend. Our vessel was a beautiful ship of about four hundred tons, copper-fastened, and built at Bombay of Malabar teak. She was freighted with cotton-wool and oil, from the Lachadive islands. We had also on board coir, jaggeree, ghee, cocoanuts, and a few cases of opium. The stowage was clumsily done, and the vessel consequently crank.

We got under way with a mere breath of wind, and for many days stood along the eastern coast of Java, without any other incident to beguile the monotony of our course than the occasional meeting with some of the small grabs of the Archipelago to which we were bound.

One evening, leaning over the taffrail, I observed a very singular, isolated cloud, to the N.W. It was remarkable, as well for its color, as from its being the first we had seen since our departure from Batavia. I watched it attentively until sunset, when it spread all at once to the eastward and westward, girting in the horizon with a narrow strip of vapor, and looking like a long line of low beach. My notice was soon afterwards attracted by the dusky-red appearance of the moon, and the peculiar character of the sea. The latter was undergoing a rapid change, and the water seemed more than usually transparent. Although I could distinctly see the bottom, yet, heaving the lead, I found the ship in fifteen fathoms. The air now became intolerably hot, and was loaded with spiral exhalations similar to those arising from heat iron. As night came on, every breath of wind died away, and more entire calm it is impossible to conceive. The flame of a candle burned upon the poop without the least perceptible motion, and a long hair, held between the finger and thumb, hung without the possibility of detecting a vibration. However, as the captain said he could perceive no indication of danger, and as we were drifting in bodily to shore, he ordered the sails to be furled, and the anchor let go. No watch was set, and the crew, consisting principally of Malays, stretched themselves deliberately upon deck. I went below—not without a full presentiment of evil. Indeed, every appearance warranted me in apprehending a Simoom. I told the captain my fears; but he paid no attention to what I said, and left me without deigning to give a reply. My uneasiness, however, prevented me from sleeping, and about midnight I went upon deck. As I placed my foot upon the upper step of the companion-ladder, I was startled by a loud, humming noise, like that occasioned by the rapid revolution of a mill-wheel, and before I could ascertain its meaning, I found the ship quivering to its centre. In the next instant, a wilderness of foam hurled us upon our beam-ends, and, rushing over us fore and aft, swept the entire decks from stem to stern.

The extreme fury of the blast proved, in a great measure, the salvation of the ship. Although completely water-logged, yet, as her masts had gone by the board, she rose, after a minute, heavily from the sea, and, staggering awhile beneath the immense pressure of the tempest, finally righted.

By what miracle I escaped destruction, it is impossible to say. Stunned by the shock of the water, I found myself, upon recovery, jammed in between the stern-post and rudder. With great difficulty I gained my feet, and looking dizzily around, was, at first, struck with the idea of our being among breakers; so terrific, beyond the wildest imagination, was the whirlpool of mountainous and foaming ocean within which we were engulfed. After a while, I heard the voice of an old Swede, who had shipped with us at the moment of our leaving port. I hallooed to him with all my strength, and presently he came reeling aft. We soon discovered that we were the sole survivors of the accident. All on deck, with the exception of ourselves, had been swept overboard; the captain and mates must have perished as they slept, for the cabins were deluged with water. Without assistance, we could expect to do little for the security of the ship, and our exertions were at first paralyzed by the momentary expectation of going down. Our cable had, of course, parted like pack-thread, at the first breath of the hurricane, or we should have been instantaneously overwhelmed. We scudded with frightful velocity before the sea, and the water made clear breaches over us. The framework of our stern was shattered excessively, and, in almost every respect, we had received considerable injury; but to our extreme joy we found the pumps unchoked, and that we had made no great shifting of our ballast. The main fury of the blast had already blown over, and we apprehended little danger from the violence of the wind; but we looked forward to its total cessation with dismay; well believing, that, in our shattered condition, we should inevitably perish in the tremendous swell which would ensue. But this very just apprehension seemed by no means likely to be soon verified. For five entire days and nights—during which our only subsistence was a small quantity of jaggeree, procured with great difficulty from the forecastle—the hulk flew at a rate defying computation, before rapidly succeeding flaws of wind, which, without equalling the first violence of the Simoom, were still more terrific than any tempest I had before encountered. Our course for the first four days was, with trifling variations, S.E. and by S.; and we must have run down the coast of New Holland. On the fifth day the cold became extreme, although the wind had hauled round a point more to the northward. The sun arose with a sickly yellow lustre, and clambered a very few degrees above the horizon—emitting no decisive light. There were no clouds apparent, yet the wind was upon the increase, and blew with a fitful and unsteady fury. About noon, as nearly as we could guess, our attention was again arrested by the appearance of the sun. It gave out no light, properly so called, but a dull and sullen glow without reflection, as if all its rays were polarized. Just before sinking within the turgid sea, its central fires suddenly went out, as if hurriedly extinguished by some unaccountable power. It was a dim, sliverlike rim, alone, as it rushed down the unfathomable ocean.

We waited in vain for the arrival of the sixth day—that day to me has not arrived—to the Swede, never did arrive. Thenceforward we were enshrouded in patchy darkness, so that we could not have seen an object at twenty paces from the ship. Eternal night continued to envelop us, all unrelieved by the phosphoric sea-brilliancy to which we had been accustomed in the tropics. We observed too, that, although the tempest continued to rage with unabated violence, there was no longer to be discovered the usual appearance of surf, or foam, which had hitherto attended us. All around were horror, and thick gloom, and a black sweltering desert of ebony. Superstitious terror crept by degrees into the spirit of the old Swede, and my own soul was wrapped up in silent wonder. We neglected all care of the ship, as worse than useless, and securing ourselves, as well as possible, to the stump of the mizen-mast, looked out bitterly into the world of ocean. We had no means of calculating time, nor could we form any guess of our situation. We were, however, well aware of having made farther to the southward than any previous navigators, and felt great amazement at not meeting with the usual impediments of ice. In the meantime every moment threatened to be our last—every mountainous billow hurried to overwhelm us. The swell surpassed anything I had imagined possible, and that we were not instantly buried is a miracle. My companion spoke of the lightness of our cargo, and reminded me of the excellent qualities of our ship; but I could not help feeling the utter hopelessness of hope itself, and prepared myself gloomily for that death which I thought nothing could defer beyond an hour, as, with every knot of way the ship made, the swelling of the black stupendous seas became more dismally appalling. At times we gasped for breath at an elevation beyond the albatross—at times became dizzy with the velocity of our descent into some watery hell, where the air grew stagnant, and no sound disturbed the slumbers of the kraken.

We were at the bottom of one of these abysses, when a quick scream from my companion broke fearfully upon the night. "See! see!" cried he, shrieking in my ears, "Almighty God! see! see!" As he spoke, I became aware of a dull, sullen glare of red light which streamed down the sides of the vast chasm where we lay, and threw a fitful brilliancy upon our deck. Casting my eyes upwards, I beheld a spectacle which froze the current of my blood. At a terrific height directly above us, and upon the very verge of the precipitous descent, hovered a gigantic ship of, perhaps, four thousand tons. Although upreared upon the summit of a wave more than a hundred times her own altitude, her apparent size exceeded that of any ship of the line or East Indiaman in existence. Her huge hull was of a deep dingy black, unrelieved by any of the customary carvings of a ship. A single row of brass cannon

protruded from her open ports, and dashed from their polished sur-
faces the fires of innumerable battle-lanterns, which swung to and fro
about her rigging. But what mainly inspired us with horror and astonishment, was that she bore up under a press of sail in the very teeth of
that supernatural sea, and of that ungovernable hurricane. When we
first discovered her, her bows were alone to be seen, as she rose slowly
from the dim and horrible gulf beyond her. For a moment of intense
terror she paused upon the giddy pinnacle, as if in contemplation of
her own sublimity, then trembled and tottered, and—came down.

At this instant, I know not what sudden self-possession came over
my spirit. Staggering as far aft as I could, I awaited fearlessly the ruin
that was to overwhelm. Our own vessel was at length ceasing from
her struggles, and sinking with her head to the sea. The shock of the
descending mass struck her, consequently, in that portion of her frame
which was already under water, and the inevitable result was to hurl
me, with irresistible violence, upon the rigging of the stranger.

As I fell, the ship hove in stays, and went about; and to the confusion
ensuing I attributed my escape from the notice of the crew. With little
difficulty I made my way unperceived to the main hatchway, which
was partially open, and soon found an opportunity of secreting myself
in the hold. Why I did so I can hardly tell. An indefinite sense of awe,
which at first sight of the navigators of the ship had taken hold of my
mind, was perhaps the principle of my concealment. I was unwilling
to trust myself with a race of people who had offered, to the cursory
glance I had taken, so many points of vague novelty, doubt, and apprehension. I therefore thought proper to contrive a hiding-place in the
hold. This I did by removing a small portion of the shifting-boards, in
such a manner as to afford me a convenient retreat between the huge
timbers of the ship.

I had scarcely completed my work, when a footstep in the hold forced me to make use of it. A man passed by my place of concealment with a feeble and unsteady gait. I could not see his face, but had an opportunity of observing his general appearance. There was about it an evidence of great age and infirmity. His knees tottered beneath a load of years, and his entire frame quivered under the burthen. He muttered to himself, in a low broken tone, some words of a language which I could not understand, and groped in a corner among a pile of singular-looking instruments, and decayed charts of navigation. His manner was a wild mixture of the peevishness of second childhood, and the solemn dignity of a God. He at length went on deck, and I saw him no more.

A feeling, for which I have no name, has taken possession of my soul—a sensation which will admit of no analysis, to which the lessons of bygone times are inadequate, and for which I fear futurity itself will offer me no key. To a mind constituted like my own, the latter consideration is an evil. I shall never—I know that I shall never—be satisfied with regard to the nature of my conceptions. Yet it is not wonderful that these conceptions are indefinite, since they have their origin in sources so utterly novel. A new sense—a new entity is added to my soul.

It is long since I first trod the deck of this terrible ship, and the rays of my destiny are, I think, gathering to a focus. Incomprehensible men! Wrapped up in meditations of a kind which I cannot divine, they pass me by unnoticed. Concealment is utter folly on my part, for the people will not see. It was but just now that I passed directly before the eyes of the mate—it was no long while ago that I ventured into the captain's own private cabin, and took thence the materials with which I write, and have written. I shall from time to time continue this Journal. It is true that I may not find an opportunity of transmitting it to the world, but I will not fail to make the endeavour. At the last moment I will enclose the MS. in a bottle, and cast it within the sea.

An incident has occurred which has given me new room for meditation. Are such things the operation of ungoverned Chance? I had ventured upon deck and thrown myself down, without attracting any notice, among a pile of ratlin-stuff and old sails in the bottom of the yawl. While musing upon the singularity of my fate, I unwittingly daubed with a tarbrush the edges of a neatly-folded studding-sail which lay near me on a barrel. The studding-sail is now bent upon the ship, and the thoughtless touches of the brush are spread out into the word DISCOVERY.

I have made many observations lately upon the structure of the vessel. Although well armed, she is not, I think, a ship of war. Her rigging, build, and general equipment, all negative a supposition of this kind. What she is not, I can easily perceive—what she is I fear it is impossible to say. I know not how it is, but in scrutinizing her strange model and singular cast of spars, her huge size and overgrown suits of canvas, her severely simple bow and antiquated stern, there will occasionally flash across my mind a sensation of familiar things, and there is always mixed up with such indistinct shadows of recollection, an unaccountable memory of old foreign chronicles and ages long ago.

I have been looking at the timbers of the ship. She is built of a material to which I am a stranger. There is a peculiar character about the wood which strikes me as rendering it unfit for the purpose to which it has been applied. I mean its extreme porousness, considered independently by the worm-eaten condition which is a consequence of navigation in these seas, and apart from the rottenness attendant upon age. It will appear perhaps an observation somewhat over-curious, but this wood would have every characteristic of Spanish oak, if Spanish oak were distended by any unnatural means.

In reading the above sentence a curious apothegm of an old weather-beaten Dutch navigator comes full upon my recollection. "It is as sure," he was wont to say, when any doubt was entertained of his veracity, "as sure as there is a sea where the ship itself will grow in bulk like the living body of the seaman."

About an hour ago, I made bold to thrust myself among a group of the crew. They paid me no manner of attention, and, although I stood in the very midst of them all, seemed utterly unconscious of my presence. Like the one I had at first seen in the hold, they all bore about them the marks of a hoary old age. Their knees trembled with infirmity; their shoulders were bent double with decrepitude; their shriveled skins rattled in the wind; their voices were low, tremulous and broken; their eyes glistened with the rheum of years; and their gray hairs streamed terribly in the tempest. Around them, on every part of the deck, lay scattered mathematical instruments of the most quaint and obsolete construction.

I mentioned some time ago the bending of a studding-sail. From that period the ship, being thrown dead off the wind, has continued her terrific course due south, with every rag of canvas packed upon her, from her trucks to her lower studding-sail booms, and rolling every moment her top-gallant yard-arms into the most appalling hell of water which it can enter into the mind of a man to imagine. I have just left the deck, where I find it impossible to maintain a footing, although the crew seem to experience little inconvenience. It appears to me a miracle of miracles that our enormous bulk is not swallowed up at once and forever. We are surely doomed to hover continually upon the brink of Eternity, without taking a final plunge into the abyss. From billows a thousand times more stupendous than any I have ever seen, we glide away with the facility of the arrowy sea-gull; and the colossal waters rear their heads above us like demons of the deep, but like demons confined to simple threats and forbidden to destroy. I am led to attribute these frequent escapes to the only natural cause which can account for such effect. I must suppose the ship to be within the influence of some strong current, or impetuous under-tow.

I have seen the captain face to face, and in his own cabin—but, as I expected, he paid me no attention. Although in his appearance there is, to a casual observer, nothing which might bespeak him more or less than man—still a feeling of irrepressible reverence and awe mingled with the sensation of wonder with which I regarded him. In stature he is nearly my own height; that is, about five feet eight inches. He is of a well-knit and compact frame of body, neither robust nor remarkably otherwise. But it is the singularity of the expression which reigns upon the face—it is the intense, the wonderful, the thrilling evidence of old age, so utter, so extreme, which excites within my spirit a sense—a sentiment ineffable. His forehead, although little wrinkled, seems to bear upon it the stamp of a myriad of years. His gray hairs are records of the past, and his grayer eyes are Sybils of the future. The cabin floor was thickly strewn with strange, iron-clasped folios, and mouldering instruments of science, and obsolete long-forgotten charts. His head was bowed down upon his hands, and he pored, with a fiery unquiet eye, over a paper which I took to be a commission, and which, at all events, bore the signature of a monarch. He muttered to himself, as did the first seaman whom I saw in the hold, some low peevish syllables of a foreign tongue, and although the speaker was close at my elbow, his voice seemed to reach my ears from the distance of a mile.

The ship and all in it are imbued with the spirit of Eld. The crew glide to and fro like the ghosts of buried centuries; their eyes have an eager and uneasy meaning; and when their fingers fall athwart my path in the wild glare of the battle-lanterns, I feel as I have never felt before, although I have been all my life a dealer in antiquities, and have imbibed the shadows of fallen columns at Balbec, and Tadmor, and Persepolis, until my very soul has become a ruin.

When I look around me I feel ashamed of my former apprehensions. If I trembled at the blast which has hitherto attended us, shall I not stand aghast at a warring of wind and ocean, to convey any idea of which the words tornado and simoom are trivial and ineffective? All in the immediate vicinity of the ship is the blackness of eternal night, and a chaos of foamless water; but, about a league on either side of us, may be seen, indistinctly and at intervals, stupendous ramparts of ice, towering away into the desolate sky, and looking like the walls of the universe.

As I imagined, the ship proves to be in a current; if that appellation can properly be given to a tide which, howling and shrieking by the white ice, thunders on to the southward with a velocity like the headlong dashing of a cataract.

To conceive the horror of my sensations is, I presume, utterly impossible; yet a curiosity to penetrate the mysteries of these awful regions, predominates even over my despair, and will reconcile me to the most hideous aspect of death. It is evident that we are hurrying onwards to some exciting knowledge—some never-to-be-imparted secret, whose attainment is destruction. Perhaps this current leads us to the southern pole itself. It must be confessed that a supposition apparently so wild has every probability in its favor.

The crew pace the deck with unquiet and tremulous step; but there is upon their countenances an expression more of the eagerness of hope than of the apathy of despair.

In the meantime the wind is still in our poop, and, as we carry a crowd of canvas, the ship is at times lifted bodily from out the sea— Oh, horror upon horror! the ice opens suddenly to the right, and to the left, and we are whirling dizzily, in immense concentric circles, round and round the borders of a gigantic amphitheatre, the summit of whose walls is lost in the darkness and the distance. But little time will be left me to ponder upon my destiny—the circles rapidly grow small—we are plunging madly within the grasp of the whirlpool—and amid a roaring, and bellowing, and thundering of ocean and of tempest, the ship is quivering, oh God! and—going down.

NOTE. The "MS. Found in a Bottle," was originally published in 1831, and it was not until many years afterwards that I became acquainted with the maps of Mercator, in which the ocean is represented as rushing, by four mouths, into the (northern) Polar Gulf, to be absorbed into the bowels of the earth; the Pole itself being represented by a black rock, towering to a prodigious height.

12

THE MERCHANTS' CUP

DAVID W. BONE

"Fatty" Reid burst into the half-deck with a whoop of exultation. "Come out, boys," he yelled. "Come out and see what luck! The *James Flint* comin' down the river, loaded and ready for sea! Who-oop! What price the *Hilda* now for the Merchants' Cup?"

"Oh, come off," said big Jones. "Come off with your Merchants' Cup. Th' *James Flint*'s a sure thing, and she wasn't more than half-loaded when we were up at Crockett on Sunday!"

"Well, there she comes anyway! *James Flint*, sure enough! Gracie's house-flag up, and the Stars and Stripes!"

We hustled on deck and looked over by the Sacramento's mouth. "Fatty" was right. A big barque was towing down beyond San Pedro. The *James Flint*! Nothing else in 'Frisco harbour had spars like hers; no ship was as trim and clean as the big Yankee clipper that Bully Nathan commanded. The sails were all aloft, the boats aboard. She was ready to put to sea.

Our cries brought the captain and mate on deck, and the sight of the outward-bounder made old man Burke's face beam like a nor'west moon.

"A chance for ye now, byes," he shouted. "An open race, bedad! Ye've nothin' t' be afraid of if th' *James Flint* goes t' sea by Saturday!"

Great was our joy at the prospect of the Yankee's sailing. The 'Frisco Merchants' Cup was to be rowed for on Saturday. It was a mile-and-half race for ships' boats, and three wins held the Cup for good. Twice, on previous years, the *Hilda*'s trim gig had shot over the line—a handsome winner. If we won again, the Cup was ours for keeps! But there were strong opponents to be met this time. The *James Flint* was the most formidable. It was open word that Bully Nathan was keen on winning the trophy. Every one knew that he had deliberately sought out boatmen when the whalers came in from the north. Those who had seen the Yankee's crew at work in their snaky carvel-built boat said that no one else was in it. What chance had we boys in our clinker-built against the thews and sinews of trained whalemen? It was no wonder that we slapped our thighs at the prospect of a more open race.

Still, even with the Yankee gone, there were others in the running. There was the *Rhondda* that held the Cup for the year, having won when we were somewhere off the Horn; then the *Hedwig Rickmers*—a Bremen four-master—which had not before competed, but whose green-painted gig was out for practice morning and night. We felt easy about the *Rhondda* (for had we not, time and again, shown them our stern on the long pull from Green St. to the outer anchorage?), but the Germans were different. Try as we might, we could never pull off a spurt with them. No one knew for certain what they could do, only old Schenke, their skipper, and he held his tongue wisely.

The *James Flint* came around the bend, and our eager eyes followed her as she steered after the tug. She was making for the outer anchorage, where the laden ships lie in readiness for a good start off.

"Th' wind's 'bout west outside," said Jones. "A 'dead muzzler'! She'll not put t' sea tonight, even if she has all her 'crowd' aboard."

"No, worse luck! Mebbe she'll lie over till Saturday after all. They say Bully's dead set on getting th' Cup. He might hang back. . . . Some excuse—short-handed or something!" Gregson was the one for "croaking."

"No hands?" said Fatty. "Huh! How could he be short-handed when everybody knows that Daly's boardin'-house is chock-full of fightin' Dutchmen? No, no! It'll be the sack for Mister Bully B. Nathan if he lets a capful o' fair wind go by and his anchor down. Gracie's agents'll watch that!"

"Well! He's here for th' night, anyway. . . . There goes her mud-hook!"

We watched her great anchor go hurtling from the bows and heard the roar of chain cable as she paid out and swung round to the tide.

"Come roun', yo' boys dere! Yo' doan' want no tea, eh?" The cook, beating tattoo on a saucepan lid, called us back to affairs of the moment, and we sat down to our scanty meal in high spirits, talking— all at one time—of our chances of the Cup.

The *Hilda* had been three months at San Francisco, waiting for the wheat crop and a profitable charter. We had come up from Australia, and most of our crew, having little wages due to them, had deserted soon after our arrival. Only we apprentices and the sail-maker remained, and we had work enough to set our muscles up in the heavy harbour jobs. Trimming coal and shovelling ballast may not be scientific training, but it is grand work for the back and shoulders.

We were in good trim for rowing. The old man had given us every opportunity, and nothing he could do was wanting to make us fit. Day and daily we had set our stroke up by the long pull from the anchorage to the wharves, old Burke coaching and encouraging, checking and speeding us, 'till we worked well together. Only last Sunday he had taken us out of our way, up the creek, to where we could see the flag at the *Rhondda*'s masthead. The old man said nothing, but well we knew he was thinking of how the square of blue silk, with Californian emblem worked in white, would look at his trim little *Hilda*'s fore-truck! This flag accompanied the Cup, and now (if only the Yankee and his hired whalemen were safely at sea) we had hopes of seeing it at our masthead again.

Tea over—still excited talk went on. Some one recalled the last time we had overhauled and passed the *Rhondda*'s gig.

"It's all very well your bucking about beating the *Rhondda*," said Gregson; "but don't think we're going to have it all our own way! Mebbe they were 'playing 'possum' when we came by that time!"

"Maybe," said Jones. "There's Peters and H. Dobson in her crew. Good men! Both rowed in the Worcester boat that left the Conways' at the start, three years ago. . . . And what about the *Rickmers*? . . . No, no! It won't do to be too cocksure! . . . Eh, Takia?"

Takia was our cox'n, a small wiry Jap. Nothing great in inches, but a demon for good steering and timing a stroke. He was serving his apprenticeship with us and had been a year in the *Hilda*. Brute strength was not one of his points, but none was keener or more active in the rigging than our little Jap.

He smiled,—he always smiled,—he found it the easiest way of speaking English. "Oh, yes," he said. "Little cocksu'—good! Too much cocksu'—no good!"

We laughed at the wisdom of the East.

"Talk about being cocky," said Gregson; "you should hear Captain Schenke bragging about the way he brought the *Hedwig Rickmers* out. I heard 'em and the old man at it in the ship-chandler's yesterday. Hot! . . . Look here, you chaps! I don't think the old man cares so much to win the Cup as to beat Schenke! The big 'squarehead' is always ramming it down Burke's throat how he brought his barque out from Liverpool in a hundred and five days, while the *Hilda* took ten days more on her last run out!"

"That's so, I guess," said Jones. (Jones had the Yankee "touch.") "Old Burke would dearly love to put a spoke in his wheel, but it'll take some doing. They say that Schenke has got a friend down from Sacramento—gym.-instructor or something to a college up there. He'll be training the 'Dutchy' crew like blazes. They'll give us a hot time, I'll bet!"

Gregson rose to go on deck. "Oh, well," he said, "it won't be so bad if the *James Flint* only lifts his hook by Saturday. Here's one bloomin' *hombre* that funks racin' a fancy whaler! . . . An' doesn't care who knows it, either!"

Thursday passed—and now Friday—still there was no sign of the wind changing, and the big Yankee barque lay quietly at anchor over by the Presidio.

When the butcher came off from the shore with the day's stores, we eagerly questioned him about the prospects of the *James Flint's* sailing. "*Huh*! I guess yew're nat the only 'citizens' that air concarned 'bout that!" he said. "They're talkin' 'bout nuthin' else on every 'lime-juicer' in the Bay! . . . An' th' *Rickmers*! Gee! Schenkie's had his eye glued ter th' long telescope ever since daybreak, watchin' fer th' *Flint* heavin' up anchor!"

The butcher had varied information to give us. Now it was that Bully Nathan had telegraphed to his New York owners for permission to remain in port over Sunday. Then again, Bully was on the point of being dismissed his ship for not taking full advantage of a puff of nor'-west wind that came and went on Thursday night.

. . . The *Flint* was short of men! . . . The Flint had a full crew aboard! Rumours and rumours! "All sorts o' talk," said the butcher; "but I know this fer certain—she's got all her stores aboard. Gosh! I guess—she—has! I don't like to wish nobody no harm, boyes, but I hope Bully Nathan's first chop'll choke him, fer th' way he done me over the beef! . . . Scorch 'im!"

In the forenoon we dropped the gig and put out for practice. Old Burke and the mate came after us in the dinghy, the old man shouting instruction and encouragement through his megaphone as we rowed a course or spurted hard for a furious three minutes. Others were out on the same ploy, and the backwaters of the Bay had each a lash of oars to stir their tideless depths. Near us the green boat of the *Rickmers* thrashed up and down in style. Time and again we drew across—"just for a friendly spurt"—but the "Dutchies" were not giving anything away, and sheered off as we approached. We spent an hour or more at practice and were rowing leisurely back to the ship when the green boat overhauled us, then slowed to her skipper's orders.

"How you vass, Cabtin Burke?" said Schenke, an enormous fair-headed Teuton, powerful-looking, but run sadly to fat in his elder years. "You t'ink you get a chanst now, *hein*? . . . Now de Yankee is goin' avay!" He pointed over to the Presidio, where the *Flint* lay at anchor. We followed the line of his fat forefinger. At anchor, yes, but the anchor nearly a-weigh. Her flags were hoisted, the blue peter fluttering at the fore, and the *Active* tug was passing a hawser aboard, getting ready to tow her out. The smoke from the tugboat's funnel was whirling and blowing over the low forts that guard the Golden Gates. Good luck! A fine nor'-west breeze had come that would lift our dreaded rival far to the south'ard on her way round Cape Horn!

Schenke saw the pleased look with which old Burke regarded the Yankee's preparations for departure.

"Goot bizness, eh?" he said. "You t'ink you fly de flack on de *Hilda* nex' *Sonndag*, Cabtin? Veil! Ah wish you goot look, but you dond't got it all de same!"

"Oh, well, Captain Schenke, we can but thry," said the old man. "We can but thry, sorr! . . . Shure, she's a foine boat—that o' yours. . . . An' likely-looking lads, too!" No one could but admire the well-set figures of the German crew as they stroked easily beside us.

"*Schweinehunden*," said Schenke brutally. We noticed more than one stolid face darkling as they glanced aside. Schenke had the name of a "hard case." "*Schweinehunden*," he said again. "Dey dond't like de hard vork, Cabtin. . . . Dey dond't like it—but ve takes der Coop, all de same! Dey pulls goot und strong, oder"—he rasped a short sentence in rapid Low German—"Shermans dond't be beat by no durn lime-juicer, *nein!*"

Old Burke grinned. "Cocky as ever, Captain Schenke! Bedad now, since ye had the luck of ye're last passage there's no limit to ye!"

"Luck! Luck! Alvays de luck mit you, Cabtin!"

"An' whatt ilse? . . . Sure, if I hadn't struck a bilt of calms an' had more than me share of head winds off the Horn, I'd have given ye a day or two mesilf!"

"Ho! Ho! Ho! *Das ist gut!*" The green boat rocked with Schenke's merriment. He laughed from his feet up—every inch of him shook with emotion. "Ho! Ho! Hoo! *Das ist ganz gut.* You t'ink you beat de *Hedwig Rickmers* too, Cabtin? You beat 'm mit dot putty leetle barque? You beat 'm mit de *Hilda, nichtwahr?*"

"Well, no," said our old man. "I don't exactly say I beat the *Rick-mers*, but if I had the luck o' winds that ye had, bedad, I'd crack th' *Hilda* out in a hundred an' five days too!"

"Now, dot is not drue, Cabtin! *Aber ganz und gar nicht!* You know you haf bedder look von de vind as Ah got. Ah sail mein sheep! Ah dond't vait for de fair winds nor not'ings!"

"No," said Burke, "but ye get 'em, all the same. Everybody knows ye've th' divil's own luck, Schenke!"

"Und so you vas! Look now, Cabtin Burke. You t'nk you got so fast a sheep as mein, eh? Vell! Ah gif you a chanst to make money. Ah bet you feefty dollars to tventig, Ah take mein sheep home quicker as you vass!"

"Done wit' ye," said stout old 'Paddy' Burke, though well he know the big German barque could sail round the little *Hilda*. "Fifty dollars to twenty, Captain Schenke, an' moind ye've said it!"

The green boat sheered off and forged ahead, Schenke laughing and waving his hand derisively. When they had pulled out of earshot, the old man turned ruefully to the mate: "Five pounds clean t'rown away, mister! Foine I know the *Rickmers* can baate us, but I wasn't goin' t' let that ould 'squarehead' have it all his own way! Divil th' fear!"

We swung under the *Hilda*'s stern and hooked on to the gangway. The old man stepped out, climbed a pace or two, then came back.

"Look ye here, byes," he said, "I'll give ye foive dollars a man—an' a day's 'liberty' t' spind it—if ye only baate th' 'Dutchmen.' . . . Let th' Cup go where it will!"

The Bay of San Francisco is certainly one of the finest natural harbours in the world, let Sydney and Rio and Falmouth all contest the claim. Land-locked to every wind that blows, with only a narrow channel open to the sea, the navies of the world could lie peacefully together in its sheltered waters. The coast that environs the harbour abounds in natural beauties, but of all the wooded creeks—fair stretches of undulating downs—or stately curves of winding river, none surpasses the little bay formed by the turn of Benita, the northern postern of the Golden Gates. Here is the little township of Sancilito, with its pretty white houses nestling among the dark green of the deeply wooded slopes. In the bay there is good anchorage for a limited number of vessels, and fortunate were they who manned the tall ships that lay there, swinging ebb and flood, waiting for a burthen of golden grain.

On Saturday the little bay was crowded by a muster of varied craft. The ships at anchor were "dressed" to the mastheads with gaily-coloured flags. Huge ferry-boats passed slowly up and down, their tiers of decks crowded with sightseers. Tug-boats and launches darted about, clearing the course, or convoying racing boats to the starting lines. Ships' boats of all kinds were massed together close inshore: gigs and pinnaces, lean whaleboats, squat dinghys, even high-sided ocean lifeboats with their sombre broad belts of ribbed cork. A gay scene of colour and animation. A fine turn-out to see the fortune of the Merchants' Cup!

At two the Regatta began. A race for longshore craft showed that the boarding-house "crimps" were as skillful at boatman's work as at inducing sailormen to desert their ships. Then two out-riggers flashed by, contesting a heat for a College race. We in the *Hilda's* gig lay handily at the starting line and soon were called out. There were nine entries for the Cup, and the judges had decided to run three heats. We were drawn in the first, and, together with the *Ardlea's* and *Compton's* gigs, went out to be inspected. The boats had to race in sea-service conditions, no lightening was allowed. At the challenge of the judges we showed our gear. "Spare oar—right! Rowlocks—right! Sea-anchor—right! Bottom boards and stern grating—right. Painter, ten fathoms; hemp. . . . A bit short there, *Compton*! Eh? . . . Oh—all right," said the official, and we manoeuvred into position, our sterns held in by the guard-boats. Some of the ships' captains had engaged a steam-launch to follow the heats, and old Burke was there with his trumpet, shouting encouragement already.

"Air yew ready?"

A pause: then, pistol shot! We struck water and laid out! Our task was not difficult. The *Ardlea*'s gig was broad-bowed and heavy; they had no chance; but the *Compton*'s gave us a stiff pull to more than midway. Had they been like us, three months at boat-work, we had not pulled so easily up to the mark, but their ship was just in from Liverpool, and they were in poor condition for a mile and a half at pressure. We won easily, and scarce had cheered the losers before the launch came fussing up.

"Come aboard, Takia," shouted old Burke. "Ye come down wit' me an' see what shape the German makes. He's drawn wit' th' *Rhondda* in this heat!"

Takia bundled aboard the launch and we hauled inshore to watch the race. There was a delay at the start. Schenke, *nichts verstehen*, as he said, was for sending his boat away without a painter or spare gear. He was pulled up by the judges, and had to borrow.

Now they were ready. The *Rickmers* outside, *Rhondda* in the middle berth, and the neat little *Slieve Donard* inshore. At the start the *Rhonddas* came fair away from the German boat, but even at the distance we could see that the "Dutchmen" were well in hand. At midway the *Rhondda* was leading by a length, still going strong, but they had shot their bolt, and the green boat was surely pulling up. The *Slieve Donard*, after an unsteady course, had given up. Soon we could hear old Schenke roaring oaths and orders, as his launch came flying on in the wake of the speeding boats.

The Germans spurted.

We yelled encouragement to the *Rhonddas*. "Give 'em beans, old sons! . . ."

"*Rhondda! Rhondda!* . . . Shake 'er up" Gallantly the white boat strove to keep her place, but the greens were too strong. With a rush, they took the lead and held it to the finish, though two lengths from the line their stroke faltered, the swing was gone, and they were dabbling feebly when the shot rang out.

"A grand race," said every one around. "A grand race"—but old Burke had something to say when he steamed up to put our cox'n among us. "Byes, byes," he said, "if there had been twinty yards more the *Rhondda* would have won. Now d'ye moind, Takia, ye divil . . . d'ye moind! Keep th' byes in hand till I give ye th' wurrd! . . . An' whin ye get th' wurrd, byes! . . . Oh, Saints! Shake her up when ye get th' wurrd!"

The third heat was closely contested. All three boats, two Liverpool barques and a Nova Scotiaman, came on steadily together. A clean race, rowed from start to finish, and the *Tuebrook* winning by a short length.

The afternoon was well spent when we stripped for the final, and took up our positions on the line. How big and muscular the Germans looked! How well the green boat sat the water! With what inward quakings we noted the clean fine lines of stem and stern! . . . Of the *Tuebrook* we had no fear. We knew they could never stand the pace the Germans would set. Could we?

Old Burke, though in a fever of excitement when we came to the line, had little to say. "Keep the byes in hand, Takia—till ye get th' wurrd," was all he muttered. We swung our oar-blades forward.

"Ready?" The starter challenged us.

Suddenly Takia yelped! We struck and lay back as the shot rang out! A stroke gained! Takia had taken the flash; the others the report!

The Jap's clever start gave us confidence and a lead. Big Jones at stroke worked us up to better the advantage. The green boat sheered a little, then steadied and came on, keeping to us, though nearly a length astern. The *Tuebrook* had made a bad start, but was thrashing away pluckily in the rear.

So we hammered at it for a third of the course, when Takia took charge. Since his famous start he had left us to take stroke as Jones pressed us, but now he saw signs of the waver that comes after the first furious burst—shifting grip or change of foothold.

"'Troke!—'troke!—'trok!*" he muttered, and steadied the pace. "'*Troke!—'troke!—'troke!*" in monotone, good for soothing tension.

Past midway the green boat came away. The ring of the German's rowlocks rose to treble pitch. Slowly they drew up, working at top speed. Now they were level—level! and Takia still droning "'*troke!—'troke!—'troke!*"—as if the lead was ours!

Wild outcry came from the crowd as the green boat forged ahead! Deep roars from Schenke somewhere in the rear! Now, labouring still to Takia's '*troke!—'troke!* we had the foam of the Germans' stern wash at our blades! *"Come away, Hildas!"* . . . *"Shake her up, there!"* . . . *"Hilda-h! Hilda-h!"*—Takia took no outward heed of the cries. He was staring stolidly ahead, bending to the pulse of the boat. No outward heed—but '*troke!—'troke!* came faster from his lips. We strained, almost holding the Germans' ensign at level with our bow pennant.

Loud over the wild yells of the crowd we heard the voice we knew—old Burke's bull-roar: *"Let 'er rip, Taki'! Let 'er rip, bye!"*

Takia's eyes gleamed as he sped us up—up—up! '*Troke* became a yelp like a wounded dog's. He crouched, standing, in the sternsheets, and lashed us up to a furious thrash of oars! Still quicker! . . . The eyes of him glared at each of us, as if daring us to fail! The yelp became a scream as we drew level—the Germans still at top speed. *"Up! Up! Up!"* yells Takia, little yellow devil with a white froth at his lips! *"Up! Up! Up!"* swaying unsteadily to meet the furious urging.

The ring of the German rowlocks deepens—deepens—we see the green bow at our blades again. Her number two falters—jars—recovers again—and pulls stubbornly on. Their "shot" is fired! They can do no more! Done!

And so are we! Takia drops the yoke ropes and leans forward on the gunwale! Oars jar together! Big Jones bends forward with his mouth wide—wide! Done!

But not before a hush—a solitary pistol shot—then roar of voices and shrilling of steamer syrens tell us that the Cup is ours!

A month later there was a stir in the western seaports. No longer the ships lay swinging idly at their moorings. The harvest of grain was ready for the carriers, and every day sail was spread to the free wind outside the Golden Gates, and laden ships went speeding on their homeward voyages. The days of boat-races and pleasant time-passing harbour jobs were gone; it was now work—work—to get the ship ready for her burden, and, swaying the great sails aloft, to rig harness for the power that was to bear us home. From early morning till late evening we were kept hard at it; for Captain Burke and the mate were as keen on getting the *Hilda* to sea after her long stay in port as they were on jockeying us up to win the Cup. Often, when we turned to in the morning, we would find a new shipmate ready to bear a hand with us. The old man believed in picking up a likely man when he offered. Long experience of Pacific ports had taught him how difficult it is to get a crew at the last moment.

So when at length the cargo was stowed, we were quite ready to go to sea, while many others—the *Hedwig Rickmers* among them—were waiting for men.

On the day before sailing a number of the ship captains were gathered together in the chandler's store, talking of freights and passages, and speculating on the runs they hoped to make. Burke and Schenke were the loudest talkers, for we were both bound to Falmouth "for orders," and the *Rickmers* would probably sail three days after we had gone.

"Vat 'bout dot bett you make mit me, Cabtin?" said Schenke. "Dot is all recht, no?"

"Oh, yess," answered the old man, but without enthusiasm. "That stands."

"Hoo! Hoo! Hoo! Tventig dollars to feefty—dot you goes home quicker as me, no?" Schenke turned to the other men. "Vat you trinks, yentlmen? Ah tinks Ah sbend der tventig dollars now—so sure Ah vass."

The others laughed. "Man, man," said Findlayson of the *Rhondda*. "You don't tell me Burke's been fool enough to take that bet. Hoo! You haven't the ghost of a chance, Burke."

"Och, ye never know," said the now doleful sportsman. "Ye never know ye'er luck."

"Look here, Cabtin," said Schenke (good-humoured by the unspoken tribute to his vessel's sailing powers)—"Ah gif you a chanst. Ah make de bett dis vay—look. Ve goes to Falmouth—you *und* me, *hein*? Now, de first who comes on de shore vins de money. Dot vill gif you t'ree days' start, no?"

"That's more like it," said the other captains. "I wish you luck, Burke," said Findlayson. "Good luck—you'll need it too—if you are to be home before the big German."

So the bet was made.

At daybreak next morning we put out to sea. The good luck that the *Rhondda* wished us came our way from the very first. When the tug left us we set sail to a fine fair wind, and soon were bowling along in style. We found the nor'-east Trades with little seeking; strong Trades, too, that lifted us to the Line almost before the harbour dust was blown from our masts and spars. There calms fell on us for a few days, but we drifted south in the right current, and in less than forty days had run into the "westerlies" and were bearing away for the Horn.

Old Burke was "cracking on" for all the *Hilda* could carry canvas. Every morning when he came on deck the first question to the mate would be: "Any ships in sight, mister?" . . . "Any ships astern," he meant, for his first glance was always to where the big green four-master might be expected to heave in sight. Then, when nothing was reported, he would begin his day-long strut up and down the poop, whistling "Garryowen" and rubbing his hands.

Nor was the joy at our good progress his alone. We in the half-deck knew of the bet, and were keen that the ship which carried the Merchants' Cup should not be overhauled by the runner-up! We had made a fetish of the trophy so hardly won. The Cup itself was safely stowed in the ship's strong chest, but the old man had let us have custody of the flag. Big Jones had particular charge of it; and it had been a custom while in 'Frisco to exhibit it on the Saturday nights to admiring and envious friends from other ships. This custom we continued when at sea. True, there were no visitors to set us up and swear what lusty chaps we were, but we could frank one another and say, "If you hadn't done this or that, we would never have won the race."

On a breezy Saturday evening we were busy at these rites. The *Hilda* was doing well before a steady nor'-west wind, but the weather—though nothing misty—was dark as a pall. Thick clouds overcast the sky, and there seemed no dividing line between the darkling sea and the windy banks that shrouded the horizon. A dirty night was in prospect; the weather would thicken later; but that made the modest comforts of the half-deck seem more inviting by comparison; and we came together for our weekly "sing-song"—all but Gregson, whose turn it was to stand the lookout on the fo'c'sle-head.

The flag was brought out and hung up—Jones standing by to see that no pipe-lights were brought near—and we ranted at "Ye Mariners of England" till the mate sent word that further din would mean a "work-up" job for all of us.

Little we thought that we mariners would soon be facing dangers as great as any we so glibly sang about. Even as we sang, the *Hilda* was speeding on a fatal course! Across her track the almost submerged hull of a derelict lay drifting. Black night veiled the danger from the keenest eyes.

A frenzied order from the poop put a stunning period to our merriment. "Helm up, f'r God's sake! . . . *Up!*—oh God!—*Up! Up!*" A furious impact dashed us to the deck. Staggering, bruised, and bleeding, we struggled to our feet. Outside the yells of fear-stricken men mingled with hoarse orders, the crash of spars hurtling from aloft vied with the thunder of canvas, as the doomed barque swung round broadside to the wind and sea.

Even in that dread moment Jones had heed of his precious flag. As we flew to the door, he tore the flag down, stuffing it in his jumper as he joined us at the boats.

There was no time to hoist out the life-boats—it was pinnace and gig or nothing. Already the bows were low in the water. "She goes. She goes!" yelled some one. "Oh, Christ! She's going!"

We bore frantically on the tackles that linked the gig, swung her out, and lowered by the run; the mate had the pinnace in the water, men were swarming into her. As the gig struck water, the barque heeled to the rail awash. We crowded in, old Burke the last to leave her, and pushed off. Our once stately *Hilda* reeled in a swirl of broken water, and the deep sea took her!

Sailor work! No more than ten minutes between "Ye Mariners" and the foundering of our barque!

We lay awhile with hearts too full for words; then the pinnace drew near, and the mate called the men. All there but one! "Gregson!" . . . No Gregson! The bosun knew. He had seen what was Gregson lying still under the wreck of the topmost spars.

The captain and mate conferred long together. We had no sail in the gig, but the larger boat was fully equipped. "It's the only chance, mister," said Burke at last. "No food—no water! We can't hold out for long. Get sail on your boat and stand an hour or two to the east'ard. Ye may fall in with a ship; she w-was right in th' track whin she s-struck. We can but lie to in th' gig an' pray that a ship comes by."

"Aye, aye, sir." They stepped the mast and hoisted sail. "Good-bye all: God bless ye, captain," they said as the canvas swelled. "Keep heart!" For a time we heard their voices shouting us God-speed—then silence came!

Daybreak!

Thank God the bitter night was past. Out of the east the long-looked-for light grew on us, as we lay to sea-anchor, lurching unsteadily in the teeth of wind and driving rain. At the first grey break we scanned the now misty horizon. There was no sign of the pinnace; no God-sent sail in all the dreary round!

We crouched on the bottom boards of the little gig and gave way to gloomy thoughts. What else could be when we were alone and adrift on the broad Pacific, without food or water, in a tiny gig already perilously deep with the burden of eight of us? What a difference to the gay day when we manned the same little boat and set out in pride to the contest! Here was the same spare oar that we held up to the judges—the long oar that Jones was now swaying over the stern, keeping her head to the wind and sea! Out there in the tumbling water the sea-anchor held its place; the ten fathoms of good hemp "painter" was straining at the bows!

The same boat! The same gear! The same crew, but how different! A crew of bent heads and wearied limbs! Listless-eyed, despairing! A ghastly crew, with black care riding in the heaving boat with us!

Poor old Burke had hardly spoken since his last order to the mate to sail the pinnace to the east in search of help. When anything was put to him, he would say, "Aye, aye, b'ye," and take no further heed. He was utterly crushed by the disaster that had come so suddenly on the heels of his "good luck." He sat staring stonily ahead, deaf to our hopes and fears.

Water we had in plenty as the day wore on. The rain-soaked clothes of us were sufficient for the time, but soon hunger came and added a physical pain to the torture of our doubt. Again and again we stood up on the reeling thwarts and looked wildly around the sea-line. No pinnace—no ship—nothing! Nothing, only sea and sky, and circling sea-birds that came to mock at our misery with their plaintive cries.

A bitter night! A no less cruel day! Dark came on us again, chill and windy, and the salt spray cutting at us like a whiplash.

Boo-m-m!

Big Jones stood up in the stern-sheets, swaying unsteadily. "D'ye hear anything there? . . . Like a gun?"

A gun? Gun? . . . Nothing new! . . . We had been hearing guns, seeing sails—in our minds—all the day! All day . . . guns . . . and sail! *Boom-m-m-m!*

"Gun! Oh God . . . a gun! Capt'n, a gun, d'ye hear! Hay—Hay-H. Out oars, there! A gun!" Hoarse in excitement Jones shook the old man and called at his ear. "Aye, aye, b'ye. Aye, aye," said the broken old man, seeming without understanding.

Jones ceased trying to rouse him, and, running out the steering oar, called on us to haul the sea-anchor aboard. We lay to our oars, listening for a further gunfire.

Whooo-o. . . . Boom-m-m.

A rocket! They were looking for us then! The pinnace must have been picked up! A cheer—what a cheer!—came brokenly from our lips; and we lashed furiously at the oars, steering to where a glare in the mist had come with the last report.

Roused by the thrash of our oars, the old man sat up. "Whatt now, b'ye? Whatt now?"

"Ship firin' rockets, sir," said Jones. "Rockets . . . no mistake." As he spoke, another coloured streamer went flaming through the eastern sky. "Give way, there! We'll miss her if she's running south! Give way, all!" The glare of the rocket put heart into our broken old skipper. "Steady now, b'yes," he said, with something of his old enthusiasm.

We laboured steadily at the oars, but our strength was gone. The sea too, that we had thought moderate when lying to sea-anchor, came at us broadside on and set our light boat to a furious dance. Wave crests broke and lashed aboard, the reeling boat was soon awash, and the spare men had to bale frantically to keep her afloat. But terror of the ship running south from us nerved our wearied arms, and we kept doggedly swinging the oars. Soon we made out the vessel's sidelight—the gleam of her starboard light, that showed that she was hauled to the wind, not running south as we had feared. They could not see on such a night, we had nothing to make a signal, but the faint green flame gave us heart in our distress.

The old man, himself again, was now steering, giving us Big Jones to bear at the oars. As we drew on we made out the loom of the vessel's sails—a big ship under topsails only, and sailing slowly to the west. We pulled down wind to cross her course, shouting together as we rowed. Would they never hear? . . . Again! . . . Again!

Suddenly there came a hail from the ship, a roar of orders, rattle of blocks and gear, the yards swung round and she layed up in the wind, while the ghostly glare of a blue light lit up the sea around.

A crowd of men were gathered at the waist, now shouting and cheering as we laboured painfully into the circle of vivid light. Among them a big man (huge he looked in that uncanny glare) roared encouragement in hoarse gutturals.

Old Schenke? The *Hedwig Rickmers?*

Aye—Schenke! But a different Schenke to the big, blustering, overbearing "Square-head" we had known in 'Frisco. Schenke as kind as a brother—a brother of the sea indeed. Big, fat, honest Schenke, passing his huge arm through that of our broken old skipper, leading him aft to his own bed, and silencing his faltering story by words of cheer. "*Ach, du lieber Gott!* It is all right, no? All right, Cabtin, now you come on board. Ah know all 'bout it! . . . Ah pick de oder boat up in de morning, und dey tells me. You come af mit me, Cabtin. . . . Goot, no?"

~~~~~~

"Ninety-six days, Schenke, and here we are at the mouth of the Channel!" Old Burke had a note of regret in the saying. "Ninety-six days! Sure, this ship o' yours can sail. With a bit o' luck, now, ye'll be in Falmouth under the hundred."

"So. If de vind holds goot. Oh, de *Hedwig Rickmers* is a goot sheep, no? But if Ah dond't get de crew of de poor lettle *Hilda* to work mein sheep, Ah dond't t'ink ve comes home so quick as hundert days, no?'"

"God bless us, man. Shure, it's the least they cud do, now. An' you kaaping' us in food an' drink an' clothes, bedad—all the time."

"Vat Ah do, Cabtin. Ah leaf you starfe, no?"

"Oh. Some men would have put into the Falklands and landed—"

"Und spoil a goot bassage, eh? Ach nein. More better to go on. You know dese men Ah get in 'Frisco is no goot. Dem 'hoodlums,' they dond't know de sailorman vork. But your beoble is all recht, eh! Gott! If Ah dond't haf dem here, it is small sail ve can carry on de sheep."

"Och, now, ye just say that, Schenke, ye just say that! But it's glad I am if we're any use t' ye."

"Hundert days to Falmouth, eh?" Schenke grinned as he said it. "Vat 'bout dot bett now, Cabtin?"

"Oh that," said Burke queerly. "You win, of course. I'm not quite broke yet, Captain Schenke. I'll pay the twenty dollars all right."

"No, no. De bett is not von. No? De bett vass—'who is de first on shore come,' *Heim*? Goot. Ven de sheep comes to Falmouth ve goes on shore, you und me, together. Like dis, eh?" He seized Burke by the arm and made a motion that they two should thus step out together.

Burke, shamefacedly, said: "Aye, aye, b'ye."

"Ah dond't care about de bett," continued the big German. "De bett is noting, but, look here, Cabtin—Ah tell you Ah look to vin dot Merchants' Cup. *Gott!* Ah vass *verricht* ven your boys come in first. *Ach so!* Und now de Cup iss at de bottom of de Pacific." He sighed regretfully. "*Gott!* I van't t' be de first Sherman to vin dot Cup too!"

The mate of the *Rickmers* came on the poop and said something to his captain. Schenke turned to the old man in some wonderment. . . . "Vat dis is, eh? My mate tell me dot your boys is want to speak mit me. Vat it is, Cabtin? No troubles I hope?"

Burke looked as surprised as the other. "Send them up, Heinrich," he said. We, the crew of the *Hilda*'s gig, filed on to the poop, looking as hot and uncomfortable as proper sailorfolk should do when they come on a deputation. Jones headed us, and he carried a parcel under his arm.

"Captain Schenke," he said. "We are all here—the crew of the *Hilda*'s gig, that you picked up when—when—we were in a bad way. All here but poor Gregson."

The big lad's voice broke as he spoke of his lost watchmate. "An, if he was here he would want t' thank ye too for the way you've done by us. I can't say any more, Captain Schenke—but we want you to take a small present from us—the crew of the *Hilda*'s gig." He held out the parcel.

Only half understanding the lad's broken words, Schenke took the parcel and opened it. "*Ach Gott. Lieber Gott,*" he said, and turned to show the gift to old Burke. Tears stood in the big "squarehead's" eyes; stood, and rolled unchecked down his fat cheeks. Tears of pleasure! Tears of pity! Stretched between his hands was a weather-beaten flag, its white emblem stained and begrimed by sea-water!

A tattered square of blue silk—the flag of the Merchants' Cup!

13

OWEN CHASE'S NARRATIVE

OWEN CHASE

I have not been able to recur to the scenes which are now to become the subject of description, although a considerable time has elapsed, without feeling a mingled emotion of horror and astonishment at the almost incredible destiny that has preserved me and my surviving companions from a terrible death. Frequently, in my reflections on the subject, even after this lapse of time, I find myself shedding tears of gratitude for our deliverance, and blessing God, by whose divine aid and protection we were conducted through a series of unparalleled suffering and distress, and restored to the bosoms of our families and friends. There is no knowing what a stretch of pain and misery the human mind is capable of contemplating, when it is wrought upon by the anxieties of preservation; nor what pangs and weaknesses the body is able to endure, until they are visited upon it; and when at last deliverance comes, when the dream of hope is realized, unspeakable gratitude takes possession of the soul, and tears of joy choke the utterance. We require to be taught in the school of some signal suffering, privation, and despair, the great lessons of constant dependence upon an almighty forbearance and mercy. In the midst of the wide ocean, at night, when the sight of the heavens was shut out, and the dark tempest came upon us, then it was that we felt ourselves ready to exclaim, "Heaven have mercy upon us, for nought but that can save us now." But I proceed to the recital. On the 20th of November (cruising in latitude 0° 40' S., longitude 119° 0' W.), a shoal of whales was discovered off the lee-bow.

The weather at this time was extremely fine and clear, and it was about 8 o'clock in the morning that the man at the mast-head gave the usual cry of, "There she blows." The ship was immediately put away, and we ran down in the direction for them. When we had got within half a mile of the place where they were observed, all our boats were lowered down, manned, and we started in pursuit of them. The ship, in the meantime, was brought to the wind, and the main-top-sail hove aback, to wait for us. I had the harpoon in the second boat; the captain preceded me in the first. When I arrived at the spot where we calculated they were, nothing was at first to be seen. We lay on our oars in anxious expectation of discovering them come up somewhere near us. Presently one rose, and spouted a short distance ahead of my boat; I made all speed towards it, came up with, and struck it; feeling the harpoon in him, he threw himself, in agony, over towards the boat (which at that time was up alongside of him), and, giving a severe blow with his tail, struck the boat near the edge of the water, amidships, and stove a hole in her. I immediately took up the boat hatchet, and cut the line, to disengage the boat from the whale, which by this time was running off with great velocity. I succeeded in getting clear of him, with the loss of the harpoon and line; and finding the water to pour fast in the boat, I hastily stuffed three or four of our jackets in the hole, ordered one man to keep constantly bailing, and the rest to pull immediately for the ship; we succeeded in keeping the boat free, and shortly gained the ship. The captain and the second mate, in the other two boats, kept up the pursuit, and soon struck another whale. They being at this time a considerable distance to leeward, I went forward, braced around the mainyard, and put the ship off in a direction for them; the boat which had been stove was immediately hoisted in, and after examining the hole, I found that I could, by nailing a piece of canvas over it, get her ready to join in a fresh pursuit, sooner than by lowering down the other remaining boat which belonged to the ship.

I accordingly turned her over upon the quarter, and was in the act of nailing on the canvas, when I observed a very large spermaceti whale, as well as I could judge about eighty-five feet in length; he broke water about twenty rods off our weather-bow, and was lying quietly, with his head in a direction for the ship. He spouted two or three times, and then disappeared. In less than two or three seconds he came up again, about the length of the ship off, and made directly for us, at the rate of about three knots. The ship was then going with about the same velocity. His appearance and attitude gave us at first no alarm; but while I stood watching his movements, and observing him but a ship's length off, coming down for us with great celerity, I involuntarily ordered the boy at the helm to put it hard up; intending to sheer off and avoid him. The words were scarcely out of my mouth, before he came down upon us with full speed, and struck the ship with his head, just forward of the fore-chains; he gave us such an appalling and tremendous jar, as nearly threw us all on our faces. The ship brought up as suddenly and violently as if she had struck a rock, and trembled for a few seconds like a leaf.

We looked at each other with perfect amazement, deprived almost of the power of speech. Many minutes elapsed before we were able to realize the dreadful accident; during which time he passed under the ship, grazing her keel as he went along, came up alongside of her to leeward, and lay on the top of the water (apparently stunned with the violence of the blow) for the space of a minute; he then suddenly started off, in a direction to leeward. After a few moments' reflection, and recovering, in some measure, from the sudden consternation that had seized us, I of course concluded that he had stove a hole in the ship, and that it would be necessary to set the pumps going. Accordingly they were rigged, but had not been in operation more than one minute before I perceived the head of the ship to be gradually settling down in the water; I then ordered the signal to be set for the other boats, which, scarcely had I dispatched, before I again discovered the whale, apparently in convulsions, on the top of the water, about one hundred rods to leeward. He was enveloped in the foam of the sea, that his continual and violent thrashing about in the water had created around him, and I could distinctly see him smite his jaws together, as if distracted with rage and fury. He remained a short time in this situation, and then started off with great velocity, across the bows of the ship, to windward. By this time the ship had settled down a considerable distance in the water, and I gave her up for lost.

I, however, ordered the pumps to be kept constantly going, and endeavoured to collect my thoughts for the occasion. I turned to the boats, two of which we then had with the ship, and with an intention of clearing them away, and getting all things ready to embark in them, if there should be no other resource left; and while my attention was thus engaged for a moment, I was aroused with the cry of a man at the hatchway, "Here he is—he is making for us again." I turned around, and saw him about one hundred rods directly ahead of us, coming down apparently with twice his ordinary speed, and to me at that moment, it appeared with tenfold fury and vengeance in his aspect. The surf flew in all directions about him, and his course towards us was marked by a white foam of a rod in width, which he made with the continual violent thrashing of his tail; his head was about half out of the water, and in that way he came upon, and again struck the ship. I was in hopes when I descried him making for us, that by a dexterous movement of putting the ship away immediately, I should be able to cross the line of his approach, before he could get up to us, and thus avoid what I knew, if he should strike us again, would prove our inevitable destruction.

I bawled out to the helmsman, "Hard up!" but she had not fallen off more than a point, before we took the second shock. I should judge the speed of the ship to have been at this time about three knots, and that of the whale about six. He struck her to windward, directly under the cathead, and completely stove in her bows. He passed under the ship again, went off to leeward, and we saw no more of him. Our situation at this junction can be more readily imagined than described. The shock to our feelings was such, as I am sure none can have an adequate conception of that were not there: the misfortune befell us at a moment when we least dreamt of any accident, and from the pleasing anticipations we had formed, of realizing the certain profits of our labour, we were dejected by a sudden, most mysterious, and overwhelming calamity. Not a moment, however, was to be lost in endeavouring to provide for the extremity to which it was now certain we were reduced. We were more than a thousand miles from the nearest land, and with nothing but a light open boat, as the resource of safety for myself and companions. I ordered the men to cease pumping, and every one to provide for himself; seizing a hatchet at the same time, I cut away the lashings of the spare boat, which lay bottom up across two spars directly over the quarter deck, and cried out to those near me to take her as she came down. They did so accordingly, and bore her on their shoulders as far as the waist of the ship. The steward had in the meantime gone down into the cabin twice, and saved two quadrants, two practical navigators, and the captain's trunk and mine; all of which were hastily thrown into the boat, as she lay on the deck, with the two compasses which I snatched from the binnacle. He attempted to descend again; but the water by this time had rushed in, and he returned without being able to effect his purpose. By the time we had got the boat to the waist, the ship had filled with water, and was going down on her beam-ends: we shoved our boat as quickly as possible from the plank-shear into the water, all hands jumping in her at the same time, and launched off clear of the ship. We were scarcely two boat lengths distant from her, when she fell over to windward, and settled down in the water.

Amazement and despair now wholly took possession of us. We contemplated the frightful situation the ship lay in, and thought with horror upon the sudden and dreadful calamity that had overtaken us. We looked upon each other, as if to gather some consolatory sensation from an interchange of sentiments, but every countenance was marked with the paleness of despair. Not a word was spoken for several minutes by any of us; all appeared to be bound in a spell of stupid consternation; and from the time we were first attacked by the whale, to the period of the fall of the ship, and of our leaving her in the boat, more than ten minutes could not certainly have elapsed! God only knows in what way, or by what means, we were enabled to accomplish in that short time what we did; the cutting away and transporting the boat from where she was deposited would of itself, in ordinary circumstances, have consumed as much time as that, if the whole ship's crew had been employed in it. My companions had not saved a single article but what they had on their backs; but to me it was a source of infinite satisfaction, if any such could be gathered from the horrors of our gloomy situation, that we had been fortunate enough to have preserved our compasses, navigators, and quadrants. After the first shock of my feelings was over, I enthusiastically contemplated them as the probable instruments of our salvation; without them all would have been dark and hopeless. Gracious God! What a picture of distress and suffering now presented itself to my imagination. The crew of the ship were saved, consisting of twenty human souls. All that remained to conduct these twenty beings through the stormy terrors of the ocean, perhaps many thousand miles, were three open light boats.

The prospect of obtaining any provisions or water from the ship, to subsist upon during the time, was at least now doubtful. How many long and watchful nights, thought I, are to be passed? How many tedious days of partial starvation are to be endured, before the least relief or mitigation of our sufferings can be reasonably anticipated. We lay at this time in our boat, about two ship lengths off from the wreck, in perfect silence, calmly contemplating her situation, and absorbed in our own melancholy reflections, when the other boats were discovered rowing up to us. They had but shortly before discovered that some accident had befallen us, but of the nature of which they were entirely ignorant. The sudden and mysterious disappearance of the ship was first discovered by the boat-steerer in the captain's boat, and with a horror-struck countenance and voice, he suddenly exclaimed, "Oh, my God! Where is the ship?"

Their operations upon this were instantly suspended, and a general cry of horror and despair burst from the lips of every man, as their looks were directed for her, in vain, over every part of the ocean. They immediately made all haste towards us. The captain's boat was the first that reached us. He stopped about a boat's length off, but had no power to utter a single syllable: he was so completely overpowered with the spectacle before him that he sat down in his boat, pale and speechless. I could scarcely recognize his countenance, he appeared to be so much altered, awed, and overcome with the oppression of his feelings, and the dreadful reality that lay before him. He was in a short time however enabled to address the inquiry to me, "My God, Mr. Chase, what is the matter?" I answered, "We have been stove by a whale." I then briefly told him the story. After a few moments' reflection he observed that we must cut away her masts, and endeavour to get something out of her to eat. Our thoughts were now all accordingly bent on endeavours to save from the wreck whatever we might possibly want, and for this purpose we rowed up and got on to her. Search was made for every means of gaining access to her hold; and for this purpose the lanyards were cut loose, and with our hatchets we commenced to cut away the masts, that she might right up again, and enable us to scuttle her decks. In doing which we were occupied about three-quarters of an hour, owing to our having no axes, nor indeed any other instruments, but the small hatchets belonging to the boats. After her masts were gone she came up about two-thirds of the way upon an even keel. While we were employed about the masts the captain took his quadrant, shoved off from the ship, and got an observation. We found ourselves in latitude 0° 40' S., longitude 119° W. We now commenced to cut a hole through the planks, directly above two large casks of bread, which most fortunately were between decks, in the waist of the ship, and which being in the upper side, when she upset, we had strong hopes was not wet. It turned out according to our wishes, and from these casks we obtained six hundred pounds of hard bread. Other parts of the deck were then scuttled, and we got without difficulty as much fresh water as we dared to take in the boats, so that each was supplied with about sixty-five gallons; we got also from one of the lockers a musket, a small canister of powder, a couple of files, two rasps, about two pounds of boat nails, and a few turtles.

In the afternoon the wind came on to blow a strong breeze; and having obtained every thing that occurred to us could then be got out, we began to make arrangements for our safety during the night. A boat's line was made fast to the ship, and to the other end of it one of the boats was moored, at about fifty fathoms to leeward; another boat was then attached to the first one, about eight fathoms astern; and the third boat, the like distance astern of her. Night came on just as we had finished our operations; and such a night as it was to us! so full of feverish and distracting inquietude, that we were deprived entirely of rest. The wreck was constantly before my eyes. I could not, by any effort, chase away the horrors of the preceding day from my mind: they haunted me the live-long night. My companions—some of them were like sick women; they had no idea of the extent of their deplorable situation. One or two slept unconcernedly, while others wasted the night in unavailing murmurs. I now had full leisure to examine, with some degree of coolness, the dreadful circumstances of our disaster. The scenes of yesterday passed in such quick succession in my mind that it was not until after many hours of severe reflection that I was about to discard the idea of the catastrophe as a dream. Alas! It was one from which there was no awaking; it was too certainly true, that but yesterday we had existed as it were, and in one short moment had been cut off from all the hopes and prospects of the living! I have no language to paint out the horrors of our situation. To shed tears was indeed altogether unavailing, and withal unmanly; yet I was not able to deny myself the relief they served to afford me. After several hours of idle sorrow and repining I began to reflect upon the accident, and endeavoured to realize by what unaccountable destiny or design (which I could not at first determine) this sudden and most deadly attack had been made upon us: by an animal, too, never before suspected of premeditated violence, and proverbial for its insensibility and inoffensiveness.

Every fact seemed to warrant me in concluding that it was anything but chance which directed his operations; he made two several attacks upon the ship, at a short interval between them, both of which, according to their direction, were calculated to do us the most injury, by being made ahead, and thereby combining the speed of the two objects for the shock; to effect which, the exact manoeuvres which he made were necessary. His aspect was most horrible, and such as indicated resentment and fury. He came directly from the shoal which we had just before entered, and in which we had struck three of his companions, as if fired with revenge for their sufferings. But to this it may be observed, that the mode of fighting which they always adopt is either with repeated strokes of their tails, or snapping of their jaws together; and that a case, precisely similar to this one, has never been heard of amongst the oldest and most experienced whalers. To this I would answer, that the structure and strength of the whale's head is admirably designed for this mode of attack; the most prominent part of which is almost as hard and as tough as iron; indeed, I can compare it to nothing else but the inside of a horse's hoof, upon which a lance or harpoon would not make the slightest impression. The eyes and ears are removed nearly one-third the length of the whole fish, from the front part of the head, and are not in the least degree endangered in this mode of attack. At all events, the whole circumstances taken together, all happening before my own eyes, and producing, at the time, impressions in my mind of decided, calculating mischief on the part of the whale (many of which impressions I cannot now recall) induce me to be satisfied that I am correct in my opinion. It is certainly, in all its bearings, a hitherto unheard of circumstance, and constitutes, perhaps, the most extraordinary one in the annals of the fishery.

14

THE WHITE WHALE

HERMAN MELVILLE

FIRST DAY

That night, in the mid-watch, when the old man—as his wont at
intervals—stepped forth from the scuttle in which he leaned, and went
to his pivot-hole, he suddenly thrust out his face fiercely, snuffing up
the sea air as a sagacious ship's dog will, in drawing nigh to some barbarous isle. He declared that a whale must be near. Soon that peculiar
odor, sometimes to a great distance given forth by the living Sperm
Whale, was palpable to all the watch; nor was any mariner surprised
when, after inspecting the compass, and then the dog-vane, and then
ascertaining the precise bearing of the odor as nearly as possible, Ahab
rapidly ordered the ship's course to be slightly altered, and the sail to
be shortened.

The acute policy dictating these movements was sufficiently vindi-
cated at daybreak by the sight of a long sleek on the sea directly and
lengthwise ahead, smooth as oil, and resembling in the pleated watery

wrinkles bordering it, the polished metallic-like marks of some swift tide-rip, at the mouth of a deep, rapid stream.

"Man the mastheads! Call all hands!"

Thundering with the butts of three clubbed handspikes on the forecastle deck, Daggoo roused the sleepers with such judgment claps that they seemed to exhale from the scuttle, so instantaneously did they appear with their clothes in their hands.

"What d'ye see?" cried Ahab, flattening his face to the sky.

"Nothing, nothing, sir!" was the sound hailing down in reply.

"T'gallant-sails! stunsails alow and aloft, and on both sides!"

All sail being set, he now cast loose the life-line, reserved for swaying him to the main royal-mast head; and in a few moments they were hoisting him thither, when, while but two-thirds of the way aloft, and while peering ahead through the horizontal vacancy between the main-top-sail and top-gallant-sail, he raised a gull-like cry in the air, "There she blows!—there she blows! A hump like a snowhill! It is Moby Dick!"

Fired by the cry which seemed simultaneously taken up by the three look-outs, the men on deck rushed to the rigging to behold the famous whale they had so long been pursuing. Ahab had now gained his final perch, some feet above the other look-outs, Tashtego standing just beneath him on the cap of the top-gallant-mast, so that the Indian's head was almost on a level with Ahab's heel. From this height the whale was now seen some mile or so ahead, at every roll of the sea revealing his high sparkling hump, and regularly jetting his silent spout into the air. To the credulous mariners it seemed the same silent spout they had so long ago beheld in the moonlit Atlantic and Indian Oceans.

"And did none of ye see it before?" cried Ahab, hailing the perched men all around him.

"I saw him almost that same instant, sir, that Captain Ahab did, and I cried out," said Tashtego.

"Not the same instant; not the same—no, the doubloon is mine, Fate reserved the doubloon for me. *I* only; none of ye could have raised the White Whale first. There she blows! there she blows!—there she blows! There again!—there again!" he cried, in long-drawn, lingering, methodic tones, attuned to the gradual prolongings of the whale's visible jets. "He's going to sound! In stunsails! Down top-gallant-sails! stand by three boats. Mr. Starbuck, remember, stay on board, and keep the ship. Helm there! Luff, luff a point! So; steady, man, steady! There go flukes! No, no; only black water! All ready the boats there? Stand by, stand by! Lower me, Mr. Starbuck; lower, lower,—quick, quicker!" and he slid through the air to the deck.

"He is heading straight to leeward, sir," cried Stubb, "right away from us; cannot have seen the ship yet."

"Be dumb, man! Stand by the braces! Hard down the helm!—brace up! Shiver her!—shiver her! So; well that! Boats, boats!"

Soon all the boats but Starbuck's were dropped; all the boat-sails set—all the paddles plying; with rippling swiftness, shooting to leeward; and Ahab heading the onset. A pale, death-glimmer lit up Fedallah's sunken eyes; a hideous motion gnawed his mouth.

Like noiseless nautilus shells, their light prows sped through the sea; but only slowly they neared the foe. As they neared him, the ocean grew still more smooth; seemed drawing a carpet over its waves; seemed a noon-meadow, so serenely it spread. At length the breathless hunter came so nigh his seemingly unsuspecting prey, that his entire dazzling hump was distinctly visible, sliding along the sea as if an isolated thing, and continually set in a revolving ring of finest, fleecy, greenish foam. He saw the vast involved wrinkles of the slightly projecting head beyond. Before it, far out on the soft Turkish-rugged waters, went the glistening white shadow from his broad, milky forehead, a musical rippling playfully accompanying the shade; and behind, the blue waters interchangeably flowed over into the moving valley of his steady wake; and on either hand bright bubbles arose and danced by his side. But these were broken again by the light toes of hundreds of gay fowl softly feathering the sea, alternate with their fitful flight; and like to some flag-staff rising from the painted hull of an argosy, the tall but shattered pole of a recent lance projected from the White Whale's back; and at intervals one of the cloud of soft-toed fowls hovering, and to and fro skimming like a canopy over the fish, silently perched and rocked on this pole, the long tail feathers streaming like pennons.

A gentle joyousness—a mighty mildness of repose in swiftness, invested the gliding whale. Not the white bull Jupiter swimming away with ravished Europa clinging to his graceful horns; his lovely, leering eyes sideways intent upon the maid; with smooth bewitching fleetness, rippling straight for the nuptial bower in Crete; not Jove, not that great majesty Supreme! did surpass the glorified White Whale as he so divinely swam.

On each soft side—coincident with the parted swell, that but once leaving him, then flowed so wide away—on each bright side, the whale shed off enticings. No wonder there had been some among the hunters who namelessly transported and allured by all this serenity, had ventured to assail it; but had fatally found that quietude but the vesture of tornadoes. Yet calm, enticing calm, oh, whale! thou glidest on, to all who for the first time eye thee, no matter how many in that same way thou may'st have bejuggled and destroyed before.

And thus, through the serene tranquilities of the tropical sea, among waves whose hand-clappings were suspended by exceeding rapture, Moby Dick moved on, still withholding from sight the full terrors of his submerged trunk, entirely hiding the wretched hideousness of his jaw. But soon the fore part of him slowly rose from the water; for an instant his whole marbleized body formed a high arch, like

Virginia's Natural Bridge, and warningly waving his bannered flukes in the air; the grand god revealed himself, sounded, and went out of sight. Hoveringly halting, and dipping on the wing, the white sea-fowls longingly lingered over the agitated pool that he left.

With oars apeak, and paddles down, the sheets of their sails adrift, the three boats now stilly floated, awaiting Moby Dick's reappearance.

"An hour," said Ahab, standing rooted in his boat's stern, and he gazed beyond the whale's place, towards the dim blue spaces and wide wooing vacancies to leeward. It was only an instant; for again his eyes seemed whirling round in his head as he swept the watery circle. The breeze now freshened; the sea began to swell.

"The birds!—the birds!" cried Tashtego.

In long Indian file, as when herons take wing, the white birds were now all flying towards Ahab's boat; and when within a few yards began fluttering over the water there, wheeling round and round, with joyous, expectant cries. Their vision was keener than man's; Ahab could discover no sign in the sea. But suddenly as he peered down and down into its depths, he profoundly saw a white living spot no bigger than a white weasel, with wonderful celerity uprising, and magnifying as it rose, till it turned, and then there were plainly revealed two long crooked rows of white, glistening teeth, floating up from the undiscoverable bottom. It was Moby Dick's open mouth and scrolled jaw; his vast, shadowed bulk still half blending with the blue of the sea. The glittering mouth yawned beneath the boat like an open-doored marble tomb; and giving one sidelong sweep with his steering oar, Ahab whirled the craft aside from this tremendous apparition. Then, calling upon Fedallah to change places with him, he went forward to the bows, and seizing Perth's harpoon, commanded his crew to grasp their oars and stand by to stern.

Now, by reason of this timely spinning round the boat upon its axis, its bow, by anticipation, was made to face the whale's head while yet under water. But as if perceiving this stratagem, Moby Dick, with that malicious intelligence ascribed to him, sidelingly transplanted himself, as it were, in an instant, shooting his plated head lengthwise beneath the boat.

Through and through; through every plank and each rib, it thrilled for an instant, the whale obliquely lying on his back, in the manner of a biting shark, slowly and feelingly taking its bows full within his mouth, so that the long, narrow, scrolled lower jaw curled high up into the open air, and one of the teeth caught in a row-lock. The bluish pearl-white of the inside of the jaw was within six inches of Ahab's head, and reached higher than that. In this attitude the White Whale now shook the slight cedar as a mildly cruel cat her mouse. With unastonished eyes Fedallah gazed and crossed his arms; but the tiger-yellow crew were tumbling over each other's heads to gain the uttermost stern.

And now, while both elastic gunwales were springing in and out, as the whale dallied with the doomed craft in this devilish way; and from his body being submerged beneath the boat, he could not be darted at from the bows, for the bows were almost inside of him, as it were; and while the other boats involuntarily paused, as before a quick crisis impossible to withstand, then it was that monomaniac Ahab, furious with this tantalizing vicinity of his foe, which placed him all alive and helpless in the very jaws he hated; frenzied with all this, he seized the long bone with his naked hands, and wildly strove to wrench it from its gripe. As now he thus vainly strove, the jaw slipped from him; the frail gunwales bent in, collapsed, and snapped, as both jaws, like an enormous shears, sliding further aft, bit the craft completely in twain, and locked themselves fast again in the sea, midway between the two floating wrecks. These floated aside, the broken ends drooping, the crew at the stern-wreck clinging to the gunwales, and striving to hold fast to the oars to lash them across.

At that preluding moment, ere the boat was yet snapped, Ahab, the first to perceive the whale's intent, by the crafty upraising of his head, a movement that loosed his hold for the time; at that moment his hand had made one final effort to push the boat out of the bite. But only slipping further into the whale's mouth, and tilting over sideways as it slipped, the boat had shaken off his hold on the jaw; spilled him out of it, as he leaned to the push; and so he fell flat-faced upon the sea.

Ripplingly withdrawing from his prey, Moby Dick now lay at a little distance, vertically thrusting his oblong white head up and down in the billows; and at the same time slowly revolving his whole spindled body; so that when his vast wrinkled forehead rose—some twenty or more feet out of the water—the now rising swells, with all their confluent waves, dazzling broke against it; vindictively tossing their shivered spray still higher into the air. So, in a gale, the but half baffled channel billows only recoil from the base of the Eddystone, triumphantly to overleap its summit with their scud.

But soon resuming his horizontal attitude, Moby Dick swam swiftly round and round the wrecked crew; sideways churning the water in his vengeful wake, as if lashing himself up to still another and more deadly assault. The sight of the splintered boat seemed to madden him, as the blood of grapes and mulberries cast before Antiochus's elephants in the book of Maccabees. Meanwhile Ahab half smothered in the foam of the whale's insolent tail, and too much of a cripple to swim,—though he could still keep afloat, even in the heart of such a whirlpool as that; helpless Ahab's head was seen, like a tossed bubble which the least chance shock might burst. From the boat's fragmentary stern, Fedallah incuriously and mildly eyed him; the clinging crew, at the other drifting end, could not succor him; more than enough was it for them to look to themselves. For so revolvingly appalling was the

White Whale's aspect, and so planetarily swift the ever-contracting circles he made, that he seemed horizontally swooping upon them. And though the other boats, unharmed, still hovered hard by, still they dared not pull into the eddy to strike, lest that should be the signal for the instant destruction of the jeopardized castaways, Ahab and all; nor in that case could they themselves hope to escape. With straining eyes then, they remained on the outer edge of the direful zone, whose center had now become the old man's head.

Meantime, from the beginning all this had been descried from the ship's mast-heads; and squaring her yards, she had borne down upon the scene; and was now so nigh, that Ahab in the water hailed her;— "Sail on the"—but that moment a breaking sea dashed on him from Moby Dick, and whelmed him for the time. But struggling out of it again, and chancing to rise on a towering crest, he shouted,—"Sail on the whale!—Drive him off!"

The *Pequod*'s prows were pointed; and breaking up the charmed circle, she effectually parted the White Whale from his victim. As he sullenly swam off, the boats flew to the rescue.

Dragged into Stubb's boat with bloodshot, blinded eyes, the white brine caking in his wrinkles; the long tension of Ahab's bodily strength did crack, and helplessly he yielded to his body's doom: for a time, lying all crushed in the bottom of Stubb's boat, like one trodden under foot of herds of elephants. Far inland, nameless wails came from him, as desolate sounds from out ravines.

But this intensity of his physical prostration did but so much the more abbreviate it. In an instant's compass, great hearts sometimes condense to one deep pang, the sum-total of those shallow pains kindly diffused through feebler men's whole lives. And so, such hearts, though summary in each one suffering; still, if the gods decree it, in their life-time aggregate a whole age of woe, wholly made up of instantaneous intensities; for even in their pointless centers, those noble natures contain the entire circumferences of inferior souls.

"The harpoon," said Ahab, half-way rising, and draggingly leaning on one bended arm—"is it safe?"

"Aye, sir, for it was not darted; this is it," said Stubb, showing it.

"Lay it before me;—any missing men?"

"One, two, three, four, five;—there were five oars, sir, and here are five men."

"That's good.—Help me, man; I wish to stand. So, so, I see him! there! there! going to leeward still; what a leaping spout!—Hands off from me! The eternal sap runs up in Ahab's bones again! Set the sail; out oars; the helm!"

It is often the case that when a boat is stove, its crew, being picked up by another boat, help to work that second boat; and the chase is thus continued with what is called double-banked oars. It was thus now. But the added power of the boat did not equal the added power of the whale, for he seemed to have treble-banked his every fin; swimming with a velocity which plainly showed, that if now, under these circumstances, pushed on, the chase would prove an indefinitely prolonged, if not a hopeless one; nor could any crew endure for so long a period, such an unintermitted, intense straining at the oar; a thing barely tolerable only in some one brief vicissitude. The ship itself, then, as it sometimes happens, offered the most promising intermediate means of overtaking the chase. Accordingly, the boats now made for her, and were soon swayed up to their cranes—the two parts of the wrecked boat having been previously secured by her—and then hoisting everything to her side, and stacking her canvas high up, and sideways outstretching it with stun-sails, like the double-jointed wings of an albatross; the *Pequod* bore down in the leeward wake of Moby Dick. At the well known, methodic intervals, the whale's glittering spout was regularly announced from the manned mast-heads; and when he would be reported as just gone down, Ahab would take the time, and then pacing the deck, binnaclewatch in hand, so soon as the last second of the allotted hour expired, his voice was heard.—"Whose is the doubloon now? D'ye see him?" and if the reply was, "No, sir!" straightway he commanded them to lift him to his perch. In this way the day wore on; Ahab, now aloft and motionless; anon, unrestingly pacing the planks.

As he was thus walking, uttering no sound, except to hail the men aloft, or to bid them hoist a sail still higher, or to spread one to a still greater breadth—thus to and fro pacing, beneath his slouched hat, at every turn he passed his own wrecked boat, which had been dropped upon the quarter-deck, and lay there reversed; broken bow to shattered stern. At last he paused before it; and as in an already over-clouded sky fresh troops of clouds will sometimes sail across, so over the old man's face there now stole some such added gloom as this.

Stubb saw him pause; and perhaps intending, not vainly, though, to evince his own unabated fortitude, and thus keep up a valiant place in his Captain's mind, he advanced, and eyeing the wreck exclaimed— "The thistle the ass refused; it pricked his mouth too keenly, sir; ha! ha!"

"What soulless thing is this that laughs before a wreck? Man, man! did I not know thee brave as fearless fire (and as mechanical) I could swear thou wert a poltroon. Groan nor laugh should be heard before a wreck."

"Aye, sir," said Starbuck, drawing near, "'tis a solemn sight; an omen, and an ill one."

"Omen? omen?—the dictionary! If the gods think to speak outright to man, they will honorably speak outright; not shake their heads, and give an old wives' darkling hint.—Begone! Ye two are the opposite poles of one thing; Starbuck is Stubb revered, and Stubb is Starbuck; and ye two are all mankind; and Ahab stands alone among the millions of the peopled earth, nor gods nor men his neighbors! Cold, cold—I shiver!—How now? Aloft there! D'ye see him? Sing out for every spout, though he spout ten times a second!"

The day was nearly done; only the hem of his golden robe was rustling. Soon, it was almost dark, but the lookout men still remained unset.

"Can't see the spout now, sir; too dark"—cried a voice from the air.

"How heading when last seen?"

"As before, sir,—straight to leeward."

"Good! he will travel slower now 'tis night. Down royals and top-gallant stun-sails, Mr. Starbuck. We must not run over him before morning; he's making a passage now, and may heave-to a while. Helm there! keep her full before the wind!—Aloft! come down!—Mr. Stubb, send a fresh hand to the fore-mast head and see it manned till morning."— Then advancing towards the doubloon in the mainmast—"Men, this gold is mine, for I earned it; but I shall let it abide here till the White Whale is dead; and then, whosoever of ye first raises him, upon the day he shall be killed, this gold is that man's; and if on that day I shall again raise him, then ten times its sum shall be divided among all of ye! Away now!—the deck is thine, sir."

And so saying, he placed himself half-way within the scuttle, and slouching his hat, stood there till dawn, except when at intervals rousing himself to see how the night wore on.

SECOND DAY

At daybreak, the three mast-heads were punctually manned afresh.

"D'ye see him?" cried Ahab after allowing a little space for the light to spread.

"See nothing, sir."

"Turn up all hands and make sail! he travels faster than I thought for;—the top-gallant sails!—aye, they should have been kept on her all night. But no matter—'tis but resting for the rush."

Here be it said, that this pertinacious pursuit of one particular whale, continued through day into night, and through night into day, is a thing by no means unprecedented in the South Sea fishery. For such is the wonderful skill, prescience of experience, and invincible confidence acquired by some great natural geniuses among the Nantucket commanders, that from the simple observation of a whale when last described, they will, under certain given circumstances, pretty accurately foretell both the direction in which he will continue to swim for a time, while out of sight, as well as his probable rate of progression during that period. And, in these cases, somewhat as a pilot, when about losing sight of a coast, whose general trending he well knows, and which he desires shortly to return to again, but at some further point; like as this pilot stands by his compass, and takes the precise bearing of the cape at present visible, in order the more certainly to hit aright the remote, unseen headland, eventually to be visited: so does the fisherman, at his compass, with the whale; for after being chased, and diligently marked, through several hours of daylight, then, when night obscures the fish, the creature's future wake through darkness is almost as established to the sagacious mind of the hunter, as the pilot's coast is to him. So that to this hunter's wondrous skill, the proverbial evanescence of a thing writ in water, a wake, is to all desired purposes well-nigh as reliable as the steadfast land. And as the mighty iron Leviathan of the modern railway is so familiarly known in its every pace, that, with watches in their hands, men time his rate as doctors that of a baby's pulse; and lightly say of it, "the up train or the down train will reach such or such a spot, at such or such an hour," even so, almost, there are occasions when these Nantucketers time that other Leviathan of the deep, according to the observed humor of his speed; and say to themselves, "So many hours hence this whale will have gone two hundred miles, will have about reached this or that degree of latitude or longitude." But to render this acuteness at all successful in the end, the wind and the sea must be the whaleman's allies; for of what present avail to the becalmed or windbound mariner is the skill that assures him he is exactly ninety-three leagues and a quarter from his port? Inferable from these statements are many collateral subtle matters touching the chase of whales.

The ship tore on; leaving such a furrow in the sea as when a cannon-ball, missent, becomes a ploughshare and turns up the level field.

"By salt and hemp!" cried Stubb, "but this swift motion of the deck creeps up one's legs and tingles at the heart. This ship and I are two brave fellows!—Ha! ha! Some one take me up, and launch me, spine-wise, on the sea,—for by live-oaks! My spine's a keel. Ha, ha! we go the gait that leaves no dust behind!"

"There she blows—she blows!—she blows!—right ahead!" was now the mast-head cry.

"Aye, aye!" cried Stubb; "I knew it—ye can't escape—blow on and split your spout, O whale! the mad fiend himself is after ye! Blow your trump—blister your lungs!—Ahab will dam off your blood, as a miller shuts his water-gate upon the stream!"

And Stubb did but speak out for well-nigh all that crew. The frenzies of the chase had by this time worked them bubblingly up, like old wine worked anew. Whatever pale fears and forebodings some of them might have felt before; these were not only now kept out of sight through the growing awe of Ahab, but they were broken up, and on all sides routed, as timid prairie hares that scatter before the bounding bison. The hand of Fate had snatched all their souls; and by the stirring perils of the previous day; the rack of the past night's suspense;

the fixed, unfearing, blind, reckless way in which their wild craft went plunging towards its flying mark; by all these things, their hearts were bowled along. The wind that made great bellies of their sails, and rushed the vessel on by arms invisible as irresistible; this seemed the symbol of that unseen agency which so enslaved them to the race.

They were one man, not thirty. For as the one ship that held them all; though it was put together of all contrasting things—oak, and maple, and pine wood; iron, and pitch, and hemp—yet all these ran into each other in the one concrete hull, which shot on its way, both balanced and directed by the long central keel; even so, all the individualities of the crew. This man's valor, that man's fear; guilt and guiltiness, all varieties were welded into oneness, and were all directed to that fatal goal which Ahab their one lord and keel did point to.

The rigging lived. The mast-heads, like the tops of tall palms, were outspreadingly tufted with arms and legs. Clinging to a spar with one hand, some reached forth the other with impatient wavings; others, shading their eyes from the vivid sunlight, sat far out on the rocking yards; all the spars in full bearing of mortals, ready and ripe for their fate. Ah! how they still strove through that infinite blueness to seek out the thing that might destroy them!

"Why sing ye not out for him, if ye see him?" cried Ahab, when, after the lapse of some minutes since the first cry, no more had been heard. "Sway me up, men; ye have been deceived; not Moby Dick casts one odd jet that way, and then disappears."

It was even so; in their headlong eagerness, the men had mistaken some other thing for the whale-spout, as the event itself soon proved; for hardly had Ahab reached his perch; hardly was the rope belayed to its pin on deck, when he struck the key-note to an orchestra, that made the air vibrate as with the combined discharges of rifles. The triumphant halloo of thirty buckskin lungs was heard, as—much nearer to

the ship than the place of the imaginary jet, less than a mile ahead—
Moby Dick bodily burst into view! For not by any calm and indolent
spoutings; not by the peaceable gush of that mystic fountain in his
head, did the White Whale now reveal his vicinity; but by the far more
wondrous phenomenon of breaching. Rising with his utmost velocity from the further depths, the Sperm Whale thus booms his entire
bulk into the pure element of air, and piling up a mountain of dazzling foam, shows his place to the distance of seven miles and more. In
those moments, the torn, enraged waves he shakes off seem his mane;
in some cases this breaching is his act of defiance.

"There she breaches! there she breaches!" was the cry, as in his
immeasurable bravadoes the White Whale tossed himself salmon-like
to Heaven. So suddenly seen in the blue plain of the sea, and relieved
against the still bluer margin of the sky, the spray that he raised, for the
moment, intolerably glittered and glared like a glacier; and stood there
gradually fading and fading away from its first sparkling intensity, to
the dim mistiness of an advancing shower in a vale.

"Aye, breach your last to the sun, Moby Dick!" cried Ahab, "thy
hour and thy harpoon are at hand!—Down! down all of ye, but one
man at the fore. The boats!—stand by!"

Unmindful of the tedious rope-ladders of the shrouds, the men,
like shooting starts, slid to the deck by the isolated backstays and halyards; while Ahab, less dartingly, but still rapidly, was dropped from
his perch.

"Lower away," he cried, so soon as he had reached his boat—a spare
one, rigged the afternoon previous. "Mr. Starbuck, the ship is thine—
keep away from the boats but keep near them. Lower, all!"

As if to strike a quick terror into them, by this time being the first
assailant himself, Moby Dick had turned, and was now coming for the
three crews. Ahab's boat was central; and cheering his men, he told

them he would take the whale head-and-head,—that is pull straight up to his forehead,—a not uncommon thing; for when within a certain limit, such a course excludes the coming onset from the whale's sidelong vision. But ere that close limit was gained, and while yet all three boats were plain as the ship's three masts to his eye; the White Whale churning himself into furious speed, almost in an instant as it were, rushing among the boats with open jaws, and a lashing tail, offered appalling battle on every side; and heedless of the irons darted at him from every boat, seemed only intent on annihilating each separate plank of which those boats were made. But skilfully maneuvered, incessantly wheeling like trained chargers in the field; the boats for a while eluded him, though, at times, but by a plank's breadth; while all the time, Ahab's unearthly slogan tore every other cry but his to shreds.

But at last in his untraceable evolutions, the White Whale so crossed and re-crossed, and in a thousand ways entangled the slack of the three lines now fast to him, that they foreshortened, and, of themselves, warped the devoted boats towards the planted irons in him; though now for a moment the whale drew aside a little, as if to rally for a more tremendous charge. Seizing that opportunity, Ahab first paid out more line: and then was rapidly hauling and jerking in upon it again—hoping that way to disencumber it of some snarls—when lo!—a sight more savage than the embattled teeth of sharks!

Caught and twisted—corkscrewed in the mazes of the line—loose harpoons and lances, with all their bristling barbs and points, came flashing and dripping up to the chocks in the bows of Ahab's boat. Only one thing could be done. Seizing the boat-knife, he critically reached within—through—and then, without—the rays of steel; dragged in the line beyond, passed it, inboard, to the bowsman, and then, twice sundering the rope near the chocks—dropped the intercepted fagot of steel into the sea; and was all fast again. That instant, the White Whale made a sudden rush among the remaining tangles of the other lines; by so doing, irresistibly dragged the more involved boats of Stubb and Flask towards his flukes; dashed them together like two rolling husks on a surf-beaten beach, and then, diving down into the sea, disappeared in a boiling maelstrom, in which, for a space, the odorous cedar chips of the wrecks danced round and round, like the grated nutmeg in a swiftly stirred bowl of punch.

While the two crews were yet circling in the waters, reaching out after the revolving line-tubs, oars, and other floating furniture, while aslope little Flask bobbed up and down like an empty vial, twitching his legs upwards to escape the dreaded jaws of sharks; and Stubb was lustily singing out for someone to ladle him up; and while the old man's line—now parting—admitted of his pulling into the creamy pool to rescue whom he could;—in that wild simultaneousness of a thousand concreted perils,—Ahab's yet unstricken boat seemed drawn up toward Heaven by invisible wires,—as arrow-like, shooting perpendicularly from the sea, the White Whale dashed his broad forehead against its bottom, and sent it, turning over and over, into the air; till it fell again—gunwale downwards—and Ahab and his men struggled out from under it, like seals from a seaside cave.

The first uprising momentum of the whale—modifying its direction as he struck the surface—involuntarily launched him along it, to a little distance from the center of the destruction he had made; and with his back to it, he now lay for a moment slowly feeling with his flukes from side to side; and whenever a stray oar, bit of plank, the least chip or crumb of the boats touched his skin, his tail swiftly drew back and came sideways, smiting the sea. But soon, as if satisfied that his work for that time was done, he pushed his plaited forehead through the ocean, and trailing after him the intertangled lines, continued his leeward way at a traveler's method pace.

As before, the attentive ship having descried the whole fight, again came bearing down to the rescue, and dropping a boat, picked up the floating mariners, tubs, oars, and whatever else could be caught at, and safely landed them on her decks. Some sprained shoulders, wrists, and ankles; livid contusions; wrenched harpoons and lances: inextricable intricacies of rope; shattered oars and planks; all these were there; but no fatal or even serious ill seemed to have befallen anyone. As with Fedallah the day before, so Ahab was now found grimly clinging to his boat's broken half, which afforded a comparatively easy float; nor did it so exhaust him as the previous day's mishap.

But when he was helped to the deck, all eyes were fastened upon him; as instead of standing by himself he still half-hung upon the shoulder of Starbuck, who had thus far been the foremost to assist him. His ivory leg had been snapped off, leaving but one short sharp splinter.

"Aye, aye, Starbuck, 'tis sweet to lean sometimes, be the leaner who he will; and would old Ahab had leaned oftener than he has."

"The ferrule has not stood, sir," said the carpenter, now coming up; "I put good work into that leg."

"But no bones broken, sir, I hope," said Stubb with true concern.

"Aye! and all splintered to pieces, Stubb—d'ye see it.—But even with a broken bone, old Ahab is untouched; and I account no living bone of mine one jot more me, than this dead one that's lost. Nor White Whale, nor man, nor fiend, can so much as graze old Ahab in his own proper and inaccessible being. Can any lead touch yonder floor, any mast scrape yonder roof?—Aloft there! which way?"

"Dead to leeward, sir."

"Up helm, then; pile on the sail again, ship keepers! down the rest of the spare boats and rig them—Mr. Starbuck, away, and muster the boat's crews."

"Let me first help thee towards the bulwarks, sir."

"Oh, oh, oh! how this splinter gores me now! Accursed fate! that the unconquerable captain in the soul should have such a craven mate!"

"Sir?"

"My body, man, not thee. Give me something for a cane—there, that shivered lance will do. Muster the men. Surely I have not seen him yet. By heaven, it cannot be!—missing?—quick! call them all."

The old man's hinted thought was true. Upon mustering the company, the Parsee was not there.

"The Parsee!" cried Stubb—"he must have been caught in—"

"The black vomit wrench thee!—run all of ye above, alow, cabin, forecastle—find him—not gone—not gone!"

But quickly they returned to him with the tidings that the Parsee was nowhere to be found.

"Aye, sir," said Stubb—"caught among the tangles of your line—I thought I saw him dragging under."

"*My* line? *my* line? Gone?—gone? What means that little word?— What death-knell rings in it, that old Ahab shakes as if he were the belfry. The harpoon, too!—toss over the litter there,—d'ye see it?— the forged iron, men, the White Whale's—no, no, no,—blistered fool! this hand did dart it!—'tis in the fish—Aloft there! Keep him nailed— Quick!—all hands to the rigging of the boats—collect the oars— harpooneers!—the irons, the irons!—hoist the royals higher—a pull on the sheets!—helm there! steady, steady for your life! I'll ten times girdle the unmeasured globe; yea and dive straight through it, but I'll slay him yet!"

"Great God! but for one single instant show thyself," cried Starbuck; "never never wilt thou capture him, old man.—In Jesus' name no more of this, that's worse than devil's madness. Two days chased; twice stove to splinters; thy very leg once more snatched from under thee; thy evil shadow gone—all good angels mobbing thee with warnings:—what more wouldst thou have?—Shall we keep chasing this murderous fish till he swamps the last man? Shall we be dragged by him to the bottom of the sea? Shall we be towed by him to the infernal world? Oh, oh!—Impiety and blasphemy to hunt him more!"

"Starbuck, of late I've felt strangely moved to thee; ever since that hour we both saw—thou know'st what, in one another's eyes. But in this matter of the whale, be the front of thy face to me as the palm of this hand—a lipless, unfeatured blank. Ahab is for ever Ahab, man. This whole act's immutably decreed. 'Twas rehearsed by thee and me a billion years before this ocean rolled. Fool! I am the Fates' lieutenant; I act under orders. Look thou, underling! that thou obeyest mine.—Stand round me, men. Ye see an old man cut down to the stump; leaning on a shivered lance; propped up on a lonely foot. 'Tis Ahab—his body's part; but Ahab's soul's a centipede, that moves upon a hundred legs. I feel strained, half stranded, as ropes that tow dismasted frigates in a gale; and I may look so. But ere I break, ye'll hear me crack; and till ye hear *that*, know that Ahab's hawser tows his purpose yet. Believe ye, men, in the things called omens? Then laugh aloud, and cry encore! For ere they drown, drowning things will twice rise to the surface; then rise again, to sink for evermore. So with Moby Dick—two days he's floated—tomorrow will be the third. Aye, man, he'll rise once more—but only to spout his last! D'ye feel brave men, brave?"

"As fearless fire," cried Stubb.

"And as mechanical," muttered Ahab. Then as the men went forward, he muttered on:—"The things called omens! And yesterday I talked the same to Starbuck there, concerning my broken boat. Oh! how valiantly I seek to drive out of others' hearts what's clinched so fast in mine!—The Parsee—the Parsee!—gone, gone? And he was to go before:—but still was to be seen again ere I could perish—How's that?—There's a riddle now might baffle all the lawyers backed by the ghosts of the whole line of judges:—like a hawk's beak it pecks my brain. *I'll, I'll* solve it, though!"

When dusk descended, the whale was still in sight to leeward.

So once more the sail was shortened, and everything passed nearly as on the previous night; only, the sound of hammers, and the hum of the grindstone was heard till nearly daylight, as the men toiled by lanterns in the complete and careful rigging of the spare boats and sharpened their fresh weapons for the morrow. Meantime, of the broken keel of Ahab's wrecked craft the carpenter made him another leg; while still as on the night before, slouched Ahab stood fixed within his scuttle; his hid heliotrope glance anticipatingly gone backward on its dial; set due eastward for the earliest sun.

THIRD DAY

The morning of the third day dawned fair and fresh, and once more the solitary night-man at the fore-mast-head was relieved by crowds of the daylight look-outs, who dotted every mast and almost every spar.

"D'ye see him?" cried Ahab; but the whale was not yet in sight.

"In his infallible wake, though; but follow that wake, that's all. Helm there; steady as thou goest, and hast been going. What a lovely day again! were it a new-made world, and made for a summer-house to the angels, and this morning the first of its throwing open to them, a fairer day could not dawn upon that world. Here's food for thought, had Ahab time to think, but Ahab never thinks; he only feels, feels, feels, *that's* tingling enough for mortal man! to think's audacity. God only has that right and privilege. Thinking is, or ought to be a coolness and a calmness; and our poor hearts throb, and our poor brains beat too much for that. And yet, I've sometimes thought my brain was very calm—frozen calm, this old skull cracks so, like a glass in which the contents turn to ice, and shiver it. And still this hair is growing now; this moment growing, and heat must breed it; but no, it's like that sort of common grass that will grow anywhere, between the earthly clefts of Greenland ice or in Vesuvius lava. How the wild winds blow it; they whip it about me as the torn shreds of split sails lash the tossed ship they cling to. A vile wind that has no doubt blown ere this through prison corridors and cells, and wards of hospitals, and ventilated them, and now comes blowing hither as innocent as fleeces. Out upon it!—it's tainted. Were I the wind, I'd blow no more on such a wicked, miserable world. I'd crawl somewhere to a cave, and slink there. And yet, 'tis a noble and heroic thing, the wind! Who ever conquered it? In every fight it has the last and bitterest blow. Run tilting at it, and you but run through it. Ha! a coward wind that strikes stark naked men, but will not stand to receive a single blow. Even Ahab is a braver thing—a nobler thing than *that*. Would now the wind but had a body; but all the things that most exasperate and outrage mortal man, all these things are bodiless, but only bodiless as objects, not as agents. There's a most special, a most cunning, oh a most malicious difference! And yet, I say again, and swear it now, that there's something all glorious and gracious in the wind. These warm Trade Winds, at least, that in the clear heavens blow straight on, in strong and steadfast, vigorous mildness; and veer not from their mark, however the baser current of the sea may turn and tack, and the mightiest Mississippis of the land shift and swerve about, uncertain where to go at last. And by the eternal Poles; these same Trades that so directly blow my good ship on; these Trades, or something like them—something so unchangeable, and full as strong, blow my keeled soul along! To it! Aloft there! What d'ye see?"

"Nothing, sir."

"Nothing! and noon at hand! The doubloon goes a-begging! See the sun! Aye, aye it must be so. I've oversailed him. How, got the start?

Aye, he's chasing me now; not I, *him*—that's bad; I might have known it, too. Fool! The lines—the harpoons he's towing. Aye, aye, I have run him by last night. About! about! Come down, all of ye, but the regular lookouts! Man the braces!"

Steering as she had done, the wind had been somewhat on the *Pequod*'s quarter, so that now being pointed in the reverse direction, the braced ship sailed hard upon the breeze as she rechurned the cream in her own white wake.

"Against the wind he now steers for the open jaw," murmured Starbuck to himself, as he coiled the new-hauled main-brace upon the rail. "God keep us, but already my bones feel damp within me, and from the inside wet my flesh. I misdoubt me that I disobey my God in obeying him!"

"Stand by to sway me up!" cried Ahab, advancing to the hempen basket. "We should meet him soon."

"Aye, aye, sir," and straightway Starbuck did Ahab's bidding, and once more Ahab swung on high.

A whole hour now passed; gold-beaten out to ages. Time itself now held long breaths with keen suspense. But at last, some three points off the weather-bow, Ahab descried the spout again, and instantly from the three mast-heads three shrieks went up as if the tongues of fire had voiced it.

"Forehead to forehead I meet thee, this third time, Moby Dick! On deck there!—brace sharper up; crowd her into the wind's eye. He's too far off to lower yet, Mr. Starbuck. The sails shake! Stand over the helmsman with a topmaul! So, so; he travels fast, and I must down. But let me have one more good round look aloft here at the sea; there's time for that. An old, old sight, and yet somehow so young; aye, and not changed a wink since I first saw it, a boy, from the sand-hills of Nantucket! The same!—the same!—the same to Noah as to me. There's a soft shower to leeward. Such lovely leewardings! They must lead some-where—to something else than common land, more palmy than the palms. Leeward! the White Whale goes that way; look to windward, then; the better if the bitter quarter. But goodbye, good-bye, old mast-head! What's this?—green? aye, tiny mosses in these warped cracks. No such green weather stains on Ahab's head! There's the difference now between man's old age and matter's. But aye, old mast, we both grow old together; sound in our hulls, though, are we not, my ship? Aye, minus a leg, that's all. By heaven! this dead wood has the better of my live flesh every way. I can't compare with it; and I've known some ships made of dead trees outlast the lives of man made of the most vital stuff of vital fathers. What's that he said? he should still go before me, my pilot; and yet to be seen again? But where? Shall I have eyes at the bot-tom of the sea, supposing I descend those endless stairs? and all night I've been sailing from him, wherever he did sink to. Aye, aye, like many more thou told'st direful truth as touching thyself, O Parsee; but, Ahab, there thy shot fell short. Goodbye, mast-head—keep a good eye upon the whale, the while I'm gone. We'll talk tomorrow, nay, tonight, when the White Whale lies down there, tied by head and tail."

He gave the word; and still gazing round him, was steadily lowered through the cloven blue air to the deck.

In due time the boats were lowered; but as standing in his shallop's stern, Ahab just hovered upon the point of the descent, he waved to the mate,—who held one of the tackleropes on deck—and bade him pause.

"Starbuck!"

"Sir?"

"For the third time my soul's ship starts upon this voyage, Star-buck."

"Aye, sir, thou wilt have it so."

"Some ships sail from their ports, and ever afterwards are missing, Starbuck!"

"Truth, sir: saddest truth."

"Some men die at ebb tide; some at low water; some at the full of the flood;—and I feel now like a billow that's all one crested comb, Starbuck. I am old;—shake hands with me, man."

Their hands met; their eyes fastened; Starbuck's tears the glue.

"Oh, my captain, my captain!—noble heart—go not—go not!— see, it's a brave man that weeps; how great the agony of the persuasion then!"

"Lower away!"—cried Ahab, tossing the mate's arm from him. "Stand by the crew!"

In an instant the boat was pulling round close under the stern.

"The sharks! the sharks!" cried a voice from the low cabin window there; "O master, my master, come back!"

But Ahab heard nothing; for his own voice was highlifted then; and the boat leaped on.

Yet the voice spake true; for scarce had he pushed from the ship, when numbers of sharks, seemingly rising from out dark waters beneath the hull, maliciously snapped at the blades of the oars, every time they dipped in the water; and in this way accompanied the boat with their bites. It is a thing not uncommonly happening to the whaleboats in those swarming seas; the sharks at times apparently following them in the same prescient way that vultures hover over the banners of marching regiments in the east. But these were the first sharks that had been observed by the *Pequod* since the White Whale had been first described; and whether it was that Ahab's crew were all such tiger-yellow barbarians, and therefore their flesh more musky to the senses of the sharks—a matter sometimes well known to affect them,—however it was, they seemed to follow that one boat without molesting the others.

"Heart of wrought steel!" murmured Starbuck, gazing over the side, and following with his eyes the receding boat—"canst thou yet ring boldly to that sight?—lowering thy keel among ravening sharks, and followed by them, open-mouthed, to the chase; and this the critical third day?—For when three days flow together in one continuous intense pursuit; be sure the first is the morning, the second the noon, and the third the evening and the end of that thing—be that end what it may. Oh! my God! what is this that shoots through me, and leaves me so deadly calm, yet expectant,—fixed at the top of a shudder! Future things swim before me, as in empty outlines and skeletons; all the past is somehow grown dim. Mary, girl! thou fadest in pale glories behind me; boy! I seem to see but thy eyes grown wondrous blue. Strangest problems of life seem clearing; but clouds sweep between— Is my journey's end coming? My legs feel faint; like his who has footed it all day. Feel thy heart,—beats it yet?—Stir thyself, Starbuck!—stave it off—move, move! speak aloud!—Mast-head there! See ye my boy's hand on the hill?—Crazed;—aloft there!—keep thy keenest eye upon the boats:—mark well the whale—Ho! again!—drive off that hawk! see! he pecks—he tears the vane"—pointing to the red flag flying at the main-truck—"Ha! he soars away with it!—Where's the old man now? sees't thou that sight, oh Ahab!—shudder, shudder!"

The boats had not gone very far, when by a signal from the mast-heads—a downward pointed arm, Ahab knew that the whale had sounded; but intending to be near him at the next rising, he held on his way a little sideways from the vessel; the becharmed crew maintaining the profoundest silence, as the head-beat waves hammered and hammered against the opposing bow.

"Drive, drive in your nails, oh ye waves! To their uttermost heads drive them in! ye but strike a thing without a lid; and no coffin and no hearse can be mine:—and hemp only can kill me! Ha! ha!"

Suddenly the waters around them slowly swelled in broad circles; then quickly upheaved, as if sideways sliding from a submerged berg of ice, swiftly rising to the surface. A low rumbling sound was heard; a subterraneous hum; and then all held their breaths; as bedraggled with trailing ropes, and harpoons, and lances, a vast form shot lengthwise, but obliquely from the sea. Shrouded in a thin drooping veil of mist, it hovered for a moment in the rainbowed air; and then fell swamping back into the deep. Crushed thirty feet upwards, the waters flashed for an instant like heaps of fountains, then brokenly sank in a shower of flakes, leaving the circling surface creamed like new milk round the marble trunk of the whale.

"Give way!" cried Ahab to the oarsmen and the boats darted forward to the attack; but maddened by yesterday's fresh irons that corroded in him, Moby Dick seemed combinedly possessed by all the angels that fell from heaven. The wide tiers of welded tendons overspreading his broad white forehead, beneath the transparent skin, looked knitted together, as head on, he came churning his tail among the boats; and once more flailed them apart; spilling out the irons and lances from the two mates' boats, and dashing in one side of the upper part of their bows, but leaving Ahab's almost without a scar.

While Daggoo and Queequeg were stopping the strained planks; and as the whale swimming out from them, turned, and showed one entire flank as he shot by them again; at that moment a quick cry went up. Lashed round and round to the fish's back; pinioned in the turns upon turns in which during the past night, the whale had reeled the involutions of the lines around him, the half torn body of the Parsee was seen, his sable raiment frayed to shreds; his distended eyes turned full upon old Ahab.

The harpoon dropped from his hand.

"Befooled, befooled!"—drawing in a long lean breath—"aye, Parsee! I see thee again.—Aye, and thou goest before; and this, *this* then is the hearse that thou didst promise. But I hold thee to the last letter of thy word. Where is the second hearse? Away, mates, to the ship! Those boats are useless now; repair them if ye can in time, and return to me; if not Ahab is enough to die—"Down men! the first thing that but offers to jump from this boat I stand in, that thing I harpoon. Ye are not other men, but my arms and my legs; and so obey me.—Where's the whale? gone down again?"

But he looked too nigh the boat; for as if bent upon escaping with the corpse he bore and as if the particular place of the last encounter had been but a stage in his leeward voyage, Moby Dick was now again steadily swimming forward; and had almost passed the ship,—which thus far had been sailing in the contrary direction to him, though for the present her headway had been stopped. He seemed swimming with his utmost velocity, and now only intent upon pursuing his own straight path in the sea.

"Oh! Ahab," cried Starbuck, "not too late is it, even now, the third day, to desist. See! Moby Dick seeks thee not. It is thou, thou, that madly seekest him!"

Setting sail to the rising wind, the lonely boat was swiftly impelled to leeward, by both oars and canvas. And at last when Ahab was sliding by the vessel, so near as plainly to distinguish Starbuck's face as he leaned over the rail, he hailed him to turn the vessel about, and follow him, not too swiftly, at a judicious interval. Glancing upwards, he saw Tashtego, Queequeg, and Daggoo, eagerly mounting to the three mastheads; while the oarsmen were rocking in the two staved boats which had just been hoisted to the side, and were busily at work in repairing them. One after the other, through the port-holes, as he sped, he also caught flying glimpses of Stubb and Flask, busying themselves on deck among bundles of new irons and lances. As he saw all this; as he heard the hammers in the broken boats; far other hammers seemed driving a nail into his heart. But he rallied. And now marking that the vane or flag was gone from the main masthead, he shouted to Tashtego, who had just gained that perch, to descend again for another flag, and a hammer and nails, and so nail it to the mast.

Whether fagged by the three days' running chase, and the resistance to his swimming in the knotted hamper he bore; or whether it was some latent deceitfulness and malice in him: whichever was true, the White Whale's way now began to abate, as it seemed, from the boat so rapidly nearing him once more; though indeed the whale's last start had not been so long a one as before. And still as Ahab glided over the waves the unpitying sharks accompanied him, and so pertinaciously stuck to the boat; and so continually bit at the plying oars, that the blades became jagged and crunched, and left small splinters in the sea, at almost every dip.

"Heed them not! those teeth but give new rowlocks to your oars. Pull on! 'tis the better rest, the sharks' jaw than the yielding water."

"But at every bite, sir, the thin blades grow smaller and smaller."

"They will last long enough! pull on!—But who can tell"—he muttered—"whether these sharks swim to feast of a whale or on Ahab?—But pull on! Aye, all alive, now—we near him. The helm! take the helm; let me pass,"—and so saying, two of the oarsmen helped him forward to the bows of the still flying boat.

At length as the craft was cast to one side, and ran ranging along with the White Whale's flank, he seemed strangely oblivious of its advance—as the whale sometimes will—and Ahab was fairly within the smoky mountain mist, which thrown off from the whale's spout, curled round his great, Monadnock hump. He was even thus close to him; when, with body arched back, and both arms lengthwise highlifted to the poise, he darted his fierce iron, and his far fiercer curse into the hated whale. As both steel and curse sank to the socket, as if sucked into a morass, Moby Dick sideways writhed; spasmodically rolled his nigh flank against the bow, and, without staving a hole in it, so suddenly canted the boat over, that had it not been for the elevated part of the gunwale to which he then clung, Ahab would once more have been tossed into the sea. As it was, three of the oarsmen—who foreknew not the precise instant of the dart, and were therefore unprepared for its effects—these were flung out; but so fell, that in an instant two of them clutched the gunwale again, and rising to its level on a combing wave, hurled themselves bodily inboard again; the third man helplessly drooping astern, but still afloat and swimming.

Almost simultaneously, with a mighty volition of ungraduated, instantaneous swiftness, the White Whale darted through the weltering sea. But when Ahab cried out to the steersman to take new turns with the line, and hold it so; and commanded the crew to turn round on their seats, and tow the boat up to the mark; the moment the treacherous line felt that double strain and tug, it snapped in the empty air!

"What breaks in me? Some sinew cracks!—'tis whole again; oars! oars! Burst in upon him!"

Hearing the tremendous rush of the sea-crashing boat, the whale wheeled round to present his blank forehead at bay; but in that evolution, catching sight of the nearing black hull of the ship; seemingly seeing in it the source of all his persecutions; bethinking it—it may be—a larger and nobler foe; of a sudden, he bore down upon its advancing prow, smiting his jaws amid fiery showers of foam.

Ahab staggered; his hand smote his forehead. "I grow blind; hands! Stretch out before me that I may yet grope my way. Is't nigh?"

"The whale! The ship!" cried the cringing oarsman.

"Oars! Oars! Slope downwards to thy depths, O sea, that ere it be for ever too late, Ahab may slide this last, last time upon his mark! I see: the ship! The ship! Dash on, my men! Will ye not save my ship?"

But as the oarsmen violently forced their boat through the sledge-hammering seas, the before whale-smitten bow-ends of two planks burst through, and in an instant almost, the temporarily disabled boat lay nearly level with the waves; its half-wading, splashing crew, trying hard to stop and gap and bail out the pouring water.

Meantime, for that one beholding instant, Tashtego's mast-head hammer remained suspended in his hand; and the red flag, half-wrapping him as with a plaid, then streamed itself straight out from him, as his own forward-flowing heart; while Starbuck and Stubb, standing upon the bowsprit beneath, caught sight of the down-coming monster just as soon as he.

"The whale, the whale! Up helm, up helm! Oh, all ye sweet powers of air, now hug me close! Let not Starbuck die, if die he must, in a woman's fainting fit. Up helm, I say—ye fools, the jaw! The jaw! Is this the end of all my bursting prayers? all my lifelong fidelities? Oh, Ahab, Ahab, lo, thy work. Steady! helmsman, steady. Nay, nay! Up helm again! He turns to meet us! Oh, his unappeasable brow drives on towards one, whose duty tells him he cannot depart. My God, stand by me now!

"Stand not by me, but stand under me, whoever you are that will now help Stubb; for Stubb, too, sticks here. I grin at thee, thou grinning whale! Whoever helped Stubb, or kept Stubb awake, but Stubb's own unwinking eye? And now poor Stubb goes to bed upon a mattress that is all too soft; would it were stuffed with brushwood! I grin at thee, thou grinning whale! Look ye, sun, moon and stars! I call ye assassins of as good a fellow as ever spouted up his ghost. For all that, I would yet ring glasses with ye, would ye but hand the cup! Oh, oh, oh, oh! thou grinning whale, but there'll be plenty of gulping soon! Why fly ye not, O Ahab? For me, off shoes and jacket to it, let Stubb die in his drawers! A most moldy and oversalted death, though;—cherries! cherries! cherries! Oh, Flask, for one red cherry ere we die!"

"Cherries? I only wish that we were where they grow. Oh, Stubb, I hope my poor mother's drawn my part-pay ere this; if not, few coppers will come to her now, for the voyage is up."

From the ship's bows, nearly all the seamen now hung inactive; hammers, bits of plank, lances, and harpoons, mechanically retained in their hands, just as they had darted from their various employments; all their enchanted eyes intent upon the whale, which from side to side strangely vibrating his predestinating head, sent a broad band of overspreading semicircular foam before him as he rushed. Retribution, swift vengeance, eternal malice were in his whole aspect, and spite of all that mortal man could do, the solid white buttress of his forehead smote the ship's starboard bow, till men and timbers reeled. Some fell flat upon their faces. Like dislodged trucks, the heads of the harpooneers aloft shook on their bull-like necks. Through the breach, they heard the waters pour, as mountain torrents down a flume.

"The ship! The hearse!—the second hearse!" cried Ahab from the boat; "its wood could only be American!"

Diving beneath the settling ship, the whale ran quivering along its keel, but turning under water, swiftly shot to the surface again, far off the other bow, but within a few yards of Ahab's boat, where, for a time, he lay quiescent.

"I turn my body from the sun. What ho, Tashtego! let me hear thy hammer. Oh! ye three unsurrendered spires of mine; thou uncracked keel; and only god-bullied hull; thou firm deck, and haughty helm, and Pole-pointed prow,—death-glorious ship! Must ye then perish, and without me? Am I cut off from the last fond pride of meanest shipwrecked captains? Oh, lonely death on lonely life! Oh, now I feel my topmost greatness lies in my topmost grief. Ho, ho! from all your furthest bounds, pour ye now in, ye bold billows of my whole foregone life, and top this one piled comber of my death! Towards thee I roll, thou all-destroying but unconquering whale; to the last I grapple with thee; from hell's heart I stab at thee; for hate's sake I spit my last breath at thee. Sink all coffins and all hearses to one common pool! and since neither can be mine let me then tow to pieces, while still chasing thee, though tied to thee, thou damned whale! *Thus*, I give up the spear!"

The harpoon was darted; the stricken whale flew forward; with igniting velocity the line ran through the groove; ran foul. Ahab stooped to clear it; he did clear it; but the flying turn caught him round the neck, and voicelessly as Turkish mutes bowstring their victim, he was shot out of the boat, ere the crew knew he was gone. Next instant, the heavy eyesplice in the rope's final end flew out of the stark-empty tub, knocked down an oarsman, and smiting the sea, disappeared in its depths.

For an instant, the tranced boat's crew stood still; then turned. "The ship? Great God, where is the ship?" Soon they through dim bewildering mediums saw her sidelong facing phantom, as in the gaseous Fata Morgana; only the uppermost masts out of water; while fixed by infatuation, or fidelity, or fate, to their once lofty perches, the pagan harpooneers still maintained their sinking lookouts on the sea. And now, concentric circles seized the lone boat itself, and all its crew, and each floating oar, and every lance-pole, and spinning, animate and inanimate, all round and round in one vortex, carried the smallest chip of the *Pequod* out of sight.

But as the last whelmings intermixingly poured themselves over the sunken head of the Indian at the mainmast, leaving a few inches of the erect spar yet visible, together with long streaming yards of the flag, which calmly undulated, with ironical coincidings, over the destroying billows they almost touched;—at that instant, a red arm and a hammer hovered backwardly uplifted in the open air, in the act of nailing the flag faster and yet faster to the subsiding spar. A sky-hawk that tauntingly had followed the main-truck downwards from its natural home among the stars, pecking at the flag, and incommoding Tashtego there; this bird now chanced to intercept its broad fluttering wing between the hammer and the wood; and simultaneously feeling that ethereal thrill, the submerged savage beneath, in his death-gasp, kept his hammer frozen there; and so the bird of heaven, with unearthly shrieks, and his imperial beak thrust upwards, and his whole captive form folded in the flag of Ahab, went down with his ship, which, like Satan, would not sink to hell till she had dragged a living part of heaven along with her, and helmeted herself with it.

Now small fowls flew screaming over the yet yawning gulf; a sullen white surf beat against its steep sides; then all collapsed, and the great shroud of the sea rolled on as it rolled five thousand years ago.

15

BLUESKIN, THE PIRATE

MERLE JOHNSON

Cape May and Cape Henlopen form, as it were, the upper and lower jaws of a gigantic mouth, which disgorges from its monstrous gullet the cloudy waters of the Delaware Bay into the heaving, sparkling blue-green of the Atlantic Ocean. From Cape Henlopen as the lower jaw there juts out a long, curving fang of high, smooth-rolling sand dunes, cutting sharp and clean against the still, blue sky above— silent, naked, utterly deserted, excepting for the squat, white-walled lighthouse standing upon the crest of the highest hill. Within this curving, sheltering hook of sand hills lie the smooth waters of Lewes Harbor, and, set a little back from the shore, the quaint old town, with its dingy wooden houses of clapboard and shingle, looks sleepily out through the masts of the shipping lying at anchor in the harbor, to the purple, clean-cut, level thread of the ocean horizon beyond.

Lewes is a queer, odd, old-fashioned little town, smelling fragrant of salt marsh and sea breeze. It is rarely visited by strangers. The people who live there are the progeny of people who have lived there for many generations, and it is the very place to nurse, and preserve, and care for old legends and traditions of bygone times, until they grow from bits of gossip and news into local history of considerable size. As in the busier world men talk of last year's elections, here these old bits, and scraps, and odds and ends of history are retailed to the listener who cares to listen—traditions of the War of 1812, when Beresford's fleet lay off the harbor threatening to bombard the town; tales of the Revolution and of Earl Howe's warships, tarrying for a while in the quiet harbor before they sailed up the river to shake old Philadelphia town with the thunders of their guns at Red Bank and Fort Mifflin.

With these substantial and sober threads of real history, other and more lurid colors are interwoven into the web of local lore—legends of the dark doings of famous pirates, of their mysterious, sinister comings and goings, of treasures buried in the sand dunes and pine barrens back of the cape and along the Atlantic beach to the southward.

Of such is the story of Blueskin, the pirate.

It was in the fall and the early winter of the year 1750, and again in the summer of the year following, that the famous pirate, Blueskin, became especially identified with Lewes as a part of its traditional history.

For some time—for three or four years—rumors and reports of Blueskin's doings in the West Indies and off the Carolinas had been brought in now and then by sea captains. There was no more cruel, bloody, desperate, devilish pirate than he in all those pirate-infested waters. All kinds of wild and bloody stories were current concerning him, but it never occurred to the good folk of Lewes that such stories were some time to be a part of their own history.

But one day a schooner came drifting into Lewes harbor—shattered, wounded, her forecastle splintered, her foremast shot half away, and three great tattered holes in her mainsail. The mate with one of the crew came ashore in the boat for help and a doctor. He reported that the captain and the cook were dead and there were three wounded men aboard. The story he told to the gathering crowd brought a very peculiar thrill to those who heard it. They had fallen in with Blueskin, he said, off Fenwick's Island (some twenty or thirty miles below the capes), and the pirates had come aboard of them; but, finding that the cargo of the schooner consisted only of cypress shingles and lumber, had soon quitted their prize. Perhaps Blueskin was disappointed at not finding a more valuable capture; perhaps the spirit of deviltry was hotter in him that morning than usual; anyhow, as the pirate craft bore away she fired three broadsides at short range into the helpless coaster. The captain had been killed at the first fire, the cook had died on the way up, three of the crew were wounded, and the vessel was leaking fast, betwixt wind and water.

Such was the mate's story. It spread like wildfire, and in half an hour all the town was in a ferment. Fenwick's Island was very near home; Blueskin might come sailing into the harbor at any minute and then—! In an hour Sheriff Jones had called together most of the able-bodied men of the town, muskets and rifles were taken down from the chimney places, and every preparation was made to defend the place against the pirates, should they come into the harbor and attempt to land.

But Blueskin did not come that day, nor did he come the next or the next. But on the afternoon of the third the news went suddenly flying over the town that the pirates were inside the capes. As the report spread the people came running—men, women, and children—to the green before the tavern, where a little knot of old seamen were gathered together, looking fixedly out toward the offing, talking in low voices. Two vessels, one bark-rigged, the other and smaller a sloop, were slowly creeping up the bay, a couple of miles or so away and just inside the cape. There appeared nothing remarkable about the two crafts, but the little crowd that continued gathering upon the green stood looking out across the bay at them none the less anxiously for that. They were sailing close-hauled to the wind, the sloop following in the wake of her consort as the pilot fish follows in the wake of the shark.

But the course they held did not lie toward the harbor, but rather bore away toward the Jersey shore, and by and by it began to be apparent that Blueskin did not intend visiting the town. Nevertheless, those who stood looking did not draw a free breath until, after watching the two pirates for more than an hour and a half, they saw them—then about six miles away—suddenly put about and sail with a free wind out to sea again.

"The bloody villains have gone!" said old Captain Wolfe, shutting his telescope with a click.

But Lewes was not yet quit of Blueskin. Two days later a half-breed from Indian River bay came up, bringing the news that the pirates had sailed into the inlet—some fifteen miles below Lewes—and had careened the bark to clean her.

Perhaps Blueskin did not care to stir up the country people against him, for the half-breed reported that the pirates were doing no harm, and that what they took from the farmers of Indian River and Rehoboth they paid for with good hard money.

It was while the excitement over the pirates was at its highest fever heat that Levi West came home again.

Even in the middle of the last century the grist mill, a couple of miles from Lewes, although it was at most but fifty or sixty years old, had all a look of weather-beaten age, for the cypress shingles, of which it was built, ripen in a few years of wind and weather to a silvery, hoary gray, and the white powdering of flour lent it a look as though the dust of ages had settled upon it, making the shadows within dim, soft, mysterious. A dozen willow trees shaded with dappling, shivering ripples of shadow the road before the mill door, and the mill itself, and the long, narrow, shingle-built, one-storied, hip-roofed dwelling house. At the time of the story the mill had descended in a direct line of succession to Hiram White, the grandson of old Ephraim White, who had built it, it was said, in 1701.

Hiram White was only twenty-seven years old, but he was already in local repute as a "character." As a boy he was thought to be half-witted or "natural," and, as is the case with such unfortunates in small country towns where everybody knows everybody, he was made a common sport and jest for the keener, crueler wits of the neighborhood. Now that he was grown to the ripeness of manhood he was still looked upon as being—to use a quaint expression—"slack," or "not jest right." He was heavy, awkward, ungainly and loose-jointed, and enormously, prodigiously strong. He had a lumpish, thick-featured face, with lips heavy and loosely hanging, that gave him an air of stupidity, half droll, half pathetic. His little eyes were set far apart and flat with his face, his eyebrows were nearly white and his hair was of a sandy, colorless kind. He was singularly taciturn, lisping thickly when he did talk, and stuttering and hesitating in his speech, as though his words moved faster than his mind could follow. It was the custom for local wags to urge, or badger, or tempt him to talk, for the sake of the ready laugh that always followed the few thick, stammering words and the stupid drooping of the jaw at the end of each short speech. Perhaps Squire Hall was the only one in Lewes Hundred who misdoubted that Hiram was half-witted. He had had dealings with him and was wont to say that whoever bought Hiram White for a fool made a fool's bargain. Certainly, whether he had common wits or no, Hiram had managed his mill to pretty good purpose and was fairly well off in the world as prosperity went in southern Delaware and in those days. No doubt, had it come to the pinch, he might have bought some of his tormentors out three times over.

Hiram White had suffered quite a financial loss some six months before, through that very Blueskin who was now lurking in Indian River inlet. He had entered into a "venture" with Josiah Shippin, a Philadelphia merchant, to the tune of seven hundred pounds sterling. The money had been invested in a cargo of flour and corn meal which had been shipped to Jamaica by the bark *Nancy Lee*. The *Nancy Lee* had been captured by the pirates off Currituck Sound, the crew set adrift in the longboat, and the bark herself and all her cargo burned to the water's edge.

Five hundred of the seven hundred pounds invested in the unfortunate "venture" was money bequeathed by Hiram's father, seven years before, to Levi West.

Eleazer White had been twice married, the second time to the widow West. She had brought with her to her new home a good-looking, long-legged, black-eyed, black-haired ne'er-do-well of a son, a year or so younger than Hiram. He was a shrewd, quick-witted lad, idle, shiftless, willful, ill-trained perhaps, but as bright and keen as a pin. He was the very opposite to poor, dull Hiram. Eleazer White had never loved his son; he was ashamed of the poor, slack-witted oaf. Upon the other hand, he was very fond of Levi West, whom he always called "our Levi," and whom he treated in every way as though he were his own son. He tried to train the lad to work in the mill, and was patient beyond what the patience of most fathers would have been with his stepson's idleness and shiftlessness. "Never mind," he was used to say. "Levi'll come all right. Levi's as bright as a button."

It was one of the greatest blows of the old miller's life when Levi ran away to sea. In his last sickness the old man's mind constantly turned to his lost stepson. "Mebby he'll come back again," said he, "and if he does I want you to be good to him, Hiram. I've done my duty by you and have left you the house and mill, but I want you to promise that if Levi comes back again you'll give him a home and a shelter under this roof if he wants one." And Hiram had promised to do as his father asked.

After Eleazer died it was found that he had bequeathed five hundred pounds to his "beloved stepson, Levi West," and had left Squire Hall as trustee.

Levi West had been gone nearly nine years and not a word had been heard from him; there could be little or no doubt that he was dead.

One day Hiram came into Squire Hall's office with a letter in his hand. It was the time of the old French war, and flour and corn meal were fetching fabulous prices in the British West Indies. The letter Hiram brought with him was from a Philadelphia merchant, Josiah Shippin, with whom he had had some dealings. Mr. Shippin proposed that Hiram should join him in sending a "venture" of flour and corn meal to Kingston, Jamaica. Hiram had slept upon the letter overnight and now he brought it to the old Squire. Squire Hall read the letter, shaking his head the while. "Too much risk, Hiram!" said he. "Mr. Shippin wouldn't have asked you to go into this venture if he could have got anybody else to do so. My advice is that you let it alone. I reckon you've come to me for advice?" Hiram shook his head. "Ye haven't? What have ye come for, then?"

"Seven hundred pounds," said Hiram.

"Seven hundred pounds!" said Squire Hall. "I haven't got seven hundred pounds to lend you, Hiram."

"Five hundred been left to Levi—I got hundred—raise hundred more on mortgage," said Hiram.

"Tut, tut, Hiram," said Squire Hall, "that'll never do in the world. Suppose Levi West should come back again, what then? I'm responsible for that money. If you wanted to borrow it now for any reasonable venture, you should have it and welcome, but for such a wildcat scheme—"

"Levi never come back," said Hiram—"nine years gone—Levi's dead."

"Mebby he is," said Squire Hall, "but we don't know that."

"I'll give bond for security," said Hiram.

Squire Hall thought for a while in silence. "Very well, Hiram," said he by and by, "if you'll do that. Your father left the money, and I don't see that it's right for me to stay his son from using it. But if it is lost, Hiram, and if Levi should come back, it will go well to ruin ye."

So Hiram White invested seven hundred pounds in the Jamaica venture and every farthing of it was burned by Blueskin, off Currituck Sound.

Sally Martin was said to be the prettiest girl in Lewes Hundred, and when the rumor began to leak out that Hiram White was courting her the whole community took it as a monstrous joke. It was the common thing to greet Hiram himself with, "Hey, Hiram; how's Sally?" Hiram never made answer to such salutation, but went his way as heavily, as impassively, as dully as ever.

The joke was true. Twice a week, rain or shine, Hiram White never failed to scrape his feet upon Billy Martin's doorstep. Twice a week, on Sundays and Thursdays, he never failed to take his customary seat by the kitchen fire. He rarely said anything by way of talk; he nodded to the farmer, to his wife, to Sally and, when he chanced to be at home, to her brother, but he ventured nothing further. There he would sit from half past seven until nine o'clock, stolid, heavy, impassive, his dull eyes following now one of the family and now another, but always coming back again to Sally. It sometimes happened that she had other company—some of the young men of the neighborhood. The presence of such seemed to make no difference to Hiram; he bore whatever broad jokes might be cracked upon him, whatever grins, whatever giggling might follow those jokes, with the same patient impassiveness. There he would sit, silent, unresponsive; then, at the first stroke of nine o'clock, he would rise, shoulder his ungainly person into his overcoat, twist his head into his three-cornered hat, and with a "Good night, Sally, I be going now," would take his departure, shutting the door carefully to behind him.

Never, perhaps, was there a girl in the world had such a lover and such a courtship as Sally Martin.

It was one Thursday evening in the latter part of November, about a week after Blueskin's appearance off the capes, and while the one subject of talk was of the pirates being in Indian River inlet. The air was still and wintry; a sudden cold snap had set in and skins of ice had formed over puddles in the road; the smoke from the chimneys rose straight in the quiet air and voices sounded loud, as they do in frosty weather.

Hiram White sat by the dim light of a tallow dip, poring laboriously over some account books. It was not quite seven o'clock, and he never started for Billy Martin's before that hour. As he ran his finger slowly and hesitatingly down the column of figures, he heard the kitchen door beyond open and shut, the noise of footsteps crossing the floor and the scraping of a chair dragged forward to the hearth. Then came the sound of a basket of corncobs being emptied on the smoldering blaze and then the snapping and crackling of the reanimated fire. Hiram thought nothing of all this, excepting, in a dim sort of way, that it was Bob, the mill hand, or old Dinah, the housekeeper, and so went on with his calculations.

At last he closed the books with a snap and, smoothing down his hair, arose, took up the candle, and passed out of the room into the kitchen beyond.

A man was sitting in front of the corncob fire that flamed and blazed in the great, gaping, sooty fireplace. A rough overcoat was flung over the chair behind him and his hands were spread out to the roaring warmth. At the sound of the lifted latch and of Hiram's entrance he turned his head, and when Hiram saw his face he stood suddenly still as though turned to stone. The face, marvelously altered and changed as it was, was the face of his stepbrother, Levi West. He was not dead; he had come home again. For a time not a sound broke the dead, unbroken silence excepting the crackling of the blaze in the fireplace and the sharp ticking of the tall clock in the corner. The one face, dull and stolid, with the light of the candle shining upward over its lumpy features, looked fixedly, immovably, stonily at the other, sharp, shrewd, cunning—the red wavering light of the blaze shining upon the high cheek bones, cutting sharp on the nose and twinkling in the glassy turn of the black, ratlike eyes. Then suddenly that face cracked, broadened, spread to a grin. "I have come back again, Hi," said Levi, and at the sound of the words the speechless spell was broken.

Hiram answered never a word, but he walked to the fireplace, set the candle down upon the dusty mantelshelf among the boxes and bottles, and, drawing forward a chair upon the other side of the hearth, sat down.

His dull little eyes never moved from his stepbrother's face. There was no curiosity in his expression, no surprise, no wonder. The heavy under lip dropped a little farther open and there was more than usual of dull, expressionless stupidity upon the lumpish face; but that was all.

As was said, the face upon which he looked was strangely, marvelously changed from what it had been when he had last seen it nine years before, and, though it was still the face of Levi West, it was a very different Levi West than the shiftless ne'er-do-well who had run away to sea in the Brazilian brig that long time ago. That Levi West had been a rough, careless, happy-go-lucky fellow; thoughtless and selfish, but with nothing essentially evil or sinister in his nature. The Levi West that now sat in a rush-bottom chair at the other side of the fireplace had that stamped upon his front that might be both evil and sinister. His swart complexion was tanned to an Indian copper. On one side of his face was a curious discoloration in the skin and a long, crooked, cruel scar that ran diagonally across forehead and temple and cheek in a white, jagged seam. This discoloration was of a livid blue, about the tint of a tattoo mark. It made a patch the size of a man's hand, lying across the cheek and the side of the neck. Hiram could not keep his eyes from this mark and the white scar cutting across it.

There was an odd sort of incongruity in Levi's dress; a pair of heavy gold earrings and a dirty red handkerchief knotted loosely around his neck, beneath an open collar, displaying to its full length the lean, sinewy throat with its bony "Adam's apple," gave to his costume somewhat the smack of a sailor. He wore a coat that had once been of fine plum color—now stained and faded—too small for his lean length, and furbished with tarnished lace. Dirty cambric cuffs hung at his wrists and on his fingers were half a dozen and more rings, set with stones that shone, and glistened, and twinkled in the light of the fire. The hair at either temple was twisted into a Spanish curl, plastered flat to the cheek, and a plaited queue hung halfway down his back.

Hiram, speaking never a word, sat motionless, his dull little eyes traveling slowly up and down and around and around his stepbrother's person.

Levi did not seem to notice his scrutiny, leaning forward, now with his palms spread out to the grateful warmth, now rubbing them slowly together. But at last he suddenly whirled his chair around, rasping on the floor, and faced his stepbrother. He thrust his hand into his capacious coat pocket and brought out a pipe which he proceeded to fill from a skin of tobacco. "Well, Hi," said he, "d'ye see I've come back home again?"

"Thought you was dead," said Hiram, dully.

Levi laughed, then he drew a red-hot coal out of the fire, put it upon the bowl of the pipe and began puffing out clouds of pungent smoke. "Nay, nay," said he; "not dead—not dead by odds. But [puff] by the Eternal Holy, Hi, I played many a close game [puff] with old Davy Jones, for all that."

Hiram's look turned inquiringly toward the jagged scar and Levi caught the slow glance. "You're lookin' at this," said he, running his finger down the crooked seam. "That looks bad, but it wasn't so close as this"—laying his hand for a moment upon the livid stain. "A cooly devil off Singapore gave me that cut when we fell foul of an opium junk in the China Sea four years ago last September. This," touching the disfiguring blue patch again, "was a closer miss, Hi. A Spanish captain fired a pistol at me down off Santa Catharina. He was so nigh that the powder went under the skin and it'll never come out again.—his eyes—he had better have fired the pistol into his own head that morning. But never mind that. I reckon I'm changed, ain't I, Hi?"

He took his pipe out of his mouth and looked inquiringly at Hiram, who nodded.

Levi laughed. "Devil doubt it," said he, "but whether I'm changed or no, I'll take my affidavy that you are the same old half-witted Hi that you used to be. I remember dad used to say that you hadn't no more than enough wits to keep you out of the rain. And, talking of dad, Hi, I hearn tell he's been dead now these nine years gone. D'ye know what I've come home for?"

Hiram shook his head.

"I've come for that five hundred pounds that dad left me when he died, for I hearn tell of that, too."

Hiram sat quite still for a second or two and then he said, "I put that money out to venture and lost it all."

Levi's face fell and he took his pipe out of his mouth, regarding Hiram sharply and keenly. "What d'ye mean?" said he presently.

"I thought you was dead—and I put—seven hundred pounds—into *Nancy Lee*—and Blueskin burned her—off Currituck."

"Burned her off Currituck!" repeated Levi. Then suddenly a light seemed to break upon his comprehension. "Burned by Blueskin!" he repeated, and thereupon flung himself back in his chair and burst into a short, boisterous fit of laughter. "Well, by the Holy Eternal, Hi, if that isn't a piece of your tarnal luck. Burned by Blueskin, was it?" He paused for a moment, as though turning it over in his mind. Then he laughed again. "All the same," said he presently, "d'ye see, I can't suffer for Blueskin's doings. The money was willed to me, fair and true, and you have got to pay it, Hiram White, burn or sink, Blueskin or no Blueskin." Again he puffed for a moment or two in reflective silence. "All the same, Hi," said he, once more resuming the thread of talk, "I don't reckon to be too hard on you. You be only half-witted, any-way, and I sha'n't be too hard on you. I give you a month to raise that money, and while you're doing it I'll jest hang around here. I've been in trouble, Hi, d'ye see. I'm under a cloud and so I want to keep here, as quiet as may be. I'll tell ye how it came about: I had a set-to with a land pirate in Philadelphia, and somebody got hurt. That's the reason I'm here now, and don't you say anything about it. Do you understand?"

16

THE ADVENTURES OF CAPTAIN HORN

FRANK STOCKTON

Early in the spring of the year 1884 the three-masted schooner *Castor*, from San Francisco to Valparaiso, was struck by a tornado off the coast of Peru. The storm, which rose with frightful suddenness, was of short duration, but it left the *Castor* a helpless wreck. Her masts had snapped off and gone overboard, her rudder-post had been shattered by falling wreckage, and she was rolling in the trough of the sea, with her floating masts and spars thumping and bumping her sides.

The *Castor* was an American merchant-vessel, commanded by Captain Philip Horn, an experienced navigator of about thirty-five years of age. Besides a valuable cargo, she carried three passengers—two ladies and a boy. One of these, Mrs. William Cliff, a lady past middle age, was going to Valparaiso to settle some business affairs of her late husband, a New England merchant. The other lady was Miss Edna Markham, a school-teacher who had just passed her twenty-fifth year, although she looked older. She was on her way to Valparaiso to take an important position in an American seminary. Ralph, a boy of fifteen, was her brother, and she was taking him with her simply because she did not want to leave him alone in San Francisco. These two had no near relations, and the education of the brother depended upon the exertions of the sister. Valparaiso was not the place she would have selected for a boy's education, but there they could be together, and, under the circumstances, that was a point of prime importance.

But when the storm had passed, and the sky was clear, and the mad waves had subsided into a rolling swell, there seemed no reason to believe that any one on board the *Castor* would ever reach Valparaiso. The vessel had been badly strained by the wrenching of the masts, her sides had been battered by the floating wreckage, and she was taking in water rapidly. Fortunately, no one had been injured by the storm, and although the Captain found it would be a useless waste of time and labor to attempt to work the pumps, he was convinced, after a careful examination, that the ship would float some hours, and that there would, therefore, be time for those on board to make an effort to save not only their lives, but some of their property.

All the boats had been blown from their davits, but one of them was floating, apparently uninjured, a short distance to leeward, one of the heavy blocks by which it had been suspended having caught in the cordage of the topmast, so that it was securely moored. Another boat, a small one, was seen, bottom upward, about an eighth of a mile to leeward. Two seamen, each pushing an oar before him, swam out to the nearest boat, and having got on board of her, and freed her from her entanglements, they rowed out to the capsized boat, and towed it to the schooner. When this boat had been righted and bailed out, it was found to be in good condition.

The sea had become almost quiet, and there was time enough to do everything orderly and properly, and in less than three hours after the vessel had been struck, the two boats, containing all the crew and the passengers, besides a goodly quantity of provisions and water, and such valuables, clothing, rugs, and wraps as room could be found for, were pulling away from the wreck.

The Captain, who, with his passengers, was in the larger boat, was aware that he was off the coast of Peru, but that was all he certainly knew of his position. The storm had struck the ship in the morning, before he had taken his daily observation, and his room, which was on deck, had been carried away, as well as every nautical instrument on board. He did not believe that the storm had taken him far out of his course, but of this he could not be sure. All that he knew with certainty was that to the eastward lay the land, and eastward, therefore, they pulled, a little compass attached to the Captain's watch-guard being their only guide.

For the rest of that day and that night, and the next day and the next night, the two boats moved eastward, the people on board suffering but little inconvenience, except from the labor of continuous rowing, at which everybody, excepting the two ladies, took part, even Ralph Markham being willing to show how much of a man he could be with an oar in his hand.

The weather was fine, and the sea was almost smooth, and as the Captain had rigged up in his boat a tent-like covering of canvas for the ladies, they were, as they repeatedly declared, far more comfortable than they had any right to expect. They were both women of resource and courage. Mrs. Cliff, tall, thin in face, with her gray hair brushed plainly over her temples, was a woman of strong frame, who would have been perfectly willing to take an oar, had it been necessary. To

Miss Markham this boat trip would have been a positive pleasure, had it not been for the unfortunate circumstances which made it necessary.

On the morning of the third day land was sighted, but it was afternoon before they reached it. Here they found themselves on a portion of the coast where the foot-hills of the great mountains stretch themselves almost down to the edge of the ocean. To all appearances, the shore was barren and uninhabited.

The two boats rowed along the coast a mile or two to the southward, but could find no good landing-place, but reaching a spot less encumbered with rocks than any other portion of the coast they had seen, Captain Horn determined to try to beach his boat there. The landing was accomplished in safety, although with some difficulty, and that night was passed in a little encampment in the shelter of some rocks scarcely a hundred yards from the sea.

The next morning Captain Horn took counsel with his mates, and considered the situation. They were on an uninhabited portion of the coast, and it was not believed that there was any town or settlement near enough to be reached by walking over such wild country, especially with ladies in the party. It was, therefore, determined to seek succor by means of the sea. They might be near one of the towns or villages along the coast of Peru, and, in any case, a boat manned by the best oarsmen of the party, and loaded as lightly as possible, might hope, in the course of a day or two, to reach some port from which a vessel might be sent out to take off the remainder of the party.

But first Captain Horn ordered a thorough investigation to be made of the surrounding country, and in an hour or two a place was found which he believed would answer very well for a camping-ground until assistance should arrive. This was on a little plateau about a quarter of a mile back from the ocean, and surrounded on three sides by precipices, and on the side toward the sea the ground sloped gradually downward. To this camping-ground all of the provisions and goods were carried, excepting what would be needed by the boating party.

When this work had been accomplished, Captain Horn appointed his first mate to command the expedition, deciding to remain himself in the camp. When volunteers were called for, it astonished the Captain to see how many of the sailors desired to go.

The larger boat pulled six oars, and seven men, besides the mate Rynders, were selected to go in her. As soon as she could be made ready she was launched and started southward on her voyage of discovery, the mate having first taken such good observation of the landmarks that he felt sure he would have no difficulty in finding the spot where he left his companions. The people in the little camp on the bluff now consisted of Captain Horn, the two ladies, the boy Ralph, three sailors,—one an Englishman, and the other two Americans from Cape Cod,—and a jet-black native African, known as Maka.

Captain Horn had not cared to keep many men with him in the camp, because there they would have little to do, and all the strong arms that could be spared would be needed in the boat. The three sailors he had retained were men of intelligence, on whom he believed he could rely in case of emergency, and Maka was kept because he was a cook. He had been one of the cargo of a slave-ship which had been captured by a British cruiser several years before, when on its way to Cuba, and the unfortunate negroes had been landed in British Guiana. It was impossible to return them to Africa, because none of them could speak English, or in any way give an idea as to what tribes they belonged, and if they should be landed anywhere in Africa except among their friends, they would be immediately reënslaved. For some years they lived in Guiana, in a little colony by themselves, and then, a few of them having learned some English, they made their way to Panama, where they obtained employment as laborers on the great canal. Maka, who was possessed of better intelligence than most of his fellows, improved a good deal in his English, and learned to cook very well, and having wandered to San Francisco, had been employed for two or three voyages by Captain Horn. Maka was a faithful and willing servant, and if he had been able to express himself more intelligibly, his merits might have been better appreciated.

The morning after the departure of the boat, Captain Horn, in company with the Englishman, Davis, each armed with a gun, set out on a tour of investigation, hoping to be able to ascend the rocky hills at the back of the camp, and find some elevated point commanding a view over the ocean. After a good deal of hard climbing they reached such a point, but the Captain found that the main object was really out of his reach. He could now plainly see that a high rocky point to the southward, which stretched some distance out to sea, would cut off all view of the approach of rescuers coming from that direction, until they were within a mile or two of his landing-place. Back from the sea the hills grew higher, until they blended into the lofty stretches of the Andes, this being one of the few points where the hilly country extends to the ocean.

The coast to the north curved a little oceanward, so that a much more extended view could be had in that direction, but as far as he could see by means of a little pocket-glass which the boy Ralph had lent him, the Captain could discover no signs of habitation, and in this direction the land seemed to be a flat desert. When he returned to camp, about noon, he had made up his mind that the proper thing to do was to make himself and his companions as comfortable as possible and patiently await the return of his mate with succor.

Captain Horn was very well satisfied with his present place of encampment. Although rain is unknown in this western portion of Peru, which is, therefore, in general desolate and barren, there are parts of the country that are irrigated by streams which flow from the snow-capped peaks of the Andes, and one of these fertile spots the Captain seemed to have happened upon. On the plateau there grew a few bushes, while the face of the rock in places was entirely covered by hanging vines. This fertility greatly puzzled Captain Horn, for nowhere was to be seen any stream of water, or signs of there ever having been any. But they had with them water enough to last for several days, and provisions for a much longer time, and the captain felt little concern on this account.

As for lodgings, there were none excepting the small tent which he had put up for the ladies, but a few nights in the open air in that dry climate would not hurt the male portion of the party.

In the course of the afternoon, the two American sailors came to Captain Horn and asked permission to go to look for game. The Captain had small hopes of their finding anything suitable for food, but feeling sure that if they should be successful, every one would be glad of a little fresh meat, he gave his permission, at the same time requesting the men to do their best in the way of observation, if they should get up high enough to survey the country, and discover some signs of habitation, if such existed in that barren region. It would be a great relief to the captain to feel that there was some spot of refuge to which, by land or water, his party might make its way in case the water and provisions gave out before the return of the mate.

As to the men who went off in the boat, the Captain expected to see but a few of them again. One or two might return with the mate, in such vessel as he should obtain in which to come for them, but the most of them, if they reached a seaport, would scatter, after the manner of seamen.

The two sailors departed, promising, if they could not bring back fish or fowl, to return before dark, with a report of the lay of the land.

It was very well that Maka did not have to depend on these hunters for the evening meal, for night came without them, and the next morning they had not returned. The Captain was very much troubled. The men must be lost, or they had met with some accident. There could be no other reason for their continued absence. They had each a gun, and plenty of powder and shot, but they had taken only provisions enough for a single meal.

Davis offered to go up the hills to look for the missing men. He had lived for some years in the bush in Australia, and he thought that there was a good chance of his discovering their tracks. But the Captain shook his head.

"You are just as likely to get lost, or to fall over a rock, as anybody else," he said, "and it is better to have two men lost than three. But there is one thing that you can do. You can go down to the beach, and make your way southward as far as possible. There you can find your way back, and if you take a gun, and fire it every now and then, you may attract the attention of Shirley and Burke, if they are on the hills above, and perhaps they may even be able to see you as you walk along. If they are alive, they will probably see or hear you, and fire in answer. It is a very strange thing that we have not heard a shot from them."

Ralph begged to accompany the Englishman, for he was getting very restless, and longed for a ramble and scramble. But neither the Captain nor his sister would consent to this, and Davis started off alone.

"If you can round the point down there," said the Captain to him, "do it, for you may see a town or houses not far away on the other side. But don't take any risks. At all events, make your calculations so that you will be back here before dark."

The Captain and Ralph assisted the two ladies to a ledge of rock near the camp from which they could watch the Englishman on his way. They saw him reach the beach, and after going on a short distance he fired his gun, after which he pressed forward, now and then stopping to fire again. Even from their inconsiderable elevation they could see him until he must have been more than a mile away, and he soon after vanished from their view.

As on the previous day darkness came without the two American sailors, so now it came without the Englishman, and in the morning he had not returned. Of course, every mind was filled with anxiety in regard to the three sailors, but Captain Horn's soul was racked with apprehensions of which he did not speak. The conviction forced itself upon him that the men had been killed by wild beasts. He could imagine no other reason why Davis should not have returned. He had been ordered not to leave the beach, and, therefore, could not lose his way. He was a wary, careful man, used to exploring rough country, and he was not likely to take any chances of disabling himself by a fall while on such an expedition.

Although he knew that the great jaguar was found in Peru, as well as the puma and black bear, the captain had not supposed it likely that any of these creatures frequented the barren western slopes of the mountains, but he now reflected that there were lions in the deserts of Africa, and that the beasts of prey in South America might also be found in its deserts.

A great responsibility now rested upon Captain Horn. He was the only man left in camp who could be depended upon as a defender,— for Maka was known to be a coward, and Ralph was only a boy,—and it was with a shrinking of the heart that he asked himself what would be the consequences if a couple of jaguars or other ferocious beasts were to appear upon that unprotected plateau in the night, or even in the daytime. He had two guns, but he was only one man. These thoughts were not cheerful, but the Captain's face showed no signs of alarm, or even unusual anxiety, and, with a smile on his handsome brown countenance, he bade the ladies good morning as if he were saluting them upon a quarter-deck.

"I have been thinking all night about those three men," said Miss Markham, "and I have imagined something which may have happened. Isn't it possible that they may have discovered at a distance some inland settlement which could not be seen by the party in the boat, and that they thought it their duty to push their way to it, and so get assistance for us? In that case, you know, they would probably be a long time coming back."

"That is possible," said the Captain, glad to hear a hopeful supposition, but in his heart he had no faith in it whatever. If Davis had seen a village, or even a house, he would have come back to report it, and if the others had found human habitation, they would have had ample time to return, either by land or by sea.

The restless Ralph, who had chafed a good deal because he had not been allowed to leave the plateau in search of adventure, now found a vent for his surplus energy, for the Captain appointed him fire-maker. The camp fuel was not abundant, consisting of nothing but some dead branches and twigs from the few bushes in the neighborhood. These Ralph collected with great energy, and Maka had nothing to complain of in regard to fuel for his cooking.

Toward the end of that afternoon, Ralph prepared to make a fire for the supper, and he determined to change the position of the fireplace and bring it nearer the rocks, where he thought it would burn better. It did burn better—so well, indeed, that some of the dry leaves of the vines that there covered the face of the rocks took fire. Ralph watched with interest the dry leaves blaze and the green ones splutter, and then he thought it would be a pity to scorch those vines, which were among the few green things about them, and he tried to put out the fire. But this he could not do, and, when he called Maka, the negro was not able to help him. The fire had worked its way back of the green vines, and seemed to have found good fuel, for it was soon crackling away at a great rate, attracting the rest of the party.

"Can't we put it out?" cried Miss Markham. "It is a pity to ruin those beautiful vines."

The Captain smiled and shook his head. "We cannot waste our valuable water on that conflagration," said he. "There is probably a great mass of dead vines behind the green outside. How it crackles and roars! That dead stuff must be several feet thick. All we can do is to let it burn. It cannot hurt us. It cannot reach your tent, for there are no vines over there."

The fire continued to roar and blaze, and to leap up the face of the rock.

"It is wonderful," said Mrs. Cliff, "to think how those vines must have been growing and dying, and new ones growing and dying, year after year, nobody knows how many ages."

"What is most wonderful to me," said the Captain, "is that the vines ever grew there at all, or that these bushes should be here. Nothing can grow in this region, unless it is watered by a stream from the mountains, and there is no stream here."

Miss Markham was about to offer a supposition to the effect that perhaps the precipitous wall of rock which surrounded the little plateau, and shielded it from the eastern sun, might have had a good effect upon the vegetation, when suddenly Ralph, who had a ship's biscuit on the end of a sharp stick, and was toasting it in the embers of a portion of the burnt vines, sprang back with a shout.

"Look out!" he cried. "The whole thing's coming down!" And, sure enough, in a moment a large portion of the vines, which had been clinging to the rock, fell upon the ground in a burning mass. A cloud of smoke and dust arose, and when it had cleared away the Captain and his party saw upon the perpendicular side of the rock, which was now revealed to them as if a veil had been torn away from in front of it, an enormous face cut out of the solid stone.

The great face stared down upon the little party gathered beneath it. Its chin was about eight feet above the ground, and its stony countenance extended at least that distance up the cliff. Its features were in low relief, but clear and distinct, and a smoke-blackened patch beneath one of its eyes gave it a sinister appearance. From its wide-stretching mouth a bit of half-burnt vine hung, trembling in the heated air, and this element of motion produced the impression on several of the party that the creature was about to open its lips.

Mrs. Cliff gave a little scream,—she could not help it,—and Maka sank down on his knees, his back to the rock, and covered his face with his hands. Ralph was the first to speak.

"There have been heathen around here," he said. "That's a regular idol."

"You are right," said the Captain. "That is a bit of old-time work. That face was cut by the original natives."

The two ladies were so interested, and even excited, that they seized each other by the hands. Here before their faces was a piece of sculpture doubtless done by the people of ancient Peru, that people who were discovered by Pizarro; and this great idol, or whatever it was, had perhaps never before been seen by civilized eyes. It was wonderful, and in the conjecture and exclamation of the next half-hour everything else was forgotten, even the three sailors.

Because the Captain was the Captain, it was natural that every one should look to him for some suggestion as to why this great stone face should have been carved here on this lonely and desolate rock. But he shook his head.

"I have no ideas about it," he said, "except that it must have been some sort of a landmark. It looks out toward the sea, and perhaps the ancient inhabitants put it there so that people in ships, coming near enough to the coast, should know where they were. Perhaps it was intended to act as a lighthouse to warn seamen off a dangerous coast. But I must say that I do not see how it could do that, for they would have had to come pretty close to the shore to see it, unless they had better glasses than we have."

The sun was now near the horizon, and Maka was lifted to his feet by the Captain, and ordered to stop groaning in African, and go to work to get supper on the glowing embers of the vines. He obeyed, of course, but never did he turn his face upward to that gaunt countenance, which grinned and winked and frowned whenever a bit of twig blazed up, or the coals were stirred by the trembling negro.

After supper and until the light had nearly faded from the western sky, the two ladies sat and watched that vast face upon the rocks, its features growing more and more solemn as the light decreased.

"I wish I had a long-handled broom," said Mrs. Cliff, "for if the dust and smoke and ashes of burnt leaves were brushed from off its nose and eyebrows, I believe it would have a rather gracious expression."

As for the Captain, he went walking about on the outlying portion of the plateau, listening and watching. But it was not stone faces he was thinking of. That night he did not sleep at all, but sat until daybreak, with a loaded gun across his knees, and another one lying on the ground beside him.

When Miss Markham emerged from the rude tent the next morning, and came out into the bright light of day, the first thing she saw was her brother Ralph, who looked as if he had been sweeping a chimney or cleaning out an ash-hole.

"What on earth has happened to you!" she cried. "How did you get yourself so covered with dirt and ashes?"

"I got up ever so long ago," he replied, "and as the Captain is asleep over there, and there was nobody to talk to, I thought I would go and try to find the back of his head"—pointing to the stone face above them. "But he hasn't any. He is a sham."

"What do you mean?" asked his sister.

"You see, Edna," said the boy, "I thought I would try if I could find any more faces, and so I got a bit of stone, and scratched away some of the burnt vines that had not fallen, and there I found an open place in the rock on this side of the face. Step this way, and you can see it. It's like a narrow doorway. I went and looked into it, and saw that it led back of the big face, and I went in to see what was there."

"You should never have done that, Ralph," cried his sister. "There might have been snakes in that place, or precipices, or nobody knows what. What could you expect to see in the dark?"

"It wasn't so dark as you might think," said he. "After my eyes got used to the place I could see very well. But there was nothing to see— just walls on each side. There was more of the passageway ahead of me, but I began to think of snakes myself, and as I did not have a club or anything to kill them with, I concluded I wouldn't go any farther. It isn't so very dirty in there. Most of this I got on myself scraping down the burnt vines. Here comes the Captain. He doesn't generally oversleep himself like this. If he will go with me, we will explore that crack."

When Captain Horn heard of the passage into the rock, he was much more interested than Ralph had expected him to be, and, without loss of time, he lighted a lantern and, with the boy behind him, set out to investigate it. But before entering the cleft, the captain stationed Maka at a place where he could view all the approaches to the plateau, and told him if he saw any snakes or other dangerous things approaching, to run to the opening and call him. Now, snakes were among the few things that Maka was not afraid of, and so long as he thought these were the enemies to be watched, he would make a most efficient sentinel.

When Captain Horn had cautiously advanced a couple of yards into the interior of the rock, he stopped, raised his lantern, and looked about him. The passage was about two feet wide, the floor somewhat lower than the ground outside, and the roof but a few feet above his head. It was plainly the work of man, and not a natural crevice in the rocks. Then the Captain put the lantern behind him, and stared into the gloom ahead of them. As Ralph had said, it was not so dark as might have been expected. In fact, about twenty feet forward there was a dim light on the right-hand wall.

The captain, still followed by Ralph, now moved on until they came to this lighted place, and found it was an open doorway. Both heads together, they peeped in, and saw it was an opening like a doorway into a chamber about fifteen feet square and with very high walls. They scarcely needed the lantern to examine it, for a jagged opening in the roof let in a good deal of light.

Passing into this chamber, keeping a good watch out for pitfalls as he moved on, and forgetting, in his excitement, that he might go so far that he could not hear Maka, should he call, the Captain saw to the right another open doorway, on the other side of which was another chamber, about the size of the one they had first entered. One side of this was a good deal broken away, and through a fracture three or four feet wide the light entered freely, as if from the open air. But when the two explorers peered through the ragged aperture, they did not look into the open air, but into another chamber, very much larger than the others, with high, irregular walls, but with scarcely any roof, almost the whole of the upper part being open to the sky.

A mass of broken rocks on the floor of this apartment showed that the roof had fallen in. The captain entered it and carefully examined it. A portion of the floor was level and unobstructed by rocks, and in the walls there was not the slightest sign of a doorway, except the one by which he had entered from the adjoining chamber.

"Hurrah!" cried Ralph. "Here is a suite of rooms. Isn't this grand? You and I can have that first one, Maka can sleep in the hall to keep out burglars, and Edna and Mrs. Cliff can have the middle room, and this open place here can be their garden, where they can take tea and sew. These rocks will make splendid tables and chairs."

The Captain stood, breathing hard, a sense of relief coming over him like the warmth of fire. He had thought of what Ralph had said before the boy had spoken. Here was safety from wild beasts—here was immunity from the only danger he could imagine to those under his charge. It might be days yet before the mate returned,—he knew the probable difficulties of obtaining a vessel, even when a port should be reached,—but they would be safe here from the attacks of ferocious animals, principally to be feared in the night. They might well be thankful for such a good place as this in which to await the arrival of succor, if succor came before their water gave out. There were biscuits, salt meat, tea, and other things enough to supply their wants for perhaps a week longer, provided the three sailors did not return, but the supply of water, although they were very economical of it, must give out in a day or two. "But," thought the Captain, "Rynders may be back before that, and, on the other hand, a family of jaguars might scent us out to-night."

"You are right, my boy," said he, speaking to Ralph. "Here is a suite of rooms, and we will occupy them just as you have said. They are dry and airy, and it will be far better for us to sleep here than out of doors."

As they returned, Ralph was full of talk about the grand find. But the Captain made no answers to his remarks—his mind was busy contriving some means of barricading the narrow entrance at night.

When breakfast was over, and the entrance to the rocks had been made cleaner and easier by the efforts of Maka and Ralph, the ladies were conducted to the suite of rooms which Ralph had described in such glowing terms. Both were filled with curiosity to see these apartments, especially Miss Markham, who was fairly well read in the history of South America, and who had already imagined that the vast mass of rock by which they had camped might be in reality a temple of the ancient Peruvians, to which the stone face was a sacred sentinel. But when the three apartments had been thoroughly explored she was disappointed.

"There is not a sign or architectural adornment, or anything that seems to have the least religious significance, or significance of any sort," she said. "These are nothing but three stone rooms, with their roofs more or less broken in. They do not even suggest dungeons."

As for Mrs. Cliff, she did not hesitate to say that she should prefer to sleep in the open air.

"It would be dreadful," she said, "to awaken in the night and think of those great stone walls about me."

Even Ralph remarked that, on second thought, he believed he would rather sleep out of doors, for he liked to look up and see the stars before he went to sleep.

At first the Captain was a little annoyed to find that this place of safety, the discovery of which had given him such satisfaction and relief, was looked upon with such disfavor by those who needed it so very much, but then the thought came to him, "Why should they care about a place of safety, when they have no idea of danger?" He did not now hesitate to settle the matter in the most straightforward and honest way. Having a place of refuge to offer, the time had come to speak of the danger. And so, standing in the larger apartment, and addressing his party, he told them of the fate he feared had overtaken the three sailors, and how anxious he had been lest the same fate should come upon some one or all of them.

Now vanished every spark of opposition to the Captain's proffered lodgings.

"If we should be here but one night longer," cried Mrs. Cliff, echoing the Captain's thought, "let us be safe."

In the course of the day the two rooms were made as comfortable as circumstances would allow with the blankets, shawls, and canvas which had been brought on shore, and that night they all slept in the rock chambers, the captain having made a barricade for the opening of the narrow passage with the four oars, which he brought up from the boat. Even should these be broken down by some wild beast, Captain Horn felt that, with his two guns at the end of the narrow passage, he might defend his party from the attacks of any of the savage animals of the country.

The Captain slept soundly that night, for he had had but a nap of an hour or two on the previous morning, and, with Maka stretched in the passage outside the door of his room, he knew that he would have timely warning of danger, should any come. But Mrs. Cliff did not sleep well, spending a large part of the night imagining the descent of active carnivora down the lofty and perpendicular walls of the large adjoining apartment.

The next day was passed rather wearily by most of the party in looking out for signs of a vessel with the returning mate. Ralph had made a flag which he could wave from a high point near by, in case he should see a sail, for it would be a great misfortune should Mr. Rynders pass them without knowing it.

To the Captain, however, came a new and terrible anxiety. He had looked into the water-keg, and saw that it held but a few quarts. It had not lasted as long as he had expected, for this was a thirsty climate.

The next night Mrs. Cliff slept, having been convinced that not even a cat could come down those walls. The Captain woke very early, and when he went out he found, to his amazement, that the barricade had been removed, and he could not see Maka. He thought at first that perhaps the negro had gone down to the sea-shore to get some water for washing purposes, but an hour passed, and Maka did not return. The whole party went down to the beach, for the captain insisted upon all keeping together. They shouted, they called, they did whatever they could to discover the lost African, but all without success.

They returned to camp, disheartened and depressed. This new loss had something terrible in it. What it meant no one could conjecture. There was no reason why Maka should run away, for there was no place to run to, and it was impossible that any wild beast should have removed the oars and carried off the negro.

17

THE WRECK OF THE *CITIZEN*

LEWIS HOLMES

The whale ship *Citizen*, of New Bedford, owned by J. Howland & Co., fitted for three or four years, and bound to the North Pacific on a whaling voyage, sailed from the port of New Bedford, October 29, 1851. She was commanded by Thomas Howes Norton, of Edgartown, Martha's Vineyard.

Her officers were the following, namely: first mate, Lewis H. Roey, of New Bedford; second mate, John P. Fisher, of Edgartown; third mate, Walter Smith, of New Bedford; fourth mate, William Collins, of New Bedford. Four boat steerers, namely: Abram Osborn, Jr., and John W. Norton, of Edgartown, John Blackadore and James W. Wentworth, of New Bedford.

The following were nearly all the names of her crew: Charles T. Heath, William E. Smith, Christopher Simmons, George W. Borth, Darius Aping, William Nye, Manuel Jose, Jose Joahim, Charles C.

Dyer, Charles Noyes, Edmund Clifford, George Long, Charles Adams, Bernard Mitchell, Nicholas Powers, William H. May, Alpheus Townshend, Barney R. Kehoe, Joseph E. Mears, James Dougherty, and Peter M. Cox. The whole number on board when she sailed was thirty-three persons. In addition to the above, five seamen were shipped at the Verd Islands, which made thirty-eight, all told.

As is generally the case, the majority of these were strangers, and perhaps had never seen each other's countenances until they appeared on the deck of the ship, henceforth to be their new home for months, and it may be for years.

Besides, in this number there were representatives from different and distant sections of the country, and not unfrequently an assortment of nations, and even races.

Here were gathered for the first time many a wandering youth, attracted to the seaboard by the spirit of romantic adventure, to see the world of waters, and to share in the excitement of new scenes. His wayward history, in breaking away from the wholesome restraints and watchcare of home, may be found written, perhaps, in many sorrowful hearts which he has left behind. Years may pass away before either parents or relatives shall hear again from the absent one, and it may be never. Such instances are not uncommon.

How much interest there is centred in a whale ship, as she is about to leave port! It is felt not only by those who embark their property and lives in her, but there are other attractions towards the ship. They are found in the desolateness which is felt in many home circles, in bidding adieu to husbands, sons, and brothers. When the anchor is weighed, and the sails are spread to the faithful breeze, sadness reigns in many households and in many hearts. The thoughts are not only painfully busy concerning *present* separations, but they bound forward to the future, and anticipate what may be the experience of a few years to come.

Changes! one hardly dares think of them! Amid the perils and dangers of the deep, how long will the ship's company remain unbroken? Will the *ship* ever return, and reenter her port again? Will those who have just released themselves from the embraces of friends, and wiped away the falling tear, and barred their hearts to the separation, will *they* ever return? or, if they should, will they ever see again those whom they are now leaving? These inquiries and reflections find expression only in painful emotions, sadness, and sorrow. Time will make changes, and leave its ineffaceable footprints with every passing year.

The land was lost sight of in the evening of the day upon which we sailed, with a strong south-west wind. We were accompanied out of the bay by two other outward bound whale ships—the *Columbus*, of Fairhaven, Captain Crowell, and the *Hunter*, of New Bedford, Captain Holt.

After the usual passage, with variable winds, and no particular incident of marked importance, except the ordinary and certain amount of seasickness on board, which generally attends the uninitiated in their first interviews with "old Neptune," Cape Verd Islands were made on the 4th of December.

With seasickness, homesickness follows; and then it is that many of the inexperienced, having left good homes and quiet life, wish a thousand times that they had never "learned the trade." But all such wishes are now in vain. With a new life on shipboard and in the forecastle, romance passes away, and leaves in its place the stern outlines of a living reality. Seasickness, however, is only a temporary affair; in most cases, indeed, it soon subsides, and then spirits and hope revive with recruited and invigorated health.

We took our departure from the islands on the 6th, in company with the ship *Benjamin Tucker*, Captain Sands; strong breezes, northeast trades. The first whales were seen about lat. 30° S., lon. 31° 41' W., distant about seven miles—light winds. We set signal for the *Benjamin Tucker*, four or five miles distant, to notify Captain Sands that whales were in sight—an agreement we made while sailing in company. Boats were lowered; the mate fastened to a whale, which brought the shoal to. The second mate was less successful; his boat was stoven by a whale, and his men were floating about upon scattered and broken pieces of the wreck. Other boats soon came up and rescued their companions. The ship now ran down to the boat which was fastened to the whale. The whale, however, was lost, in consequence of cutting the line in the act of lancing him. After a pursuit of an hour or more, the mate fastened to another whale, and finally secured it, though it proved to be of but little pecuniary value. At the same time the boats of the *Benjamin Tucker* captured a whale, but they could not boast of much superiority. It made them *three* barrels. Thus ended the first whaling scene on the voyage, and certainly not a very profitable day's work.

The *Citizen* was put on her course. We passed several ships— weather good. December 20, lat. 40° S., whales were raised again, but took no oil. Still in company with the *Benjamin Tucker*. On Christmas Eve, Captain Sands and his wife took tea on board of our ship, thus reviving remembrances of home and friends, though thousands of miles distant from our native port.

The next incident of more than ordinary interest was another whale scene, of sufficient excitement and peril to satisfy the most ardent and aspiring.

The *Benjamin Tucker* had luffed to, headed to the westward, with signal to the *Citizen* that whales were in sight. The ship *Columbus* was then in company. The three ships were in full pursuit of the monsters of the deep. The school was overtaken in course of an hour or two working to the leeward. At first, one of the boats was lowered from the *Citizen*, and then another, and another, until four boats were bounding over the waves, each seeking to be laid alongside of his victim, and join in the uncertain conflict. From the three ships there were twelve boats pressing forward with the utmost celerity to share in the encounter, and each emulous to bear off his prize. The fourth boat despatched from the *Citizen* fastened to a whale. He was shortly lanced, and spouted blood—a sure indication that he had received his death wound. In mortal agony, he plunged, and floundered, and mingled the warm current of his own life with the foaming waters around him. Conscious, apparently, of the authors of his sufferings, with rage and madness he at once attacked the boat, and with his ponderous jaws seized it, and in a moment bit it in two in the centre. Nor was there any time to be lost by the humble occupants of the boat. The rules of courtesy and ordinary politeness in entertaining a superior were for the time being laid entirely aside. Each seaman fled for his life—some from the stern, and others from the bow, while the cracking boards around and beneath them convinced them that the whale had every thing in his own way. Besides, the sensation was any thing but pleasant in expecting every moment to become fodder to the enraged leviathan of the deep. In quick succession those enormous jaws fell, accompanied with a deep, hollow moan or groan, which evinced intense pain, that sent a chill of terror to the stoutest hearts. They felt the feebleness of man when the monster arose in his fury and strength. A boat was soon sent to the rescue of their companions, who were swimming in every direction, to avoid contact with the enraged whale, which seemed bent on destroying every thing within his reach. He really asserted his original lordship in his own native element, and was determined to drive out all intruders. He therefore attacked the second boat, and would probably have ground it to atoms, had not a fortunate circumstance of two objects perhaps somewhat disconcerting him, and dividing his attention, turned him off from his purpose.

The captain of the *Citizen*, observing the affray from the beginning, was soon convinced that matters were taking rather a serious direction, and that not only the boats but the lives of his men were greatly imperilled. He therefore ordered the fifth boat to be instantly lowered, manned with "green hands," the command of which he himself assumed, and directed in pursuit of the whale. Five boats were now engaged in the contest, with the exception of the one stoven, and all the available crew and officers, including the captain, concentrated their efforts and energies in order to capture this "ugly customer." Just at the moment he was attacking or had already attacked the second boat, the captain's boat appeared on the ground, and from some cause best known to himself, the whale immediately left the former and assailed the latter. What the whale had already done, and what he appeared determined still to do, were by no means very flattering antecedents, and would very naturally impress the minds of "green hands," especially, that whaling, after all, was a reality, and not an imaginary affair or ordinary pastime.

On, therefore, the whale came to the captain's boat, ploughing the sea before him, jaws extended, with the fell purpose of destroying whatever he might chance to meet. As he approached near, the lance was thrust into his head and held in that position by the captain, and by this means he was kept at bay, while the boat was driven astern nearly half a mile. In this manner he was prevented from coming any nearer to the boat, the boat moving through the water as fast and as long as he pressed his head against the point of the lance. This was the only means of their defence. It was a most fortunate circumstance in a most trying situation. If the handle of the lance had broken, they would have been at the mercy of a desperate antagonist. The countenances of the boys were pallid with fear, and doubtless the very hair upon their heads stood erect.

It was a struggle for life. It was death presented to them under one of the most frightful forms. They were, however, as singularly and as suddenly relieved as they were unexpectedly attacked. The whale caught sight of the ship, as was supposed, which was running down towards the boats, and suddenly started for the new and larger object of attack. This was observed by the captain, who immediately made signal to keep the ship off the wind, which would give her more headway, and thus, if possible, escape a concussion which appeared at first sight inevitable.

The whale started on his new course towards the ship with the utmost velocity, with the intention of running into her. The consequences no one could predict; more than likely he would have either greatly disabled the ship, or even sunk her, had he struck her midships. To prevent such a catastrophe—the injury of the ship, and perhaps the ruin of the voyage—every thing now seemed to depend upon the direction of the ship and a favoring wind. Every eye was turned towards the ship; oars were resting over the gunwale of the boats, and each seaman instinctively fixed in his place, while anticipating a new encounter upon a larger scale, the results of which were fearfully problematical.

A good and merciful Providence, however, whose traces are easily discernible in the affairs of men both upon the ocean and upon the land, opportunely interfered. The ship was making considerable headway. The whale started on a bee line for the ship, but when he came up with her, in consequence of her increased speed before the wind, he fell short some ten or twelve feet from the stern. The crisis was passed. On he sped his way, dragging half of the boat still attached to the lines connected with the irons that were in his body. His death struggle was long and violent. In about half an hour he went into his "flurry, and turned up." Colors were set for the boats to return to the ship; the dead whale was brought alongside, cut in, boiled out, and seventy-five barrels of sperm oil were stowed away.

We copy the following whale incident from the *Vineyard Gazette* of October 14, 1853. The editor says,—

"We are indebted to Captain Thomas A. Norton, of this town, one of the early commanders of the whale ship *Hector*, of New Bedford, for the following interesting particulars relative to an attack upon and final capture of an ugly whale. Captain Norton was chief mate of the *Hector* at the time.

"'In October, 1832, when in lat. 12° S., lon. 80° W., the ship ninety days from port, we raised a whale. The joyful cry was given of "There she blows!" and every thing on board at once assumed an aspect of busy preparation for the capture. The boats were lowered, and chase commenced. When we got within about three ships' lengths of him, he turned and rushed furiously upon us. He struck us at the same moment we fastened to him. He stove the boat badly; but with the assistance of sails which were placed under her bottom, and constant bailing, she was kept above water. The captain, John O. Morse, came to our assistance. I told him he had better keep clear of the whale; but he said he had a very long lance, and wanted to try it upon the rascal. Captain Morse went up to the whale, when all at once he turned upon the boat, which he took in his mouth, and held it "right up on end," out of the water, and shook it all to pieces in a moment.

The men were thrown in every direction, and Captain Morse fell from a height of at least thirty feet into the water. Not being satisfied with the total destruction of the boat, he set to work and "chewed up" the boat kegs and lantern kegs, and whatever fragments of the boat he could find floating on the water. At this stage of the "fight," I told Captain Morse that if he would give me the choice of the ship's company, I would try him again. It was desperate work, to all appearance, and up to this time the vicious fellow had had it all his own way. The captain was in favor of trying him from the ship, but finally consented for us to attack him again from a boat. With a picked crew, we again approached the whale, now lying perfectly still, apparently ready for another attack, as the event proved. Seeing our approach, he darted towards us with his mouth wide open, his ponderous jaws coming together every moment with tremendous energy. We gave the word to "stern all," which was obeyed in good earnest. As we passed the ship, I heard the captain exclaim, "There goes another boat!" She did go, to be sure, through the water with all speed, but fortunately not to destruction. The monster chased us in this way for half a mile or more, during most of which time his jaws were within six or eight inches of the head of the boat. Every time he brought them together, the concussion could be heard at the distance of at least a mile. I intended to jump overboard if he caught the boat. I told Mr. Mayhew, the third mate, who held the steering oar, that the whale would turn over soon to spout, and that then would be our time to kill him. After becoming exhausted, he turned over to spout, and at the same instant we stopped the boat, and buried our lances deep in "his life." One tremendous convulsion of his frame followed, and all was still. He never troubled us more. We towed him to the ship, tried him out, and took ninety barrels of sperm oil from him.

"'When we were cutting him in, we found two irons in his body, marked with the name of the ship *Barclay*, and belonging to the mate's boat. We afterwards learned that three months before, when the same whale was in lat. 5° S., lon. 105° W., he was attacked by the mate of the ship *Barclay*, who had a desperate struggle with him, in which he lost his life.'

"Captain Norton, at the time of the adventure with this whale, had 'seen some service,' but he freely confesses that he never before nor since (though he has had his buttons bitten off his shirt by a whale) has come in contact with such an ugly customer as 'the rogue whale,' as he was termed in sailor parlance. He seemed to possess the spirit of a demon, and looked as savage as a hungry hyena. Our readers may imagine the effect such an encounter would have upon a crew of 'green hands.' During the frightful chase of the boat by the whale, their faces were of a livid whiteness, and their hair stood erect. On their arrival at the first port, they all took to the mountains, and few, if any of them, have ever been seen since."

The *Citizen* was put on her course again, with strong breezes and fair wind. About five days after, we spoke with the *Benjamin Tucker*, but Captain Sands had taken no oil. In lat. 47° S. another whale was raised; three boats were lowered in pursuit, but before he could be reached by the irons, he turned flukes, and was seen no more. Lost sight of the *Benjamin Tucker*. We shaped our course for Statan Land. In lat. 48° S. we experienced a very heavy gale from the south-west, which continued with great severity for twenty-four hours. We spoke with the bark *Oscar*, Captain Dexter, bound round the cape.

Statan Land in sight, passed seventeen ships, all bound for the cape. The *Citizen* was eleven days in doubling the cape, and experienced very heavy weather. In lat. 54° S. we raised the first right whale, but, blowing hard, could not lower. Whales were in sight several days in succession, but we could not lower, on account of rugged weather. In lat. 47° S. a ship was discovered with her boats down in pursuit of whales; came up with her; lowered for right whales, and chased them for an hour or more, but took none. At this time we spoke with the ship *Columbus* again, with one of her boats fastened to a whale. She had one boat stoven.

Passed St. Felix Islands, on the coast of Chili, and sighted the Gallipagos. In crossing the equator, it was calm for twenty-seven days, and but little progress was made during that time. On the 20th of April, 1852, after a passage of more than five months from New Bedford, we entered the port of Hilo.

Hilo is a port on the Island of Hawaii, one of the cluster of islands in the North Pacific Ocean called Sandwich Islands. They were discovered by Captains Cook and King in 1778, who gave them their present name, in honor of the first lord of the admiralty. The group consists of ten islands, but all of them are not inhabited; they extend from lat. 18° 50' to 22° 20' N., and from lon. 154° 53' to 160° 15' W., lying about one third of the distance from the western coast of Mexico to the eastern coast of China. By the census of 1849, the population of seven of the islands is given as follows: Hawaii, 27,204; Oahu, 23,145; Maui, 18,671; Kauhai, 6,941; Molokai, 3,429; Nuhua, 723; Lanai, 523; amounting to 80,641.

Most of these islands are volcanic and mountainous. In several places the volcanoes are in activity. Some of the mountains are of great height, being estimated at fifteen thousand feet.

The climate is warm, but not unhealthy, the winter being marked only by the prevalence of heavy rains between December and March. A meteorological table gives as the greatest heat during the year, 88° of Fahrenheit; as the least, 61°. Some of these islands are distinguished for the cultivation of the yam, which affords quite a valuable supply for ships.

The situation of the Sandwich Islands renders them important to vessels navigating the Northern Pacific, and especially so to whalemen. The ports of Hilo, Lahaina, Honolulu, and a few others, are the resort of a large number of whale ships, for the purpose of obtaining recruits. They may be considered as a central point, where ships meet both in the fall and spring, and from whence all matters of intelligence are transmitted to San Francisco, and from the latter place to the Atlantic States.

Formerly all ship news and letters were brought from the islands to the Atlantic States by homeward bound ships around the Horn, which required for their passages from three and a half to five months. But now, in consequence of mail communications across the isthmus to San Francisco, and from thence to the islands, letters and other public intelligence from the last-named place reach us in six weeks or two months from date.

At the port of Hilo the ship was recruited for the Arctic. We remained in port fifteen days, sailed for Honolulu, and left letters for owners and for home. We touched at another port before proceeding to the north, and there we took in an additional supply of provisions, and then directed our course towards the straits.

In lon. 180° W. we hauled to the north towards the coast of Kamtschatka. Passed Copper Island. We saw many ships on our passage thus far, but we took no whales until June.

About this time we captured two whales off shore, and found great quantities of ice. Spoke with Captain Crowell, of the ship *Columbus*, and Captain Crosby, of the ship *Cornelius Howland*.

We went into the ice with Captain Crosby, in search of whales, and soon found them; boats were lowered; pursuit commenced; several were struck; but our irons drew, and we therefore lost them.

A gale of wind coming on and increasing, we worked out of the ice as soon as possible. We were at that time, when the gale commenced, some fifteen or twenty miles in the floating and broken masses, of varied thickness and dimensions, greatly obstructing the course of the ship, and rendering her situation at times exceedingly dangerous. But by constant tacking and wearing in order to avoid concussion with the ice, or being jammed between opposite pieces, both ships were finally worked out of the ice in safety.

On the inside of Cape Thaddeus, we saw a large number of ships; spoke with several, but they reported that whales were scarce.

We now put the ship on her course for Behring Straits. We took one whale off the Bay of the Holy Cross, which made the fourth since we left port. We sailed along the coast towards the east; land frequently in sight; foggy; heard many guns from ships for their boats.

When off Plover Bay, ten miles from land, we picked up a dead whale, having no irons in him, nor anchored, and therefore a lawful prize. Many dead whales are found by ships in course of the season, and especially when ice is prevalent. They are struck by different boats, and if in the vicinity of ice, they will surely make for it, and go under it or among it; under these circumstances the lines must be cut. After some time, the badly wounded whales die, and are picked up as before stated.

We passed between St. Lawrence Island and the main land, or Indian Point. The huts of the natives were plainly seen from the ship's deck; still working our way towards the straits. At this time, we were in company with the ship *Montezuma*, Captain Tower, and the ship *Almira*, Captain Jenks. Whales were seen going towards the north, as it is usual for them to do so at this season of the year.

We anchored in St. Lawrence Bay; weather foggy. The natives came off to trade, and brought their accustomed articles for traffic, such as deer and walrus skins, furs, teeth, &c. They take in exchange needles, fancy articles, tobacco, &c.

After a few days, the fog having cleared away somewhat, we stood towards the north again; heard guns; saw whales; still in company with aforementioned ships; blowing heavy; all the ships in sight were under double-reefed topsails; beating.

Passed East Cape. Saw whales, but they were working quickly to the north; we followed them in their track with all the sail we could carry on the ship; they came to loose, floating ice, into which they went and shortly disappeared. A novel, and yet a common sight was now witnessed; the ice was covered with a vast number of walruses, which, to appearance, extended many miles.

The weather being fine for the season, the last part of June, in company with the *Almira*, Captain Jenks, we concluded we would go into the ice again, and if good fortune would have it so, we might capture a few whales.

Accidents occur not unfrequently when least expected, and sad ones, too, arise sometimes from the slightest circumstance, or inattention. Contact with icebergs, or large masses of block ice, when a ship is under sail, is highly dangerous. A momentary relaxation of vigilance on the part of the mariner may bring the ship's bows on the submerged part of an iceberg, whose sharp, needle-like points, hard as rock, instantly pierce the planks and timbers of a ship, and perhaps open a fatal leak. Many lamentable shipwrecks have doubtless resulted from this cause. In the long, heavy swell, so common in the open sea, the peril of floating ice is greatly increased, as the huge angular masses are rolled and ground against each other with a force which nothing can resist.

The striking of the *Citizen* against a mass of ice, which nearly resulted in the loss of the ship and the destruction of the voyage, was simply inattention or misunderstanding the word of command.

The man at the wheel was ordered not to "luff" the ship any more, but "steady," as she was approaching a mass of ice; indeed, ice was all around us, which would have passed us on our larboard bow, and thus we should have escaped a concussion; but instead of doing this, he put the wheel down, which brought the ship into the wind, and the consequence was, a large hole was stoven in her larboard bow; the ship began to leak badly. Casks were immediately filled with water, and placed on the starboard side of the ship, and thus in a measure heeled the ship, which brought the leak to a considerable extent out of the water; otherwise, she must have sunk in a very little time. So far as we were able, we temporarily repaired the injury, and made all possible sail on the ship, in order to seek some place of safety, where the whole extent of the damage could be ascertained.

In the present disabled and crippled condition of the ship, we felt it was exceedingly perilous and unsafe to remain even a single day in the Arctic. We therefore left the whale ground, and though our progress was slow, yet we put upon the ship all the sail she would bear, since on account of the leak she was very much heeled, and we were obliged to sail her in that condition.

Nor was it safe for our ship to be left alone to beat her way back two hundred miles or more, unaccompanied by another vessel, lest by some unforeseen circumstance,—an event not altogether improbable,—the ship might founder at sea, and all on board perish.

Captain Jenks, of the ship *Almira*, therefore, kindly proffered his services, with whatever aid he could give, and accompanied our ship nearly to the point of her destination, to the Bay of St. Lawrence, which was about two hundred miles distant from the place where the accident occurred.

When off East Cape, we obtained some plank from the ship *Citizen*, Captain Bailey, of Nantucket. We passed the heads of the bay, and, with shortened sail, we worked our way up more than thirty miles beyond the direction of any chart, our boats being sent ahead, and sounding the depth of water. We finally reached a point, and came to anchor in a little basin, or inlet, about one hundred and sixty feet from the shore, in five fathoms of water, completely landlocked.

Here in good earnest we commenced breaking out the fore hold abreast of the leak, and took out casks, shooks, &c., and careened the ship still more, which exposed at once the full extent of the damage which the ship had sustained from the ice.

It was found that several planks and timbers were badly stoven. Repairs were made with the utmost expedition; and in seven days from the time the ship went into the bay, she was out again, and on her way towards the north, as strong, and perhaps stronger than she was before.

We passed through the straits, and came to anchor north of East Cape, in company with the ship *E. Frazer*, Captain Taber, and the bark *Martha*, Captain Crocker. After lying there three or four days, we got under way and stood towards north by west, with high winds, and foggy. We heard whales blowing in the night. The next day whales were seen going north; we followed, and finally passed the "school." We changed the course of the ship, beat back, found them again, and commenced taking oil.

About the first of August, the fog having cleared away, we saw a large number of ships "cutting in" and "boiling out," actively engaged in securing a good season's work. We took several whales at this time. All were busy, and at work as fast as possible, in capturing whales, cutting and boiling. The whole scene, in which were some forty or fifty ships taking whales and stowing away oil, was one of exciting and cheering interest.

Such times as these are the whalemen's harvests.

On the 15th of August, during a heavy blow, we lost run of the whales. We spoke with several ships about this time, among which were the *Benjamin Morgan*, Captain Capel, and the *General Scott*, Captain Alexander Fisher.

From this last date to the 22d of September, we spoke with a great number of ships; sometimes whales were plenty, and at other times scarce; and the weather equally changeable; sometimes heavy blows, rainy, and foggy; and then again mild and pleasant.

Among others we spoke with Captain Henry Jernegan, and Captain John Fisher, both of whom are now no more, having finished their earthly voyages, and gone to their "long home."

18

THE CRUISE OF THE *WASP*

HENRY CABOT LODGE AND
THEODORE ROOSEVELT

A crash as when some swollen cloud
 Cracks o'er the tangled trees!
With side to side, and spar to spar,
 Whose smoking decks are these?
I know St. George's blood-red cross,
 Thou mistress of the seas,
But what is she whose streaming bars
 Roll out before the breeze?

Ah, well her iron ribs are knit,
 Whose thunders strive to quell
The bellowing throats, the blazing lips,
 That pealed the Armada's knell!

The mist was cleared,—a wreath of stars
Rose o'er the crimsoned swell,
And, wavering from its haughty peak,
The cross of England fell!—Holmes

In the war of 1812 the little American navy, including only a dozen frigates and sloops of war, won a series of victories against the English, the hitherto undoubted masters of the sea, that attracted an attention altogether out of proportion to the force of the combatants or the actual damage done. For one hundred and fifty years the English ships of war had failed to find fit rivals in those of any other European power, although they had been matched against each in turn; and when the unknown navy of the new nation growing up across the Atlantic did what no European navy had ever been able to do, not only the English and Americans, but the people of Continental Europe as well, regarded the feat as important out of all proportion to the material aspects of the case. The Americans first proved that the English could be beaten at their own game on the sea. They did what the huge fleets of France, Spain, and Holland had failed to do, and the great modern writers on naval warfare in Continental Europe—men like Jurien de la Graviere— have paid the same attention to these contests of frigates and sloops that they give to whole fleet actions of other wars.

Among the famous ships of the Americans in this war were two named the *Wasp*. The first was an eighteen-gun ship-sloop, which at the very outset of the war captured a British brig-sloop of twenty guns, after an engagement in which the British fought with great gallantry, but were knocked to pieces, while the Americans escaped comparatively unscathed. Immediately afterward a British seventy-four captured the victor. In memory of her the Americans gave the same name to one of the new sloops they were building. These sloops were stoutly made, speedy vessels which in strength and swiftness compared favorably with any ships of their class in any other navy of the day, for the American shipwrights were already as famous as the American gunners and seamen. The new *Wasp*, like her sister ships, carried twenty-two guns and a crew of one hundred and seventy men, and was ship-rigged. Twenty of her guns were 32-pound carronades, while for bow-chasers she had two "long Toms." It was in the year 1814 that the *Wasp* sailed from the United States to prey on the navy and commerce of Great Britain. Her commander was a gallant South Carolinian named Captain Johnson Blakeley. Her crew were nearly all native Americans, and were an exceptionally fine set of men. Instead of staying near the American coasts or of sailing the high seas, the *Wasp* at once headed boldly for the English Channel, to carry the war to the very doors of the enemy.

At that time the English fleets had destroyed the navies of every other power of Europe, and had obtained such complete supremacy over the French that the French fleets were kept in port. Off these ports lay the great squadrons of the English ships of the line, never, in gale or in calm, relaxing their watch upon the rival war-ships of the French emperor. So close was the blockade of the French ports, and so hopeless were the French of making headway in battle with their antagonists, that not only the great French three-deckers and two-deckers, but their frigates and sloops as well, lay harmless in their harbors, and the English ships patroled the seas unchecked in every direction. A few French privateers still slipped out now and then, and the far bolder and more formidable American privateersmen drove hither and thither across the ocean in their swift schooners and brigantines, and harried the English commerce without mercy.

The *Wasp* proceeded at once to cruise in the English Channel and off the coasts of England, France, and Spain. Here the water was traversed continually by English fleets and squadrons and single ships of war, which were sometimes convoying detachments of troops for Wellington's Peninsular army, sometimes guarding fleets of merchant vessels bound homeward, and sometimes merely cruising for foes. It was this spot, right in the teeth of the British naval power, that the *Wasp* chose for her cruising ground. Hither and thither she sailed through the narrow seas, capturing and destroying the merchantmen, and by the seamanship of her crew and the skill and vigilance of her commander, escaping the pursuit of frigate and ship of the line. Before she had been long on the ground, one June morning, while in chase of a couple of merchant ships, she spied a sloop of war, the British brig *Reindeer*, of eighteen guns and a hundred and twenty men. The *Reindeer* was a weaker ship than the *Wasp*, her guns were lighter, and her men fewer; but her commander, Captain Manners, was one of the most gallant men in the splendid British navy, and he promptly took up the gage of battle which the *Wasp* threw down.

The day was calm and nearly still; only a light wind stirred across the sea. At one o'clock the *Wasp*'s drum beat to quarters, and the sailors and marines gathered at their appointed posts. The drum of the *Reindeer* responded to the challenge, and with her sails reduced to fighting trim, her guns run out, and every man ready, she came down upon the Yankee ship. On her forecastle she had rigged a light carronade, and coming up from behind, she five times discharged this pointblank into the American sloop; then in the light air the latter luffed round, firing her guns as they bore, and the two ships engaged yard-arm to yard-arm. The guns leaped and thundered as the grimy gunners hurled them out to fire and back again to load, working like demons. For a few minutes the cannonade was tremendous, and the men in the tops could hardly see the decks for the wreck of flying splinters. Then the vessels ground together, and through the open ports the rival gunners hewed, hacked, and thrust at one another, while the black smoke curled up from between the hulls. The English were suffering terribly. Captain Manners himself was wounded, and realizing that he was doomed to defeat unless by some desperate effort he could avert it, he gave the signal to board. At the call the boarders gathered, naked to the waist, black with powder and spattered with blood, cutlas and pistol in hand. But the Americans were ready. Their marines were drawn up on deck, the pikemen stood behind the bulwarks, and the officers watched, cool and alert, every movement of the foe. Then the British sea-dogs tumbled aboard, only to perish by shot or steel. The combatants slashed and stabbed with savage fury, and the assailants were driven back. Manners sprang to their head to lead them again himself, when a ball fired by one of the sailors in the American tops crashed through his skull, and he fell, sword in hand, with his face to the foe, dying as honorable a death as ever a brave man died in fighting against odds for the flag of his country. As he fell the American officers passed the word to board. With wild cheers the fighting sailormen sprang forward, sweeping the wreck of the British force before them, and in a minute the *Reindeer* was in their possession. All of her officers, and nearly two thirds of the crew, were killed or wounded; but they had proved themselves as skilful as they were brave, and twenty-six of the Americans had been killed or wounded.

The *Wasp* set fire to her prize, and after retiring to a French port to refit, came out again to cruise. For some time she met no antagonist of her own size with which to wage war, and she had to exercise the sharpest vigilance to escape capture. Late one September afternoon, when she could see ships of war all around her, she selected one which was isolated from the others, and decided to run alongside her and try to sink her after nightfall.

Accordingly she set her sails in pursuit, and drew steadily toward her antagonist, a big eighteen-gun brig, the *Avon*, a ship more powerful than the *Reindeer*. The *Avon* kept signaling to two other British war vessels which were in sight—one an eighteen-gun brigand the other a twenty-gun ship; they were so close that the *Wasp* was afraid they would interfere before the combat could be ended. Nevertheless, Blakeley persevered, and made his attack with equal skill and daring.

It was after dark when he ran alongside his opponent, and they began forthwith to exchange furious broadsides. As the ships plunged and wallowed in the seas, the Americans could see the clusters of topmen in the rigging of their opponent, but they knew nothing of the vessel's name or of her force, save only so far as they felt it. The firing was fast and furious, but the British shot with bad aim, while the skilled American gunners hulled their opponent at almost every discharge. In a very few minutes the *Avon* was in a sinking condition, and she struck her flag and cried for quarter, having lost forty or fifty men, while but three of the Americans had fallen.

Before the *Wasp* could take possession of her opponent, however, the two war vessels to which the *Avon* had been signaling came up. One of them fired at the *Wasp*, and as the latter could not fight two new foes, she ran off easily before the wind. Neither of her new antagonists followed her, devoting themselves to picking up the crew of the sinking *Avon*.

It would be hard to find a braver feat more skilfully performed than this; for Captain Blakeley, with hostile foes all round him, had closed with and sunk one antagonist not greatly his inferior in force, suffering hardly any loss himself, while two of her friends were coming to her help.

Both before and after this the *Wasp* cruised hither and thither making prizes. Once she came across a convoy of ships bearing arms and munitions to Wellington's army, under the care of a great two-decker. Hovering about, the swift sloop evaded the two-decker's movements, and actually cut out and captured one of the transports she was guarding, making her escape unharmed. Then she sailed for the high seas. She made several other prizes, and on October 9 spoke a Swedish brig.

This was the last that was ever heard of the gallant *Wasp*. She never again appeared, and no trace of any of those aboard her was ever found. Whether she was wrecked on some desert coast, whether she foundered in some furious gale, or what befell her none ever knew. All that is certain is that she perished, and that all on board her met death in some one of the myriad forms in which it must always be faced by those who go down to the sea in ships; and when she sank there sank one of the most gallant ships of the American navy, with as brave a captain and crew as ever sailed from any port of the New World.

LIST OF SOURCES

"An American Sealer in the Russian Sea," from *Stories of Ships and the Sea*, Jack London, 1922

"The Capture: A True Account," from *The Atrocities of the Pirates*, Aaron Smith, 1824

"The Proud Narraganset's Escape," from *Yankee Ships and Yankee Sailors*, James Barnes, 1897

"Mutiny on Board the Ship *Globe* of Nantucket," from *Narrative of the Mutiny, on Board the Ship* Globe, William Lay and Cyrus M. Hussey, 1828

"On the Grand Banks," from *Captains Courageous*, Rudyard Kipling, 1897

"Yammerschooner," from *Sailing Alone around the World*, Joshua Slocum, 1900

"Young Ironsides," from *Old Ironsides*, James Fenimore Cooper, 1853

"Rounding Cape Horn," from *White-Jacket*, Herman Melville, 1850

"Loss of a Man—Superstition," from *Two Years before the Mast*, Richard Henry Dana, 1840

"A Student's Sea Story," from *Sam Lawson's Oldtown Fireside Stories*, Harriet Beech Stowe, 1881

"MS. Found in a Bottle," Edgar Alan Poe, 1831

"The Merchants' Cup," from *Broken Stowage*, David W. Bone, 1922

"Owen Chase's Narrative," from *Shipwreck of the Whaleship Essex*, Owen Chase, 1821

"The White Whale," from *Moby Dick*, Herman Melville, 1851

"Blueskin, the Pirate," from *Howard Pyle's Book of Pirates*, Merle Johnson, 1921

"The Adventures of Captain Horn," from *The Adventures of Captain Horn*, Frank Stockton, 1895

"The Wreck of the *Citizen*," from *The Arctic Whaleman*, Lewis Holmes, 1857

"The Cruise of the *Wasp*," from *Hero Tales of American History*, Henry Cabot Lodge and Theodore Roosevelt, 1895